Distinguished Service

1. *Lydia Chapin,* 1917.

Distinguished Service

LYDIA CHAPIN KIRK,

Partner in Diplomacy, 1896–1984

Lydia Chapin Kirk

Edited by Roger Kirk

With a Foreword by Robert Orris Blake

AN ADST-DACOR DIPLOMATS AND DIPLOMACY BOOK

SYRACUSE UNIVERSITY PRESS

Syracuse University Press, Syracuse, New York 13244-5160

First Edition 2007
07 08 09 10 11 12 6 5 4 3 2 1

Unless otherwise stated, all illustrations courtesy of Roger Kirk.

The paper used in this publication meets the minimum requirements of American National Standard for Information Sciences—Permanence of Paper for Printed Library Materials, ANSI Z39.48–1984.∞™

For a listing of books published and distributed by Syracuse University Press, visit our Web site at SyracuseUniversityPress.syr.edu.

ISBN-13: 978-0-8156-0891-2 ISBN-10: 0-8156-0891-8

Library of Congress Cataloging-in-Publication Data

Kirk, Lydia.
Lydia Chapin Kirk : partner in diplomacy, 1896–1984 / Lydia Chapin Kirk ; edited by Roger Kirk ; with a foreword by Robert Orris Blake. — 1st ed.
p. cm. — (ADST-DACOR diplomats and diplomacy series)
Includes index.
ISBN-13: 978-0-8156-0891-2 (hardcover : alk. paper)
1. Kirk, Lydia. 2. Kirk, Alan Goodrich, 1888–1963—Marriage. 3. Ambassadors' spouses—United States—Biography. 4. United States—Foreign relations—20th century. 5. Diplomats—England—London—Social life and customs—20th century. 6. Diplomats—Belgium—Social life and customs—20th century. 7. Diplomats—Soviet Union—Social life and customs. 8. Diplomats—Taiwan—Social life and customs—20th century. 9. Admirals' spouses—United States—Biography. 10. Women authors, American—Biography. I. Kirk, Roger, 1930– II. Title.
E748.K54A3 2007
973.91—dc22
2007019349

Manufactured in the United States of America

To Lydia Kirk,

a distinguished lady and an inspiring mother,

and to all those service wives past, present, and future

who work in supporting roles to their husbands,

to the benefit of their families and their country.

As the wife of the respected naval officer and ambassador Alan Kirk, LYDIA CHAPIN KIRK acted as a vital but unpaid partner in her husband's appointments to London, Belgium, the Soviet Union, and the Republic of China on Taiwan, serving as a witness to and occasional participant in some of the seminal events of the twentieth century. She was also a published author, with three novels and a memoir to her credit.

ROGER KIRK, born in 1930, lived in England, Belgium, and Russia with his parents, Alan and Lydia Kirk, just before and after World War II. After graduating from Princeton magna cum laude and Phi Beta Kappa in 1952 and doing his military service, he joined the U.S. State Department, later serving as U.S. ambassador to the UN organizations in Vienna and to Somalia and Romania. In 1984 and 1987 he received Presidential Awards for Outstanding Service. Since his retirement from the State Department in 1990, he has taught graduate seminars at Georgetown University, chaired the Board of the Washington International School, and lectured on international affairs. He now serves as vice chair of a Washington, D.C., think tank. In 1994 he coauthored *Romania versus the United States: Diplomacy of the Absurd.* He speaks six languages.

Contents

Illustrations

Foreword

ROBERT ORRIS BLAKE

I met Lydia Kirk in Moscow in early 1950. I was young and single, a Foreign Service officer on my second assignment. She was the wife of our ambassador, Admiral Alan Kirk. Some months later the Kirks invited me to join them in the embassy residence to help manage the place and to share meals with them when they were not dining out. Later when my wife and I were living in New York we saw a lot of the Kirks. Our families became good friends.

And so it was a delight to read *Distinguished Service: Lydia Chapin Kirk, Partner in Diplomacy, 1896–1984*. I love Mrs. Kirk's lively description of life in Moscow. Like all good autobiographers she avoids anything that can be interpreted as self-praise, so I will add a few notes about her personality. For starters, she had magnetism. When she and her handsome husband entered any room, conversation would stop and all attention would focus on them. They would usually go their own ways, and she would quickly dominate one corner with her wit and charm.

In her later years, especially after her husband's death, I came to see her as often as I could. I would invariably find her in lively conversation with fascinating friends, many of them young people. How can any of us forget her wicked chuckle and her deep, throaty voice?

Lydia Kirk had a special interest in politics and politicians, here and in other countries. In the Soviet Union it was hard to find out much about the country's secretive leaders. What were they really like and how did they relate to one another? I remember an especially interesting conversation I overheard between Mrs. Kirk and the Russian-born wife of the Swedish ambassador, who had contacts with important Soviet politicians. Mrs. Kirk was able to extract a good deal of useful information from her on that occasion, and I am sure on many others.

There was another side to Lydia Kirk that I admired: her sense of adventure. She loved exploring the most remote parts of Moscow. On the first breezy autumn day she would suggest taking "a short walk." Hours later, after trying unsuccessfully to jiggle the lock on an abandoned church, she would return to her residence, tired but triumphant.

You can see why we all loved her. Readers are lucky to get to know this wonderful lady through the pages of this book.

Preface

ROGER KIRK

My mother, the author of this memoir, shared her husband's career as naval officer and ambassador for forty-four years, from 1918 through 1962. The bulk of the memoir is devoted to her "service," as she would call it, as companion to my father in his assignment as U.S. naval attaché in London at the beginning of World War II and, after that war, as U.S. ambassador to Belgium, the Soviet Union, and finally the Republic of China on Taiwan. She also gives a brief description of her childhood in Erie, Pennsylvania, and Washington, D.C., and tells of her life as a girl and young woman in pre–World War I Paris and Washington.

Mother writes in an old-fashioned style and tells of a time when wives' roles were different than they are now. She served as helpmate to her husband and was happy in that role. She did so not only because this was "expected" of a wife, but also because she was proud to help her husband serve his country in important jobs.

Mother was also quite capable of doing things on her own, as shown by her activities when my father was away at sea. As a young married woman, she served on the National Board of the Junior League. Early in World War II she worked as a cable censor in the Navy Department, and later on she traveled as a Red Cross volunteer throughout the mid-Atlantic states, giving talks to the wives of U.S. prisoners of war. She wrote four books, one of them on the *New York Times* bestseller list for several weeks.

In her role as diplomat's spouse, Mother considered it her task to assure that, wherever she was—wartime England, Brussels immediately after the war, Moscow during the cold war, and Taipei—the household functioned smoothly and cheerfully as a source of comfort to her husband and his staff, and as a welcoming place for his contacts. She also felt she must be a worthy representative of her family and her country. Intense patriotism and pride of family were integral parts of her heritage and character.

She rarely writes about her inner feelings in her memoir; indeed, she kept these to herself throughout her life. In the milieu in which she grew up it was not customary to reveal them, and her New England heritage reinforced this tendency. She did not share them with me, with my sisters, or with anyone else as far as I know.

Mother's motivations do peek out here and there. In describing her departure from wartime England, leaving her husband there, she says, "I was determined not to cry. I wanted to show the [British neighbors who had come to say goodbye] how an American woman could behave." On learning of her husband's unexpected assignment as U.S. ambassador to Moscow at the height of the cold war in 1949, she says, "Who was I, a service woman born and bred, to object, as I could share the challenge with him?" And finally, when he was asked to go to Taiwan as ambassador to the Republic of China, ending ten years of pleasant retirement in New York, she says, "Alan had a job to do, a job that I could share, and that was that."

It was important that my mother felt this way, for the U.S. Navy and Foreign Service of those days expected their employees' wives to work hard in an unpaid supporting role. The saying that "the government got two for one" was literally correct. A wife's job was an important one and often not easy. In many ways, moves from one country to another were a greater challenge for the wife than for her husband. It was she who had to set up housekeeping and keep the children happy in a foreign land, while her husband merely moved to another American office, albeit in a different country.

An ambassador's wife—my mother's role for most of the period she chronicles—had help from household and embassy staff, but she had to be an example for all the other women. A complaining, demanding, or fearful ambassador's wife can ruin morale at a post, while an inspiring one can do wonders, especially in a difficult and isolated place.

I embarked on this project from a conviction that Mother's draft material, quite aside from its sentimental value to her family, had literary merit and was of real historical value and therefore should be preserved in a readily accessible form. It provides a firsthand picture of an era of significant social change and of the role that a talented and courageous "traditional" wife could play alongside her husband in key spots during the hot and cold wars of the forties, fifties, and sixties. The roles of diplomats' and naval officers' wives have changed, reflecting the change in women's place in our society. But service wives performed a significant, if subordinate, role in former times. This memoir illustrates that abundantly. I hope that by doing so it will help gain those earlier wives the respect they deserve in an age that tends to pity rather than admire them.

The text published here is based on autobiographical drafts my mother wrote in the 1960s and on letters she wrote to my two sisters and me both in 1949–51 from Moscow and in 1962 from Taipei. The letters from Moscow were extensively quoted in her book, *Postmarked Moscow,* published by Charles Scribner's Sons in 1952, which Simon and Schuster has graciously given me permission to draw from here.

In preparing this text, I have combined and considerably shortened my mother's drafts and letters. Although I have altered few of her words, I have supplemented them to give readers an idea of the diplomatic challenges my father was facing and to explain some names, references, and foreign phrases that Mother would have thought needed no clarification. In all these cases I have written in her style, or as she related these facts to me.

Mother's draft memoir omitted any account of two twenty-year periods in her life. One was from 1918 to 1937, roughly between her marriage and her final year in California before going to London with my father upon his assignment as U.S. naval attaché at the American Embassy there. As I was born in 1930, I have little personal knowledge to contribute, but I have filled in the story in my own words from a couple of fragments written by my mother, notes from my older sister Marian, and published biographical material. The other period was the twenty years of Mother's life that followed my father's death in 1964; I have covered this period in the final chapter. I was abroad much of that time, as I had joined the U.S. diplomatic service. My older sister was in Philadelphia, but my sister Deborah saw our mother frequently. She supplied most of the material for this section, which I have put in my own words. Both of these sections are bracketed, to clearly delineate my voice from my mother's.

I am grateful to my sisters, Marian Kirk Appel and Deborah Kirk Solbert, for their help in the project, and especially to my wife, Madeleine Yaw Kirk, for her tolerance, support, and understanding during the too-long writing and editing process. Margery Boichel Thompson, publishing director of the Association for Diplomatic Studies and Training, was of inestimable help in the editing and publishing, as was Mary Selden Evans, executive editor at Syracuse University Press.

PART ONE

Early Life, 1896–1939

1

Beginnings, 1896–1908

In 1896, the year of my birth, Erie, Pennsylvania, was a good town to live in. The streets were broad and shaded with old elms, the houses large and comfortable with yards full of fruit trees and shrubs, faithful replicas of any to be found in Connecticut from where the first white settlers had come in the early 1800s. With the houses the pioneers established a way of life and thought much akin to that they had left behind. These were not grand folk, but they were educated people, industrious and respectable, and they brought with them their preachers and teachers, their Bibles and history books, giving to each settlement order, decency, and peaceful, hard-earned prosperity.

On the heels of the first settlers came other migrations: German, Irish, Polish, Finnish. Erie became an industrial center. The men of our family owned manufactories that made steam boilers and kitchen utensils. The Erie City Iron Works, run by the Seldens, made the boilers, the Griswold Manufacturing Company the iron saucepans and skillets and waffle irons. Both families came from Connecticut within twenty miles of each other, both had close relatives still occupying old homesteads on Long Island Sound or the Connecticut River, and the bonds with New England were still very strong. Among my Griswold grandmother's forebears were two governors of Connecticut, Matthew and Roger Griswold. Governor Matthew married his cousin Ursula Wolcott, and there is a table in the Hartford Historical Museum where five past, present, and future governors of Connecticut, all Ursula's near relations, sat together: her husband, father, brother, uncle, and son.

Grandmother was a remarkable woman. About five feet four, she held herself very erect, and her white hair and heavy black brows above dark, sparkling eyes made her very striking. Thanks to her New England parentage she had an almost eighteenth-century education and a tolerance and humor within the bounds of strict principles of right and wrong. From her I inherited my love of books; the shelves in the Erie house were full of them. I loved her and I respected her, and I am proud to bear her name.

My own mother, Grace Selden, was born in 1865. I never knew her father, a descendant of Thomas Selden, an original proprietor of Hartford, Connecticut, but his pictures show him to have been a blonde, amiable-looking man, and certainly my blonde mother must have been very like him, for her pleasant, sunny nature and love of people were very different from Grandmother's somewhat shy austerity.

Without intellectual pretensions, Mother had considerable shrewdness and was an excellent judge of people. Pretty, popular, and gay (in my day, *gay* meant "lively" or "fun-loving"), a favorite with everyone, she refused all her beaus until my father, Frederic Lincoln Chapin, a dashing young naval officer attached to a patrol boat assigned to the Great Lakes, appeared on the scene and successfully wooed her.

My father was born and grew up in Kirkwood, Illinois. All Chapins are supposedly descended from English immigrant Deacon Samuel Chapin, whose statue presides over a town square in Springfield, Massachusetts. Father's branch of the family moved west to Illinois, where my grandfather became president of the Kirkwood town bank. Seeing a notice announcing examinations for the Naval Academy, Father asked permission to take them, passed, and entered Annapolis at the age of sixteen. He was a man of wide interests, an excellent linguist, and an ardent student of history.

Father's career included long tours of sea service that kept him apart from his family, a real deprivation for us and especially for my mother, who loved him very much. On his occasional tours of shore duty, doubly precious for us all, he read aloud to us children each evening before din-

2. *Lydia Chapin, aged two years, 1898.*

ner. He liked to join our weekend sightseeing and on our motor trips was remarkably patient with a car full of females. He was truly a fine man.

My grandfather Selden died a year or two before Mother was married, but his affairs were left in competent hands. Grandmother was able to keep the big house, a home for herself and a home for Mother and her children when Father was at sea. Both my brother Selden and I were born there, he on September 19, 1899, my third birthday. I had been given a kitten that morning. Later, I was told that, when I learned I had a baby brother born that day, I wanted to give him a present and took my Moo, a beloved and very dirty woolen rag, and put it in his crib. I think I remember doing this, though the touching episode may have been reported later by a doting nurse.

Mother was often away with Father, and my brother Selden and I were left to spend part of our winters and all of our summers with Grandmother

3. Lydia with her mother, Grace Selden Chapin, and her brother, Selden Chapin, 1902.

in Erie. Although our own family was not large, the Selden and Griswold relatives were often at the house. Uncle Matt Griswold had six sons, and they and their children visited back and forth with us. Those were the days of plenty, when there was always enough for another guest.

In the summer there was lots to do all day long, but, best of all, I liked the summer evenings, with my hands and face washed and my dress changed into a starched linen frock. Some evenings Grandmother and I would walk across the street to call on other muslin-dressed old ladies. They would receive me politely, and I enjoyed sitting on fat, plush-covered stools, looking at picture books while the ladies chatted with each other.

In early October 1901 Father was assigned to duty in the Navy Department in Washington, and we moved into a tall, narrow house on New Hampshire Avenue. Father bought Mother a high-wheeled, open electric carriage, with a dashboard covered in black patent leather like the dashboard of a smart horse cart and a single seat for two or three passengers. We felt very grand riding around Dupont Circle and up and down Connecticut Avenue until one rainy day, as we went zooming along, the car skidded on the wet pavement and we turned completely around. Mother was quite shaken, but I thought it great fun.

In early June of 1902 Father was asked to go to Asia as aide to Admiral Robley Evans, commander-in-chief of the Asiatic Squadron. This was a great compliment, one that could not be refused, but the cruise was a long one. He was away for two years, and it seemed as though he had really disappeared over the horizon. We moved in with Grandmother in Erie and relied on letters from him. He wrote often, telling of his adventures in China, Korea, and Japan, and of the people he met and the beautiful things he had seen and bought.

This was the year I learned to read. I was six, and it was Grandmother who taught me. She was a good teacher. The books she chose were not simple ones, but words fascinated me as she explained them, and by the end of the year I could read quite easily. Grandmother also taught me to respect books. "Books," she said, "are your friends. You must treat them carefully." She was right, for books have remained my friends throughout the years.

Finally in the spring of 1904 the welcome news arrived that Father was coming home. His ship docked in Brooklyn toward the end of April. At first brother Selden and I were very shy of this strange gentleman whom we had not seen for nearly two years, but in very little time we were quite satisfied to accept this nice, blue-eyed, brown-mustached man for our father. Mother was in seventh heaven, holding his hand all the way back to New York in the trolley.

Father stayed a week in Erie, and there were new smells in the house, whiffs of cigarettes and pipe tobacco. I was sorry when they evaporated after he left, taking Mother with him to Old Point Comfort near Norfolk, where his ship had gone for overhaul. Orders came through later in the month assigning Father to the Navy Department. All this was very exciting, even more so when Father announced he planned to buy an automobile. He had decided, after much consultation and studying of catalogues, on a White Steamer made in Cleveland, to be delivered in Erie. It came two weeks later, black and very shiny, two seats in the front, room for three in the back. On each fender there was a long, varnished wicker

4. Family car with Grace Selden Chapin, Uncle George, and driver, 1904.

basket for umbrellas and picnic gear. All the fittings, handles, lamps, hub-caps, and even the radiator were bright brass. We were quite privileged to have a car, as in 1904 there were only eight thousand cars in the United States, and the speed limit in most cities was ten miles an hour.

We moved to Washington in the autumn of 1904. In those days the city was pleasantly leisured for people like us. Politics and politicians were present in this capital city, but they were happily removed from the groups where Mother and Father found friends. Three of Mother's friends, responding to the need for a primary school for their own children, journeyed to New York, engaged teachers, and started the Potomac School on the second floor of a building on Dupont Circle. That school has since expanded greatly, moved twice, and is now on extensive grounds in nearby Virginia. It is still one of the best in the Washington area, and I was delighted to address the students on its seventy-fifth anniversary in 1979.

School opened on September 20, the day after Selden's and my joint birthday. I was eight. I felt rather fearful that first morning when Mother delivered me into the care of the teacher, Miss Hammond. I knew none of the other pupils except for Catherine Harlow, the daughter of a close friend of Mother's. We sat waiting a bit nervously, but Miss Hammond soon put us all at ease, talking to each pupil, asking questions as to our interests. By the time recess came at ten-thirty, we girls were chattering happily as we crossed into Dupont Circle. Class was dismissed at twelve-thirty. I walked home round the corner to find Mother waiting, inquiring anxiously how I liked the school. I reported that I liked it and that I liked the teacher. "I think school is going to be fun," I said.

I was right. As time went on Miss Hammond taught us that learning really could be fun. Even the arithmetic sums, my worst subject, she made interesting. As for English lessons, twice a week we were required to write a ten-minute original composition. I remember one of her subjects: "Suppose you were invisible. What would you do?" Thanks to this training there must be dozens of lawyers and diplomats, hostesses and housewives, statesmen and doctors, early graduates of the Potomac School, who can face paper and pencil without too many qualms. A nicely turned phrase in a speech or peace treaty may well be owing to the Potomac School's ten-minute compositions.

I enjoyed school but looked forward to June, when I would make my first trip with Grandmother to her childhood home, Black Hall, her Griswold family property on the banks of the Connecticut River near Old Lyme, Connecticut. Grandmother was one of seven sisters and a brother. The four unmarried sisters, Aunts Marian, Phoebe, Lizzie, and Nelly, lived together in the old Griswold house where Grandmother had grown up. Aunt Marian I knew well, for she often visited us in Erie.

When Grandmother's and my train reached Black Hall, we saw Aunt Lizzie waiting on the platform at the head of a long flight of stairs. She greeted Grandmother, then bent down over me. "I've brought the surrey. It is tied up down below. Hop in the front seat and put a rug around you. You'll feel cold after hot Washington."

Benjamin, the old horse, trotted along the three miles to the river and turned up the lane. "We are on Griswold property now," said Aunt Lizzie as she turned off the main road. "The houses we pass belong to relatives. Ours is up at the top of the hill." We went past cousin Judge Griswold's house, cousin Charlie Griswold's house, cousin Lizzie Lane's, and then up the little hill and through the picket gate to swing round in front of the aunts' house facing the water with the meadows stretching sweet and wide before it. Two-storied and rambling, it was not a very grand house.

Aunt Lizzie drove round the house and drew up as the other three aunts came out of doors. We went indoors and followed Aunt Marian upstairs. "I've put a cot for you, Lydia, in the passage room next door. There's a bath and a toilet round the corner. We put that in last autumn. It is a help not to have to go outside in the bad weather. I'll leave you now. Supper will be ready when you come down." After she had gone, Grandmother explained that there had been no indoor plumbing in the house until very recently, and there was still no electricity or gas, only lamps and candles.

Mornings were the time for chores. In the afternoon there was the never-failing fascination of the beach just across the meadows fronting the house, the beach with its sand and shells, the tide that swept in and out and covered the rocks along the shore or left the bare rocks for you to climb over. There were other afternoons, deliciously long, empty, and drowsy, when we did nothing at all. I would take a book and sit on the back porch or make long chains of flowers—daisies, hollyhocks, or lilac blossoms.

When the weather was warm we sat on the back veranda after supper; but, if it was too cool, a green cloth was spread on the dining table, a student lamp set in the center, and we drew up our chairs to read or work. I liked those lamplit evenings.

As our visit to Black Hall in the summer of 1905 came to an end, I felt very bad at leaving. I would have liked to have stayed on all summer, but Grandmother reminded me that we must be in Erie to welcome Mother and Father arriving from Washington. They came a few days later, and it was very gay in the house, with friends often coming for lunches and dinners. There were treats for us, picnics with our friends, corn roasted over a fire, and thick slices of watermelon. On one picnic a water snake glided across my bare foot. Even as I write I feel slippery and cold. I hate snakes.

We made an overnight journey in the car to Chautauqua, a lakeside resort in southwestern New York State. At the hotel in nearby

Jamestown Selden and I were given a room with what was called a Murphy bed, a yellow varnished affair that could be shut up against the wall during the day and pulled down at night. I felt very nervous lest it shut up while we were in it.

We were back in Erie for the Fourth of July celebration. I never really enjoyed the early part of the Erie July Fourths, when the men and boys threw exploding firecrackers in every direction. In those days there were no regulations on fireworks, and many people were injured every year. I felt rather like one of the family dogs that crept whimpering under the front porch. I stuck it out bravely until it was time for picnic supper. When it grew dark, we lit sparklers and small strings of lady crackers and the men launched rockets and pinwheels some distance away. The summer wore on, Father's vacation ended, and we went back to Washington.

School was as interesting as ever, and Miss Hammond was full of new ideas and programs for the coming year. At Christmas I received a splendidly bound set of Charles Dickens's works and celebrated an attack of measles by having Dickens's *Pickwick Papers* read to me. I found parts of it slow going and solaced myself with raspberry-flavored gumdrops.

I was looking forward to another visit to Black Hall, counting the days after school was over in June. This year, 1906, Grandmother wrote that my ten-year-old cousin, Matthew Griswold, would also be there. He was company, but selfishly I liked having the place to myself. Matthew was not much of a reader, and I had discovered Sir Walter Scott's *Ivanhoe* in the hall bookcase. All too soon the time came for us to return to Erie, and another summer passed much like the previous ones, except the boys were more willing to join in on our games. Privately I thought we had more fun without them.

The coming winter, 1906–7, was our last in Washington as Father was again due for sea. He left in the spring, and we went back to Erie after a fine summer visit to Black Hall. Father could not come home for Christmas. We missed him, but he arrived soon after New Year's with very, very exciting news. He had been appointed naval attaché to our embassy in Paris and all of us were to leave for France six weeks later.

After considerable discussion Grandmother was persuaded to go with us. Veenie, our old nurse, was to go also, so we would be quite a party.

In Erie I had French lessons from a Mademoiselle Charpentier, who painfully guided me through *L'Histoire de France* in words of one and two strange-sounding syllables. She was a missionary in her own way, for she made those kings and queens of France very real to me. She did what she could to prepare me for the enchantment of France and, just before I left, showed me her dearest possession. It was a postcard addressed to her by one of her small pupils. It read, "Mademoiselle, Erie, Pennsylvania," and it had reached her without trouble. Alone, in herself, she upheld the honor of her nation in our city.

Time grew short. Trunks were brought down, a great many of them. Finally, in February, all was ready, trunks and boxes packed. Andrew, our young chauffeur, would follow once we became established.

2

Paris, 1908–1911

In February 1908, we set off by train from Erie to New York, seen off by friends and relatives at the Erie station. I was eleven, my brother Selden eight. The government arranged passage to France for Mother and Father, Grandmother, nurse Veenie, Selden, and myself, on the old *St. Louis* steamship of the American line. Never a very elegant vessel, she had been requisitioned as an auxiliary cruiser in the Spanish-American war ten years before, and her appearance and gait bore evidence of that ordeal. We floundered across the Atlantic in a heavy February gale, poor Father dismayed by the four seasick females in his party.

We were a dismal and rather tired group upon reaching our destination, the French port of Cherbourg, on a dark, wet, winter morning, but Father marshaled us smartly aboard the smaller boat that would take us to the dock and then installed us on a train to Paris. Arriving in Paris, we were met by a secretary of the American Embassy and driven to our hotel. That night Veenie, Selden, and I had dinner in the dining room. The food was unfamiliar but we were hungry and ate everything, though Selden made faces when they brought him warm milk.

Next day we took a walk wearing our double-breasted sailor jackets and caps with ribboned letters reading "USS *Missouri*," the name of an American battleship. We felt very strange and lost in this great, gray city. Father spoke a fair amount of French, Mother very little. Grandmother, Selden, and Veenie spoke none at all. We children decided that we did not like Paris. Father and Mother seemed to be very busy, and

Grandmother, quite tired, sat quietly in the hotel. We were no longer seasick, but we were that plague of all time, American children abroad. Forbidden to drink Paris water, a large jug of Evian mineral water had been set up on our outside balcony. At odd times Selden and I sneaked out, tipping it very gently over the rail so it splashed down on the street, only once hitting our target, a dressed-up boy walking with a priest. They looked up, but we had backed away through the open window.

On the American holiday commemorating George Washington's birthday we invited the family into the living room and gave a patriotic performance. Selden recited the story of Washington saying "I cannot tell a lie" as he confessed that he had chopped down a cherry tree in the yard. We sang patriotic songs, "My Country 'Tis of Thee" and "Columbia, the Gem of the Ocean," and I gave a spirited rendition of the poem "Paul Revere's Ride," commemorating that Revolutionary War hero's ride through the Massachusetts countryside to warn of the approaching British soldiers. We could not understand why Mother and Grandmother had tears in their eyes. I suppose they realized we were two lonely American children far from home and friends.

It was soon time to go to school. I was enrolled at the École Fenélon, where I spent every morning until twelve writing sums and dictation in purple ink with a squeaky pen. My classmates were solemn children with black cotton pinafores and ink-stained fingers. No one paid much attention to me, though one girl did offer me a bite of her chocolate at the mid-morning snack. I discovered that French arithmetic was much the same as English. So was geography when they stuck to continents and did not wander round the subdivisions of France. Gradually I began to learn French, to enter my lessons in shiny black copybooks, and to study and recite parrotwise, reeling off names and dates. Later, as my French improved, I was moved up from one class to another.

We stayed several weeks at the hotel while Mother and Father looked about for a suitable apartment. Finally they found just what they wanted, a large furnished flat at 114 Avenue Champs Elysées, Paris's parade route from the Louvre Palace to the Arc de Triomphe. It was on the corner, appropriately enough, of Avenue Washington. I occupied a room with Grandmother, each of us with a fine canopied bed. We got along well together, kept nearly the same hours, and, though it might be considered odd today for a girl of eleven to share her grandmother's bedroom, no one questioned the arrangement.

Walks to and from school and slightly rebellious afternoon strolls up the Champs Elysées were about the only exercise available to us, but the walks were not too bad, and they could be punctuated with stops to ride on the merry-go-round or watch the Punch and Judy puppet shows in the park. We were not allowed out alone; well-brought-up children never walked alone on Paris streets. I lunched with the family every day; Selden had his at school and reported that the boys drank watered wine instead of milk. Nurse Veenie was horrified, but Father said it would not do him any harm.

On Sundays we rode out, all of us, into the country, or if the weather was bad Father took us to museums. I had read stories of the executions during the Terror period of the French Revolution so always shut my eyes when we drove through the Place de la Concorde in the center of town, where the executions took place. I imagined that I could see the guillotine and poor Marie Antoinette, the deposed queen, walking up the steps to have her head cut off.

I had relatively little contact with other children, though over time I did make friends with one or two American girls. None of the French children with whom I went to school became real friends. Perhaps we were too busy. Lessons and homework left very little spare time and, when vacations came, we were whisked away to the seashore or packed into the family touring car for long motor trips.

We began to look white-faced from lack of real exercise, and Mother decided that something active must be found for us to do. I continued my walks, but each Friday, along with two other American girls, Veenie took me to an indoor ice-skating rink, the Palais de Glace (Ice Palace), an elegant place frequented by fashionable folk. At four-thirty sharp she had instructions to take us home, as that was the hour when the gay ladies arrived with their gentlemen escorts and it became no longer *comme il faut* (suitable) for young girls.

"*Ce n'est pas pour les jeunes filles*" (that is not for young girls). How often I was to hear that during the years I lived in Paris and later when

I went back there to boarding school. At eleven I had very little idea of who or what the gay ladies were who came to the Palais de Glace, but by the time I was fourteen and went back to America I knew all about them. A noticing child grew up fast in Paris, and, though my education in such matters stemmed mainly from reading history and cataloguing the mistresses of the kings of France, I could guess at certain similarities between them and the laughing young women who appeared at four-thirty with bunches of violets pinned to their furs and mustachioed gallants carrying their skates in velvet bags.

As summer approached, it was decided that Grandmother, Veenie, Selden, and I would go to Houlgate, a seaside resort on the Normandy coast, for July. We enjoyed Houlgate. Happily I found a friend, Clover Todd, the daughter of a widowed American college professor. She was a tall, dreamy girl, but we talked of books and she told me of her life in New York. We would have nothing to do with anyone else, preferring our own games and our own secrets. When the sea was calm, we went bathing together, only venturing knee-deep into the surf that pounded up the beach at high tide.

Father was also air attaché, although in 1908 our American efforts in that field were largely experimental. In early September Father was invited to an air show at the racecourse in Rheims, one hundred miles west of Paris. No sooner had he arrived at Rheims than he sent word to Mother, "This is so interesting, come up and bring the children." Greatly excited, we were packed into the car and driven to Rheims, where we spent the night. The distance trials would be held the next day, to be measured in laps flown round the racetrack. One lap around the stadium track in the air was an achievement for those early, very slow airplanes, and the prize would go to the one who did the most without landing. In the morning we drove to the racecourse, and Father took us out into the paddock to look at the various machines. Some would never get off the ground. One lay wrecked after its first attempt. It had risen twenty feet, then collapsed along with its inventor.

We lunched in the grandstand café, then took our seats for the show. The two French contenders each swung round the track several times, but then the American outdistanced them all. We counted the laps with delight and cheered when he was declared the winner. A band played "The Star Spangled Banner" and the American flag was hoisted above the stands. We followed Father out to congratulate our hero and see him receive a great gleaming cup. It was all most satisfactory.

Writing this, it seems extraordinary that my own life has spanned the years between that victorious flight round the race track at Rheims and, seventy-odd years later, skies filled with huge planes that cross continents and oceans in a matter of hours. I myself have flown across the ocean in the supersonic Concorde. As for the military potential, one dares not think about it. Perhaps, after all, we should have left the skies to the birds.

Not entirely satisfied with the École Fenélon for me, Mother and Father decided to enter me in a new school, the Cours Dieterlein, for the coming year. Like many French intermediate schools, this one ran on a system of four preparation mornings and two recitation days, one on Wednesday afternoon, one on Saturday morning. I liked my new school. The other girls paid little attention to me, but I went about my business and kept to myself at the mid-morning break for games in the courtyard. Mother and Father read in my fall art report that I had "a small talent, but large enough to encourage," so inquiries were made among the family's artistic friends. To my delight it was arranged for me to have drawing class once a week.

Veenie came to pick me up from school at twelve-thirty. We walked back past several shops, one a butcher's that displayed a calf's head outside, quite horrid with long dark lashes below closed eyes. I looked the other way. There was a paper store and a small confectioner's with delicious candies in the window. I asked Veenie for ten sous (a few cents), bought a bar of chocolate, and tried to forget the dead calf.

Running in from the street in the first weeks of 1909, I slipped and fell on the curb outside our doorway, hurting my left leg. Aside from the first painful hours when Veenie undertook to reduce the swelling by pressing on it with brown paper and a buttered steel knife, some old wives' cure her mother had brought from Germany, I enjoyed the drama and all the attention it brought me. The doctor was called in when nurse Veenie's ministrations failed. He pronounced the bone broken and sent for a surgeon to come to the house. An operating table was arranged in the bedroom, I was given whiffs of evil-smelling anesthetic while the bone was set, and my interested and now very sympathetic family looked on.

No crutches, the doctor said, lest I fall again. I must wait. I was young and the bone should heal quickly. So there I lay in bed, but after a few days I managed to hop into the library where Grandmother and I embarked on a series of card games and large jigsaw puzzles. I could read, of course, and that was a comfort. The bone took some time to mend, and I reveled in my importance. As healing progressed, I was carried downstairs each day by the butler and the young footman and lifted into the back seat of the new town car the family had purchased. This was a very smart vehicle, a small Renault, dark red with gleaming brass trimmings, and I felt very grand riding round the city, doing errands and leaving Mother's and Father's visiting cards, sorting them out from a written list and turning down the corners to show they were delivered personally.

In those days cards with one's name, position, and address were left at the house of fellow members of "society" after a dinner at their house and at those of any dinner guests one had not met before, upon one's departure for and return from holiday, and on numerous other occasions. The top left corner was the one turned down to show the card had been delivered personally—usually by the owner, in this case by the daughter of the owner. The card would be marked "ppc." if one was going away on holiday, "pp." if one was leaving for good, and so on. These cards did serve some purpose. They introduced newcomers to society, reminded them of one's own name, and kept track of who was where, all of which was important for purposes of invitations and the like. Society ladies in those days had much leisure time, as they typically did not work and had plenty of servants to do the household chores, but leaving cards was a time-consuming and often tedious task. It is no wonder Mother turned the job over to me, and I needed something to do.

That summer we stayed in town except for short weekend trips to the country. One Sunday I will never forget. We had gone to see the former royal palace of Versailles a short way out of town. Upon returning to Paris and entering the Place de la Concorde, we found it completely filled by a screaming mob of people. Even with our diplomatic license plates there was no way of getting through. The police seemed utterly helpless. It was quite terrifying. Then, minutes later, we heard the sound of horses' hooves, and out from the rue de Rivoli came the Garde Républicaine, the elite Paris municipal police detachment, at a gallop, their sabers drawn. They encircled the crowd, driving them toward the gates of the Tuileries garden next to the Place de la Concorde. The gates opened and then shut behind them. I thought the eighteenth-century French Revolution had started all over again, but later we learned it had been a demonstration against the execution of two Spanish anarchists. Angry mobs are something I hope never to see or hear again. I was very frightened.

It was soon time for school again. It was arranged that I would return to the Cours Dieterlein for the autumn term, then after Christmas have lessons in French diction with Mademoiselle Avril, an actress of some repute, and drawing instruction two mornings a week. It was an exciting program and I could hardly wait for the weeks to go by.

Mademoiselle Avril was a striking woman with dark eyes, beautifully waved brown hair, and what the papers of the day would term "a handsome bust." She had been, so it was said, the mistress of the great industrialist, Alfred Nobel, the Swede who invented dynamite and founded the Nobel Peace Prize, but she had rashly left him for an impecunious young lover and now augmented her income by giving lessons to selected pupils from diplomatic circles.

I went once a week to Mademoiselle Avril's flat, where we sat at a marble-topped table in the window of her salon looking out on a tiny pebbled garden. I learned the poems by heart, copied them down in notebooks, making pictures to illustrate my favorite pieces. I think she enjoyed working with me; I know I am grateful today for the warmth and intelligence of her instruction. I continued my lessons with her until we left Paris. Several times during the last year she remarked:

"If you wanted, Lydia, you could become an actress, a French actress. I could train you so that you could try for a Conservatoire prize [the most prestigious award for an aspiring actress]. You have the voice, perhaps later you will have the looks, but even if the looks are ordinary it will not matter. It is the voice and the talent—and even more the desire."

Then she would laugh and say: "A foolish dream, my child, for why should a young American girl want to go on the French stage? Believe me, it is not a life I would wish for you. No, in your great free country there will be great free things for you to do. Why break your heart here?"

I thought the talk very exciting and was pleased that she should think me good enough to study for the Conservatoire acting school, the goal of every French drama student, but it all seemed quite impossible and improbable when I told my family about it, and I am afraid they thought it a little foolish. As for Veenie, it confirmed her worst suspicions of the lady.

My brother's and my social lives were very limited. My parents did occasionally have parties for our contemporaries at which we organized games and went about the business in honest American fashion. We were sometimes invited to parties "for the young people" organized by friends of my parents who had children our age. These were usually not nearly as much fun. I really learned to dread the ones where we were expected to dance with rebellious young gentlemen while our elders sat against the wall and talked with each other. We thought they were talking about us, making critical remarks about our teeth, our figures, our clothes, all of which might have been improved upon. Perhaps they were, but more likely they were happily occupied with their own and their neighbor's grown-up affairs and scarcely noticed us at all. Actually my brother and I were very shy children and still felt out of place in this foreign and unfamiliar world of European juvenile society, so unlike anything we had known before.

"Did you ever get a terrible pain, Mother, right here, in your stomach, when you get to the door of a party?" my brother Selden asked one day. Even Mother, who was pretty and popular and enjoyed herself anywhere, understood what he meant, and ever after that pain has been called, in our family, the "party stomach ache." I have had it many times; it always hurts, and it is worse when it leaves your stomach and climbs into your throat so that whatever you say sounds smothered and foolish. The attacks grow more infrequent with age and experience, but they still can occur.

If we lacked some of the normal children's entertainments, there were special compensations. When the succession of royal visitors arrived in Paris, especially in spring, we would have front-row seats, a view of the processions from our own apartment windows as they passed down the Champs Elysées in front of our house. One time our own ex-president Theodore Roosevelt came to Paris as the guest of the French government, and Selden and I were taken by Father to see his reception at the station. Father brought us up to shake hands. The president leaned over and said:

"Little girl, I am delighted to meet you, for I made a trip to Panama on your father's ship. I have never forgotten him. He is one of the finest naval officers I have ever known."

Nor would I forget President Roosevelt in his frock coat, eyeglasses twinkling, his teeth shining white below his bushy brown mustache.

Evenings at home Father read to us—history books, James Fenimore Cooper, Sir Walter Scott, and Rudyard Kipling's *The Jungle Books, Kim,* and *Stalky & Co.* We had an hour of our own with him before dinner while Mother was dressing. I can still smell the spicy odor of his pipe tobacco, a special blend he made himself. He kept it in a jar on his smoking table along with the silver boxes for cigars and Turkish cigarettes, together with his pipes, straight ones, curved ones, some with amber stems, all with polished, glistening bowls of patterned wood.

Gradually I was growing from a little girl into a young lady, and the women of the family—Grandmother, Mother, and Veenie—decided in the fall of 1910, when I was fourteen, that something must be done about my figure and my complexion. After rebellious tears I was inserted into something called a "Ferris waist," a kind of junior corset of boned white muslin cloth, hideously uncomfortable and very deforming to the adolescent shape.

It was discovered I had a slight spinal curvature because of my having favored my broken leg the year before, so the doctor recommended corrective exercises at a gymnasium. To this place of torture Veenie took me twice a week. I hated everything about it, beginning with the appalling costume of light blue serge shirt and bloomers that was required of all clients. The attendants were Swedish or German, every one of them a complete sadist, and I detested being made to perform silly backbends and push-ups and horrid exercises with bar and dumbbells. At the end of the season my curvature was no better. "Lack of cooperation," the *diréctrice* said, but it is not much worse today, and I am still happy to think my spine could not be influenced by those nasty women.

My complexion required more drastic treatment, although its condition was normal for a young girl. At any rate I was sent off to a skin doctor who prodded and poked, and once stuck me with an electric needle, whereupon I had hysterics. He finally dismissed the case with a packet of lotions and salves with which I was to be anointed night and morning. But the skin doctor was nothing compared with the dentist who undertook to straighten my teeth. He must have learned something from accounts of the tortures of heretics by the fifteenth-century Inquisition, for he built a framework of gold wire in my mouth, attached top and bottom with elastic bands that snapped continually, and had me come to his office every few days to have the wires screwed tighter. It was probably essential that my teeth be straightened, and I suppose I should be grateful that the dentist brought my teeth into line, but happily other methods have been devised for the treatment of children today.

Now my hair was tied with black or brown ribbons instead of the light-colored ones at the nape of the neck, not on top like a child's, and my best dresses came from Mother's own dressmaker. I even had a pair of silk stockings, brown to match new shoes. My study schedule was fairly intense and I began to look more pasty and more in need of the skin specialist than ever, so it was evident that extra provision had to be made for outdoor exercise. Mother herself never walked a step if she could help it, Veenie was too busy, Grandmother too old, and the other children whom I knew were locked away in school.

A splendid solution was finally arrived at when Mother discovered a very nice, intelligent, and energetic woman, Mademoiselle Larronde, and together we explored old Paris three or four afternoons a week. On rainy days we did the museums, even the moldy, forgotten ones on the side streets, and some seventy years later, I take as much pleasure in visiting them as I do old friends, and I am certain I find them less changed.

5. *Sketches by Lydia Chapin, 1910.*

Another very important part of those last two years were my drawing lessons from M. Guimard, a respectable family man with a good studio in the bottom of his garden. To his studio I walked once a week, discreetly chaperoned by Veenie, who sat somewhat disapprovingly in the corner. M. Guimard was a kind man and a fair artist with an enthusiastic color sense that he indulged by painting large canvases of gypsy gatherings. We students drew and painted still-lifes of pots and flowers or of drapery thrown over a chair, and now and again M. Guimard employed a model for us or got one of his children to pose.

We had another splendid Christmas that winter. It was the last we would have in the apartment, as the lease was up in January and we were to move to a hotel until we returned to America in late February 1911, just three years after we first arrived in Paris. The grown-ups in the family were delighted at the prospect of going home, but Selden and I felt vaguely uneasy. I had been quite happy that winter in Paris, even though there was little time after lessons and walks for ordinary play or recreation. Living and growing up in Paris was an adventure in itself, and even the lessons were fun.

Selden and I had spent three years learning to live, if not with European children, then somewhat as European children, and we were not sure how we would fit in at home. I was fourteen, Selden eleven. My head was crammed with information I guessed would mean nothing to my friends in Erie. I could recite the names of the mistresses of the Anjou and Bourbon kings; I could recognize the difference between Regency and Louis XVI furniture; I could spot the cut of a Worth or Gallot gown. I could reel off by heart any amount of French poetry. My accent was impeccable, and my expression precocious.

I could translate the first passages in Caesar, do simple problems in algebra, write several paragraphs in affected nineteenth-century prose, show a satisfactory knowledge of Chaucer's tamer *Canterbury Tales,* Milton's "L'Allegro," Gray's "Elegy," and certain historical plays of Shakespeare. My drawing had improved, and, as I had a fancy to become an artist, I knew and enjoyed good paintings. The pictures in the Louvre and Luxembourg museums had become as familiar as the books on our library shelves. About music I was entirely ignorant. I had shown no musical promise as a small child. I was incapable of playing any instrument, so the family considered it useless for me to listen to other people perform. Neither Mother nor Grandmother cared for music, and the days of radio and good phonographs had not yet arrived.

As for outdoor sports, I was not good at tennis. I could swim ten breathless strokes, and, in spite of the afternoons spent at the Palais de Glace, I never managed more than a timid outer edge on my ice skates. I danced badly and I could never run very fast, but I was a tireless walker, especially if I was looking at things that interested me.

I was slightly shy, intensely self-conscious, and faintly superior in my own thinking, but I did have enough common sense to realize things might be difficult at home. I knew I would have to learn to get on with girls and boys of my own age while storing away my European experiences for my own private pleasure and enjoyment, but I was looking forward to seeing the United States again.

3

The United States and Paris, 1911–1913

Our trip home in 1911 was a March crossing, gray and dull. I spent long days on deck reading books from the ship's library and managed to survive the voyage without too many stomach qualms. We arrived in New York early one morning, brother Selden and I standing on deck with Father to see the Statue of Liberty as we sailed into the harbor. We were very excited. There would be relatives on the dock, New York cousins and friends. We realized that we were coming home, and we had no more thought for what we left behind as we watched Liberty holding aloft the torch of paradise.

Upon our arrival in New York we found dear cousin Nell Brown waiting for us despite the blustery weather. Next day we were again excited as our train passed the Erie city limits, but the town looked smaller and dirtier than we remembered, and there was smoke belching out of the tall stacks of the manufacturing plants. On the station platform relatives were waiting. It was a cold morning and there was still snow about. We had not seen proper snow for three years, and, though the drifts looked soot-covered, it made a real homecoming.

I found my friends quite changed. Many of the boys and girls I had known were off to boarding school. They came home for the Easter vacation, and I sat a little self-consciously on the sidelines, wondering what the mysterious quality they called "pep" could be, obviously a very desirable quality but not anything included in my Paris study program. Until I had really grown up myself and went back to live in Washington,

I was the friend and confidante of the "peppy" girls' beaus and admirers, the one "who would understand." Spotty young gentlemen spent long hours sitting on our front porch, pouring out their hearts, begging me to intercede with one or the other of the sixteen-year-old coquettes. It was all a little removed from the loves of Louis XV of France, but I found it passionately interesting.

The summers were long in Erie. Two or three of the boys had cars of their own and invited us to go riding, but they were the dashing ones and my own conservative family looked on them with disapproval. Others borrowed their families' cars, and we all piled into the back, each girl with a bulging food basket, bound for the shore of Lake Erie. There would be singing round a fire, and always two or three daring couples would walk alone up the beach, a conspicuous maneuver noticed by all. There was no strong drink, not even beer, though it was whispered that one of the older girls always ordered claret lemonade when invited by the boys to the country club. Most of the boys smoked cigarettes, but only one of us girls smoked. The country club on the edge of town was where we went to play a little tennis, but by and large we made our own entertainment, and it was cheerful and harmless and wholesome.

Soon after we returned from Europe Father was ordered to sea again. We felt very sorry to have him leave us, but he was given command of a battleship, the *Missouri,* whose caps we had worn on our arrival in Paris. His appointment was a great compliment, as his rank of commander would not ordinarily entitle him to a captain's command, and we were all very proud. Mother was away a great deal with Father that summer, as the fleet was based at Narragansett Bay, Rhode Island, but she returned in time to plan for our going off to boarding school in September.

Grandmother arranged a last dinner for us, all our favorite dishes, to be eaten before taking the train east to school. But even the chocolate ice cream with the marshmallow sauce in whirls on the special brown pottery plates we always used for that dessert could not make us forget that we were leaving home. We had left home often enough before, but this time, after we reached New York, Mother would put us on trains to go on alone.

Pullman travel in 1911 required a special technique. It was not considered quite nice for ladies to undress completely when they retired. There might be a wreck. Worse yet, a stranger, a man even, might mistake one's berth for his own, as they were in a line down both sides of the railroad car, distinguished only by the number on their heavy green curtains. Any number of embarrassing situations might occur, and ladies must be suitably protected against them. We therefore took off only the top layer of our clothing—dress and petticoat, not even our corsets—and donned a high-necked, long-sleeved garment of dark silk, buttoned from throat to foot, known as a Pullman wrapper. So encased, I found the nights hardly restful, especially as Grandmother warned me not to let the blankets touch my face.

Miss Porter's School in Farmington, Connecticut, was one of the oldest and finest girls' boarding schools in the country, and I am glad to see it is still flourishing. There were various groups in the school, but I did not seem to fit into any one of them. I was not unhappy or homesick, however. I was fond of my roommate Jane and enjoyed the friends she brought to our room. I made friends of my own, girls like myself who stood a little apart from the others either by choice or circumstance.

Perhaps one reason the social aspects of school life were not all that important was that I found outlets in study itself, in reading, in dramatics, and especially in my drawing and modeling. The library was for me a pleasant place of refuge. I discovered that the French *Illustration* magazine included a drama supplement with the text of the latest and often the naughtiest of the new Paris plays. These I smuggled back to my room and read with delicious pleasure.

We had little opportunity of meeting the opposite sex at Farmington aside from vacations. Weekends away were limited to one Saturday in the football season, and male callers were only permitted, by appointment, between three and five on Saturday afternoons in the fall and winter, never, never in the spring. If the weather allowed, girls and their callers took a walk, a very decorous and chilly stroll, returning for tea in one of the parlors of Main House. The headmistress's secretary, Miss Thomas, poured tea and then remained well within view at her desk in the outer hall.

I had no callers during my two years at school, for I had no admirers devoted or bold enough to face such an ordeal. What I could and did do was to write letters for some of my more inarticulate friends. Correspondence was more esteemed than today, and any girl whose daily mail included fat envelopes stamped "Yale Station" or "Harvard College, Cambridge, Mass." was apt to tell about them. She usually showed these letters to a privileged few and asked their advice about how best to answer them. Here my lively imagination made up for actual experience, and I acquired quite a reputation as a composer of light verse and titillating phrases.

I left Farmington without tears or regrets after my two years there, and yet, when I returned forty years later, I realized that it had meant more to me than I had known. In any event I was happy enough that June afternoon of 1913 to see my trunk and bags packed and strapped and then to slip into the big blue touring car in which Mother and Grandmother had so bravely motored east from Erie. Up and down the halls, in the parlors of Main House, everywhere, girls were giggling, crying, shouting. There were parents, aunts, uncles, a few courageous brothers and beaus, all scattered and scattering. Life that had been so ordered, so certain, was breaking up into colored bits like a kaleidoscope turning before our eyes. But it promised to be as bright and as unexpected as the pattern in the glass, and I could hardly wait to see what might happen next.

The summer of 1913 was gay enough. I began to feel like a young lady, and Mother bought me two pretty evening dresses at a New York Fifth Avenue shop. I was invited to pay a number of out-of-town visits. I went to Massachusetts, first to Cape Cod where a school friend's family, the Coolidges, owned a long stretch of beach on Buzzard's Bay.

Later my school roommate and I paid a visit to another friend at Manchester, Mass. I stayed so long my clean clothes ran out. I must have looked a rather creased and spotted sixteen-year-old, for I was too shy to inquire about laundry. I loved that North Shore of Massachusetts, with the sea beating against the cliffs and the waves rolling in over the Singing Beach at Manchester.

The climax of the summer was our family's visit to Newport, Rhode Island. We went to meet Father, who sailed into Newport harbor on his new ship, the *Wyoming.* We felt very proud of Father, the youngest captain in the navy and in command of its newest battleship. He looked so confident and successful, and Mother looked so pretty and happy in her white linen frock with her big straw hat and red parasol. It was a very gay few weeks. As the captain's daughter, I held the center of the stage and enjoyed it immensely. Father gave a dance for me just before the ship sailed. I wore my cherry dress and believed all the nice things attentive young ensigns said to me that night. They were very clean young men in starched white uniforms. They made a kind of game of it, one taking up where the other left off, so that I went home very happy with a whirling head.

In Erie I found things a little different that summer. I still liked sitting on the porch with Grandmother, for she was better company than anyone else in town, but some of the boys came calling of an evening. Those I had listened to the year before came to talk to me about myself as well as the other girls, and I felt I must be growing up.

Comparatively few girls went to college in 1913, and no women of my own family had ever been. Mother felt I was too young to leave school entirely, so there were long discussions as to what I should do. Father was leaving on the *Wyoming* for a European cruise, sailing in October, and Mother planned to meet him in Paris when he came there on leave. It seemed a good opportunity to take me along and to place me in school in Europe, a school where I could keep up my French.

It was therefore decided to send me to Miss Harris's in Paris, an exclusive establishment accommodating some fifteen or sixteen carefully chosen young American ladies. It was with a certain amount of cheerful conceit and mounting anticipation that I saw the time approaching when we would sail for Europe. We sailed for France in late September. A sailor's daughter, and later a sailor's wife, I never really liked the ocean. To look at from the shore, yes, or to dabble about in, but there is so much cold and dark that even a huge ship always seems lost and alone. I was glad, therefore, when at last we saw a streak of dim shoreline and it was time to pack and help Mother sort and label our belongings for the arrival at the French port of Le Havre.

It was a wet day when we docked, but it was fun to hear French again, even though the French was the complaining chatter of the porters demanding bigger tips from the tourists. At the train station in Paris there was more familiar confusion and shouting of porters. Mother was pleased to see old friends on the platform and grateful to one of them, Mr. Martin, for taking charge of our luggage and us, silencing the porters with waves of his silver-mounted umbrella, ordering them to strap our suitcases to the roof of his smart town car, arranging for the trunks to follow.

As we drove off, he said to Mother, "We have great plans, Grace. We have arranged everything. You give us the signal as soon as Lydia is in school."

Mother looked doubtfully at me, but I was anxious to see the school and not sorry when the time came for me to be delivered there three days later. As I spoke French as easily as English I had no formal classes to attend and spent most of my time working on my art with the teachers at school and in nearby studios. I did sit in on a History of Art course given by Mademoiselle Joos, the language teacher.

Mother remained in Paris awaiting Father's arrival, and on Thursdays and Sundays she came to take me out. One treat I always enjoyed was tea at the Ritz Hotel, sitting with Mother and Mrs. Martin at one of the little marble-topped tables in the garden corridor. Mrs. Martin knew all the names and gossip and could point out the fashionable folk and the demimondaines (defined as "ladies of equivocal morals" in my French dictionary, often the mistresses of rich and important persons). There was "Canada," a tall, sinuous, dark-haired woman wrapped in sables, who walked slowly between the tables, crossing her legs one over the other each time she stepped in her tight velvet dress. There was Mistinguette, ugly as a monkey with big eyes peering out from under a fringe of black hair. There was a Swede, pale and as icy cold as a snow maiden. There was Madame de C-, a crowd of lacquer-haired young men trailing after her. I tried to set some of these naughty and fascinating ladies down in my sketchbook. My schoolmates were vastly intrigued and I became quite a heroine with my pictures and stories.

The autumn wore on and pretty soon the U.S. fleet with Father's ship arrived in France and he came on leave to Paris. He and Mother were very busy, but they took me about with them, and I felt very grand to be walking out with my handsome parents. I felt even grander when I could introduce them to the girls at school.

Early in December Mother left for home to meet Father in New York when he arrived back from the Mediterranean. It would be hard for me to spend Christmas away from the family, but she planned that I would go to Switzerland with a party of girls from school. Skiing had not yet become fashionable, but there would be skating and tobogganing, and we all looked forward to the holidays.

However, one of the school directors called me into her room late one afternoon. She looked serious as she asked me to sit down beside her. She spoke to me in English.

"Mrs. Martin has just telephoned. I am afraid I have bad news for you, Lydia. Your father is very ill in New York and your mother wants you to come home at once. She is there in New York with him. Mrs. Martin tells me that her husband has made reservations for you on the French ship *Savoie* sailing on the twentieth from Le Havre. We both think you should have someone with you, and if it suits your mother we will send Miss Gardner.

"You must be brave, Lydia. Later when things are better you can come back to us. You must not worry. We must hope for the best."

Worry, hope. I could scarcely grasp what she had said. It seemed too unreal, too impossible. Even when she went on to speak of the details they meant nothing to me, nothing except that I must see Mrs. Martin, hear what she could tell me. If I was really to go home, there must be a great deal to do, clothes to be packed, tickets and money to be arranged for.

Mrs. Martin came, red-eyed and fashionably dressed. She meant to be kind, but there was little she could add to what I had been told. Mr. Martin, she assured me, would make all the steamship arrangements. I thanked Mother's friend. I am afraid my manner was stiff and strange, but I felt numb and bewildered.

Into the trunks went my pretty new clothes, my books. In a suitcase I put the gay little packages Mother had left for my Christmas. I would have had them go into the trunks with the rest, but a nice friend said no, even if I had to spend Christmas at sea, it must still be Christmas.

I cannot remember leaving or even how we reached Le Havre. Miss Gardner was a young woman, a secretary and an accountant. She was kindly enough, but I had never had much to do with her, and no one now seemed very real or close. I felt somehow as if she were dim and vague as a shadow.

We got aboard the ship. We had not sailed yet when the steward brought a cablegram to Miss Gardner's cabin.

"Tell Lydia her father died this morning."

I sat down beside Miss Gardner and took the cablegram in my hand. I sat there for minutes, and I can remember the engines starting up and the noise and shouting as we backed away from the dock. Then I went to my own cabin.

And during the night and next day I grieved in anger. I thought my faith in God and right and goodness itself was destroyed. I had never known sorrow before, I had never even seen sorrow. To have my father die, my father, so handsome, so clever, so alive. I remembered what President Roosevelt had said: "The finest naval officer I have ever known."

How could a just and wise God take my fifty-year-old father, so beloved by his family, so esteemed by his service and his country? And what a waste, what a cruel, senseless waste. There must be others, old men, sick men, foolish, wicked men, any of them could be spared, but not my father.

Each day in that week's voyage seemed something to get through, and each night only a period of waiting in my narrow bunk until the morning. Miss Gardner made a brave effort on Christmas, and we each drank a glass of tepid champagne from the half bottle the captain sent round with his compliments. I brought my packages into her cabin, undid the ribbons, and then quite suddenly I cried.

In New York dear cousin Nell Brown, Mother's favorite relative and closest friend, was waiting for me, and there was my brother Selden, tall and pale, looking very grown up, beside her. It was so good to be with Cousin Nell, very like Mother herself and so understanding of a hurt, bewildered child. She took care of me that day, bought me some simple black clothes and a hat, and with her husband, Cousin Hunter, put us on the train for Erie that night. At the station in Erie Mother was waiting in the car. Mother, who loved gay, pretty clothes, sat swathed in heavy black, a thick crepe veil over her widow's bonnet. Seeing her so strangely still and quiet I knew it must all be true, that it was not a dreadful, frightening dream from which I would wake and find myself in my bed at Miss Harris's school. And yet, as we had not been there for the funeral, the whole thing was still very hard for me to believe and impossible for me to accept. Father was so often away it seemed he must be off on a cruise, that each mail would bring letters from him, and that he would return to tell us of his adventures.

It had been a terrible shock for Mother, and I often felt it was a shock from which she never recovered, that her life was cracked as a vase is cracked, only appearing whole to the outward eye. Mother lived twenty-eight years after Father's death, always a happy, cheerful companion to her family and friends, but she never wore colors again, and she never ceased to mourn the man she loved so dearly.

As there seemed little for me to do in Erie, and as Mother felt Father would have wanted me to continue my studies in Paris, it was arranged for me to return to France in early January. Mother and Grandmother were so very patient and thoughtful. They saw to everything and made certain the Erie household ran as usual, relatives and friends came and went, and we talked about ordinary things. If we had not been wearing those black clothes, we might have persuaded ourselves that nothing had happened.

Everyone tried to be kind when I got back to Paris, and it was good to be with the other girls, all of whom were friendly and sympathetic. Now that I was there I was determined to do well. I felt on my honor to get as much as possible out of the winter. I was wiser than I realized, for it would be twenty-one years before I returned to France again. But in that early spring of 1914 I gave very little thought to the future as I walked to and from the art studio each morning. The sights and sounds and the demands of the present were quite enough.

My art teacher approved my taking modeling to help with my drawing, so I went three afternoons a week to work with a fine artist and very nice woman who taught me the magic of clay, of feeling shape grow beneath my fingers and the structure and substance that underlay surface and color. I enjoyed the modeling lessons and respected all she tried to teach about the integrity of workmanship.

"You must not cheat," she said. "When you are molding a human form, you are too near the Creator himself."

The days were scarcely long enough, there was so much to see, so much to learn, and evenings there were lessons to study, books to read. I had begun to enjoy French poetry, but my new teacher put me through my paces once a week with an hour's diction lesson in the back salon. He paced up and down in front of me, a furious little man, while I stood clutching a small handkerchief in a perspiring hand. He was a hard taskmaster, especially toward a pupil who knew French and thought she knew more than she did. He was very good for my vanity and very good for my accent. Over and over he would have me repeat a single line:

"Remember to use your head at the same time as your voice and your heart and, above all, Mademoiselle, *simplifiez*!"

Good advice for self-conscious, pretentious seventeen-year-old.

It was fine weather that spring. The chestnut trees bloomed early, and the awnings went up over the sidewalk cafés. In Paris itself and in the world outside Paris and outside France, much was happening. We saw few newspapers—there seemed to be no time to read them—but even if we had seen them we could scarcely have understood the meaning of the incidents piling up like thunderclouds on the horizon. School in Paris ended in mid-May 1914, and it was arranged for me to travel home with a friend and her family.

One evening at sea there was an iceberg alert. We got out of bed, dressed in our warmest clothes, took our life preservers down from the racks in our cabins, then waited for instructions. The engines stopped, and there was an ominous stillness. We sat huddled in our coats, waiting for word of some kind. We were very frightened. Mr. Lea, my friend's father, poured out a small drink of brandy for each of us. Long, very long minutes passed. Finally a knock on the door. Danger over. Thankfully we undressed and climbed back into bed.

Owing to relief and the brandy, we slept until bright sunshine shone through our portholes, and the rest of the voyage passed off quietly. This was before radar had been invented, so a ship had nothing but sailors with telescopes to warn of an iceberg nearby. If a ship reported icebergs in the vicinity at night, the prudent thing was to alert the passengers, stop the ship, and hope it could get out of the way before some drifting iceberg hit it. The ship's captain would have been especially cautious in this case, as the ship was in the same area where the *Titanic* had sunk after hitting an iceberg two years before.

4

At Home in the United States, 1914–1938

I was glad to get back to my friends in Erie, Pennsylvania, for a relaxing, carefree summer. I visited school friends in various nice places. It was as I was leaving Erie for Newport, Rhode Island, to stay with a Farmington classmate in late June that I read in the paper of the assassination of an Austrian archduke in Sarajevo, but it meant very little to me. Excitable Bulgars and Serbs were always flourishing pistols, even throwing bombs under royal carriages, and there seemed enough grand dukes in Europe to go round. The death of this particular duke, however, introduced serious complications, and by the time I was back in Erie in early August the First World War had begun.

It was hard to think of France at war, even though I had been brought up on talk of *La Revanche* (The Revenge) for France's defeat by Germany in 1871. I tried to picture the soldiers marching toward the front, more like a parade of brother Selden's lead soldiers than war, the German kaiser stiff and proud at the head of his stiff and proud troops, straight out of the paintings of military maneuvers.

Those German troops marched across Belgium, sacred treaties were broken, and England came to the defense of France. Naturally we at home were violently pro-Ally against the Germans. So were all our friends. Especially in the east of the United States it was fashionable to be pro-Ally, and a few impetuous young men, elegantly educated abroad, sailed to join their British or French comrades in the fight.

Obviously I could not return to Europe that fall, but I was very anxious to go on with my art studies. Mother was puzzled as to where to send me. New York City seemed full of danger for an impressionable young woman just turning eighteen. The stories of life and love in Greenwich Village, where most artists lived and worked, were alarming to careful parents, and it was thought imprudent to subject me to such an atmosphere. I had been staying on Cape Cod in Massachusetts with my good friend Isabel Coolidge from Boston, and it was her mother who suggested a solution. Why not send me to study at the Boston Art Museum? She knew a very nice woman, Mrs. Dodge, who took two to three girls into her house in Boston each winter. It was agreed, therefore, that I would board with Mrs. Dodge, and I arrived in Boston in late September.

Life in Boston was a contrast to the Paris scene, and my art classes under a certain Phillip Hale were academic and dry. Phillip Hale could draw and he could teach others to draw, yet if they lost the spark of the divine fire in doing so he would still have felt it a proper sacrifice. Good artists rather than great artists emerged from his classes. I only wish he could have let us enjoy ourselves.

Outside the class I was studying life, however. For the first time I was allowed out alone in a city. I could buy my own books, my own clothes, I could ride on trolley cars and subways, I could go to a matinee concert with a friend, to the movies even. I had begun to dream and to brood about the rights of man. My heart bled for the downtrodden masses, so that when a socialist rally was announced I decided to attend with other students from the Museum School. The light of battle shone in our eyes, but the meeting proved very tame; the speakers were a succession of dreary, uncombed men and women, and even the Red Flag ornamenting the platform and the audience's off-tune singing of the stirring socialist anthem, "The Internationale," could not keep my enthusiasm alight. I came away still full of pity for the downtrodden but wishing their champions were a gayer, cleaner lot.

The Boston Public Library offered safer scope for my sympathies and emotions. I read from the works of the famous Russian writers Chekhov and Dostoevsky. I even took seven lessons in Russian at the Berlitz School. I learned to say "brown hat and red pencil" in Russian, and to write the alphabet, but that was enough, for soon after I met up with a pale young man who initiated me into the elegant subtleties of the British authors Oscar Wilde and George Moore, and I spent my evenings copying late-nineteenth-century drawings of clowns at wine-spilled banquet tables. The pale young man brought some Harvard friends to call. Mrs. Dodge let me give them tea, and we talked earnestly and knowingly of things we knew little of.

All this while, across the ocean, the war went on its dreary, mud-stained, bloodstained way. Except for headlines and battle diagrams we knew very little about it. The first hopes of easy victory had faded, and the armies had dug in opposite each other in muddy trenches in the French countryside. Our president, Woodrow Wilson, promised us neutrality and what proved to be an uneasy peace. Throughout large sections of the United States partisan fights sprang up where there were solid blocks of pro-German and anti-interventionist sentiment, but the bulk of the American people were on the side of the Allies, especially after German submarines starting sinking merchant and passenger ships on their way to France and England.

Could we remain outside the struggle? We hoped so, and those who knew the status of our military establishment hoped so. Only the wise and the fearful really thought we would be involved in Europe. We were sympathetic, but the struggle still seemed very far away, and when I went home to Erie in the summer of 1915, I enjoyed myself for three long, carefree months before returning to Boston in the autumn.

Boston debutante balls were a trial for the shy, plain, unknown girls like myself, but the rest of life was full of interest, and working and learning and playing were great fun. I took modeling lessons from a young and talented Jewish sculptress, and I was glad to feel my fingers in clay again. In spite of the charm of pure line and the fascination of color, I believe sculpture brings a greater sensation of creation than any other art. I liked the solid satisfaction of expanding forms and measured dimensions. I did not sell any pieces, but in the first few years of my marriage I did several bas-reliefs and even a small statue or two of friends' children.

I walked in a woman's suffrage parade. We were asked to assemble on lower Beacon Street in Boston, several hundred of us headed by the indomitable ladies who had organized the demonstration. We were given sashes to pin across our breast, "Votes for Women," and hardy volunteers from each group carried banners and flags. We felt triumphant, if a trifle footsore, so much so that we were out parading again six weeks later, this time in favor of military preparedness. More and more the war seemed to be our fight even though the politicians and the Middle West shouted for peace at any price.

One day at lunch in 1916, three friends and I evolved a plan for the summer. Why not go, all four of us, to Provincetown on Cape Cod, to spend six weeks studying painting with a local artist? Our parents were consulted and gave willing consent, anything to distract us from going overseas to hold hospital basins or distribute doughnuts to Allied soldiers in the trenches.

Provincetown of those days was a kind of bohemian Greenwich Village by the Sea, but our bohemianism was distinctly amateur. We checked in at the art school in a big barn on a hill above the town. There were thirty or more regular students, girls and men, not too many men and none that looked overly attractive. In any case we were there to study art, not the opposite sex. If the men's hair had not been quite so long, their shoulders broader, and their voices deeper, we might have felt differently.

We worked hard. We grew bolder, our colors grew brighter, and we dared to forget the academic line and to dapple sunshine across the model's face, golden specks of pure, luminous paint. We looked fairly dappled ourselves, sunburned, healthy, and gaily untidy. It was all a good and gay time, and I was sorry to pack up and go home to Erie and more conventional surroundings.

I found Mother had come to a great and firm decision. Fearing lest I grow too single-minded a career woman, too wrapped up in my art and too unaware of the normal social aspects of life, she determined to leave Erie for the winter and to take an apartment in Washington where she would bring me out in society. I was just twenty, two years past the usual debutante age, but this was no handicap in Washington, where the eligible men were considerably more mature than those found in a Boston stag line.

"All very well," she said, "for you to become a serious artist, but you should see more of the world, the social world, before making your choice."

I made feeble protest but Mother was determined. My Provincetown tales convinced her that she was doing the right thing in showing me the world that she had known, and in showing me to that world. Perhaps she may have had an intimation that the world would change, that the darkening war clouds would bring storms to shatter and destroy the peace of ordered society.

We arrived in Washington to a warm welcome from our former servant, Mary Hawkins, who presented the other two black servants, Jenny the chambermaid and Crockett the butler, very elegant in a striped waistcoat, which he always wore with his livery. I felt as if I were Young Missee come back to the old plantation, and Jenny and Crockett were perfectly cast in the role of old retainers.

A friend of Mother's, Miss Squier, now a social secretary—talented, well connected, well informed—took my launching in hand. She was an old hand at the business but confided to Mother that she was considerably relieved to find her subject so attractive, well dressed, and well mannered.

In those days, and earlier, it was usual for young women of "society" to marry men a few years older than they. The parents or guardians of eighteen-year-old girls held debutante parties at which they introduced us to these somewhat older men, who had seen us, if at all, only as little girls or pimply teenagers. *Debutante,* the feminine of the French word for "starting on a career," fitted our introduction into the social scene and marriage, considered the only appropriate "career" for most of us at the time.

Debutante parties were normally held at Christmastime and in early June, when the girls' schools and colleges were on vacation and the men's work lighter. There would be several teas, dinners, and dances during the season, at which we could become familiar enough with each other to go out together, usually with at least one other couple, on more informal excursions—concerts, walks, skating, picnics, even small dinners. Eventually, it was hoped, this familiarity would lead to marriage with an "appropriate" man.

The evening of our first debutante dinner the chaperones came first, an exceedingly attractive young couple from Boston. Our tutor thought their background and his position as junior counselor in the Treasury Department gave the intellectual tone that fitted in with my own slightly bluestocking, faintly intellectual approach. In Paris, our poetry teacher had taught us to hold a small handkerchief in one hand during a difficult recitation. I held one now, a very damp one, crumpled in my left palm, but gradually things eased and I found myself talking to a big, jolly young man, a military aide at the White House; a short, hearty naval lieutenant from the Secretary of the Navy's yacht; a pale-faced, gentlemanly southerner who emerged each evening from a bank vault to oblige elegant hostesses; and a junior British Embassy officer with a thick lock of hair falling over his highborn forehead.

One admonition that Mother gave me has served me in good stead through long years of party-going: "Never stay so long you wear out your good time. Go home while you are still enjoying yourself."

Good advice, applicable to life as well. And I did enjoy those Washington dances, far more than I had enjoyed the Boston balls with their stag lines of contemptuous sophomores. These "older men" of twenty-six and thirty took a kinder and more relaxed view than did the sophomores toward the idea that a girl must have a new dancing partner every two minutes. Indeed, if a girl could talk as well as dance, they seemed quite happy to spend some time with her.

I was twenty, older than most of the other girls, and grew to feel quite superior at these parties. No such feelings, however, when I was invited to formal dinners given by Mother's friends to spice up the party with a couple of young girls and youngish men. A young man or two were provided for us, but we were not to sit in corners with them; we must make our manners to the older people, our mission being to listen, to watch, and to grace the party. These parties I truly enjoyed.

Across the Atlantic the war had been going on for nearly two years, but there were the America Firsters who wanted no part of any U.S. involvement. There were others who told of German atrocities, the tragedy of Belgians under German occupation, and the heart-rending ordeal of trench warfare.

In June Mother and I left again for Erie where I rocked on the front porch with Grandmother and found things very tame after the excitement of my Washington season. When we returned to Washington in the fall of 1916, the war news from Europe was disturbing and the Germans seemed invincible. The sinking the year before of the passenger liner *Lusitania*, with numbers of Americans aboard, had shocked many people, but it was not until early 1917, when Germany announced unrestricted submarine warfare against all shipping, including our own, that opinion hardened.

Finally, on April 6, 1917, America declared war on Germany. Mother and I went down to the Capitol and stood in the crowd as President Woodrow Wilson spoke from the steps reading the Proclamation of War. It was a solemn moment. The crowd was very still. Then as Wilson turned away there was a great cheer, though a woman standing beside me was shaken with sobs.

It was still hard to believe we were actually at war, for as the days wore on life seemed much as before. As I was recovering one Sunday afternoon in late 1917 from an attack of German measles (rubella), known with mistaken patriotism at the time as Liberty measles, my Potomac School friend Catherine Harlow came to call with her current naval beau and another young officer, Lieutenant Alan Goodrich Kirk, stationed outside Washington at the Naval Ordinance Proving Ground in Indian Head, Maryland. I found Lieutenant Kirk especially charming and was sorry he seemed prematurely bald. He told his friend, Catherine's beau, that he found me charming but thought my dress hideously unbecoming.

On next meeting his hair had grown. It was blonde and there seemed to be plenty of it. I wore a different dress and we got on very well together. The four of us met on odd weekends through the winter, although not too often, for Lieutenant Kirk's job was a demanding one and the trip to Washington nearly three hours by boat up the river.

I learned later that the Kirks, too, had been early settlers, Quakers originally from England who came to Pennsylvania in the early 1700s. During the Revolution a young Roger Kirk had left his family home to join the fighting in the Pennsylvania militia. His descendant, the father

6. *Lydia and a friend, Atlantic City, 1918.*

of my future husband Alan Kirk, had a wholesale grocery business in Philadelphia and lived with his wife and family in a fine old Victorian house in Beverly, New Jersey, on the banks of the Delaware River. Alan had followed the example of his uncle, Admiral Caspar F. Goodrich, entering the Naval Academy at sixteen as a member of the class of 1909.

Even though Alan and I saw each other several times during the winter of 1917–18, it was only in May 1918 that I took the daring step of proposing we call each other by our first names. A house party he and some friends organized in Annapolis later that month brought us much closer together. My thank-you note was quite effusive: "What a glorious

7. Lydia Chapin Kirk after her marriage, with her grandmother, her mother, and her daughter Marian, in Erie, 1919.

time we had. . . . Alan Kirk beside me . . . we thought very hard of each other and our hearts pounded under wet bathing suits in a thoroughly ridiculous and very exciting manner."

In June things seemed to be moving quite fast, too fast for a shy twenty-one-year-old, and I went off with Mother to Erie for the summer. The separation did not slow matters, however. When Alan came up to Erie for a house party over the Fourth of July holiday, he proposed, and I accepted. I was in that happy state typical of young women in my position, writing him a day or two afterward, "The house is so curiously empty and the only thing really full and overflowing is my heart—and there is no one there but you."

Alan was also happy. He wrote a friend in early August: "I am walking on air, in rosy glowing clouds, in a blissful, heaven-sent haze. . . . She loves me. . . . We are to be married next month. . . . I am as happy as I never thought I would be, and life was never sweeter." I was marrying a dedicated naval officer, however. The letter continued: "I almost went to sea last week . . . turned me down because of too much rank. . . . What a shame. . . . Lydia wants me to go to sea, not at once, but soon, so she does not tie me to the shore!"

[Here the author's manuscript breaks off and does not pick up again until her time in California in 1937–38. We do have a few letters that give occasional insights into her activities and feelings, but I have had to fill in the intervening years.

My parents' engagement was announced on August 19, 1918, and the wedding was on September 14 of that year. After a brief honeymoon in upper New York State, they moved into my father's quarters at the Indian Head Proving Ground in Maryland. In May 1919, Father was ordered to sea, and Mother, then seven months pregnant, moved into her mother's apartment in Washington and went with her to Erie for the summer. She wrote my father brave letters about missing him, and on July 6, 1919, had her baby, my sister Marian, in his absence. He did get a few days off in mid-August, and they spent a couple of weeks together in Philadelphia while his ship was in port there, leaving the baby in the care of a nurse in Erie.

There is some evidence from the letters that Mother was having to adjust her spending habits. It was hard at first, but as the years went on she became very good at frugality and passed it on to all of us children. Sea duty took its toll on her morale during 1919, but in early spring 1920 Father was transferred to Washington as executive officer of the presidential yacht *Mayflower.* A tour at the Navy Department followed, so the couple had four years together there, during which time my sister Deborah was born (June 26, 1922). Mother, remembering her art lessons in Paris, did some statues of friends' children during this period, but then dropped it.

Next Father was sent to the battleship *Maryland* on the West Coast, and he and Mother took a house in Long Beach, California. Mother

8. Alan and Lydia Kirk, Washington, 1920.

was appalled at the idea of moving to California, a place that she knew nothing about and far from her mother and the familiarity of the East Coast. The *Maryland* spent many months at sea during the two years they were in Long Beach, and Mother apparently felt a bit alone and adrift. "Cried a lot," recalls my older sister.

Mother's view of Long Beach at the time is reflected in the one brief journal entry we have. Headed "Long Beach," part of it reads as follows:]

Except for the floral display, Long Beach is the final socialist utopia. It is every bit as interesting as I have always imagined Utopia to be! Here

9. *Sculpture by Lydia, 1921.*

we have Liberty, Equality, and Fraternity, the only condition being that by municipal ordinance no man may kiss his wife on the street. I do not think Long Beach husbands will find that a deprivation.

No one by thought, word, or deed differs from anyone else in this land of plenty. The schools and libraries are full enough—"Have you got a copy of one of them there Tarzan books?" And the newspapers appear every half-hour, hysterical shrieks in pink, orange, and blue. If England declared war on the United States, you would find it on page seventeen beneath nut soufflé—a dainty dish for Thursday's hostess—although on the front page, "War veteran kills wife and child and hides bodies in trunk of car." These people are all entirely self-sufficient. We may not be interested in them. They are less so in us.

[In 1926 Father was again assigned to Washington. My parents, probably with help from Mother's mother, bought a nice house in Georgetown, 3011 P Street, for thirty thousand dollars, and spent two happy years there. Three years followed at the Naval War College in Newport, Father a student for a year and then a faculty member. With the Depression and consequent reduction in navy pay and disappearance of dividends from Mother's family's Erie City Iron Works, they had to move into a smaller house, known in the family as "the old squeeze," made more so by my birth on November 2, 1930.

Another year in Washington followed, the couple this time living with my grandmother in her house owing to shortage of funds. Father was away a certain amount, as he was assigned to a destroyer that cruised up and down the East Coast, but Mother was with her mother, in a city that Mother knew well and where she had many friends. It was a happy time, though promotions were slow and a future in the peacetime navy uncertain.

In 1932 Father was once again transferred to Long Beach for two years, but this time my parents took a house in Pasadena, then a pretty town with streets, houses, and people more like those back east. Mother liked Pasadena and made a number of friends there. Her initial apprehension, however, is illustrated by her Christmas card from the first year. As sent out, it was a drawing of the whole family in front of a small hut, Mother in a grass skirt, Marian pounding corn in an earthen bowl by her side. The caption, in French, reads, "The Kirk family, shipwrecked on the coast of California among savages and wild beasts, sends you greetings." The initial version, with the same caption, was of a group of monkeys in a tree, each with the face of one of their new California friends. Some of these friends saw the sketch and laughed about it, but Mother was fond of them by this time and decided to send out a less personal version.

As Father was typically at sea on a cruise all summer, the rest of us would return east until fall. We spent the time with Mother's mother in the family's newly built house in Black Point, Connecticut, a quiet resort on Long Island Sound, not far from the Griswold family property

10. Lydia's Christmas card of her family in "primitive" California, 1932.

in Old Lyme. In 1934 Father was again transferred to Washington, and my parents spent two quite socially active years there, living at my grandmother's once more. In 1936 Father was given command of a light cruiser in the Pacific and returned to California for three years, first at La Jolla and then Long Beach, with summers for Mother and us children at Black Point.

Mother's manuscript now resumes with a brief description of this second time in Long Beach, in 1937–38:]

11. The Kirks on USS Milwaukee, *California, 1936. Front, from left, unknown woman, Roger, Deborah, Alan, and Lydia Kirk. Official U.S. Armed Forces photograph.*

In spite of dismal memories of Long Beach in the early twenties, this time I enjoyed living there, close to the California naval base at San Pedro. Alan, attached to the staff of the commanding admiral, could come ashore each night his ship was in port. Apart from the naval families, living as we did to be near our men, I had no friends in Long Beach, but Pasadena, where we had earlier spent two happy years, was only thirty miles away. Now, with daughter Marian in college in the east and Deborah entered as a boarder at the Bishop School in La Jolla, only seven-year-old Roger would be living with us.

We gave and went to parties with our naval friends. The Long Beach library was surprisingly good considering the cultural level of Long Beach citizens. The shelves were full of treasures and, with comparatively empty days while my two men were away—Alan at sea and

Roger at day school—I had plenty of time for reading. I found books too for Roger when he came home in the afternoon, all the old favorites to be read aloud before supper. Every ten days or so I drove up to Pasadena to see old friends, to lunch and play tennis, and among the navy wives in Long Beach itself we exchanged informal luncheons and tea parties.

One ladies' lunch I gave occurred on the day British King Edward VIII broadcast his speech announcing his abdication to marry an American divorcee, Wallis Simpson. Several of the women had known Mrs. Simpson when she was the wife of an American naval officer. We clustered around the radio; a few were in tears while I sat stony-eyed.

Finally one lady asked, "What do you think will be the end of these two people?"

"Quite clearly," I answered, "the back pages of *Vogue* fashion magazine."

How right I was, though some of the guests may have thought me hardhearted.

After a short, pleasant summer in Black Point, Roger and I returned to Long Beach. Alan's sea duty was coming to an end and new orders would be issued when the fleet returned from the usual post-Christmas cruise. We made the most of our last months in California, giving a farewell dance for our naval and Pasadena friends, a very fine party spiced by a glorious punch, which led one couple to drive the thirty miles back to Pasadena in second gear.

As there seemed little point in remaining in California while Alan was away at sea on the usual winter cruise, Roger and I left right after Christmas. In Washington my two daughters met us on the station platform, full of accounts of Christmas parties and plans for the last week of vacation. Mother had sent her car and chauffeur down, and we drove to our rented apartment, where we were welcomed by an old chambermaid of Mother's come to oblige "Miss Lydia." It was good to have my three children together again, even if for a short time. After several winters in California I enjoyed catching up with old friends, lunching and dining out, although I was eager to know what the future held for Alan.

PART TWO

London, 1939–1940

5

On the Threshold of War in England, 1939

There had been a hint of an appointment abroad, and, sure enough, Alan wrote from California in March 1939 of his assignment as U.S. naval attaché in London, the top naval officer on the American Embassy staff. He would be returning to Washington in April, and we would probably leave for England in late May or early June. This was exciting news, especially as it was followed by the word that he had been promoted to captain.

Alan's assignment to London was far from a routine one, and a real compliment. Another war by Britain and France against Germany seemed very possible. While the United States had no intention of becoming involved, the First World War had shown how hard it was to stay out. Even in the absence of war, good information on what was going on in London naval circles would be needed.

Roger and I would of course go with him to London, and we decided that when school and college closed the two girls would join us, Marian for the summer and Deborah for a year before going off to college. Meanwhile there was much to be discussed and arranged, what to take with us for a stay of probably two or three years. We would be renting a furnished house or apartment in London but wanted enough of our own belongings to make it homelike.

Another exciting piece of news was the word that we were to be included in the annual, and very formal, presentation of diplomats, aristocratic debutantes, and selected others to King George VI and Queen

Elizabeth in Buckingham Palace in early July. We had to buy appropriate dresses for me and for Marian and Deborah, as both girls were to be presented. Meticulous directions were forwarded from our embassy. I felt like a bride ordering her trousseau. My mother was just as excited about our purchases as the rest of us. She emptied her jewel case, insisting I take her pearls, a large opal pendant on a diamond chain, diamond clips, and a matching wide diamond bracelet. "Short of a tiara you can wear this in your hair," she said.

The time to leave grew closer. Then one morning what should happen but Roger came down with the mumps. No question about it, short of putting his head in a bag, he would never be allowed aboard ship. At that time there was no inoculation for mumps, so everyone who had not had it was vulnerable. There was no way a ship could allow someone with the disease to board and possibly infect other passengers. Alan would have to sail without us. We would have to wait three weeks while the wretched disease took its course and our ship, the *America*, returned to New York, as U.S. Government personnel were required to use American flag transportation.

The day finally arrived when Roger and I with bag and baggage took the train for New York. We went to the World's Fair there, an exhausting experience but highly satisfactory as far as Roger was concerned, and next day got safely aboard the *America*. Happily the voyage was a smooth one, only a few quavers for me. Roger proved a fine sailor, and the days at sea passed quickly.

A couple of hours before reaching the British port of Southampton the ship stopped to pick up the pilot who had come to guide us to the dock. We were on deck watching the proceedings when who should come up the gangway but Alan. It was a joyful meeting. He had wangled a place on the pilot's launch to sail into port with us. Alan said his car and chauffeur would be waiting on the dock, and we would start at once for London. I would find our temporary lodgings in St. James's Street in central London very comfortable. Meanwhile he had lined up an apartment for me to see in nearby Lowndes Square, hoped I would like it.

The ship edged up the channel into port. The stewards gave precedence to our luggage, a courtesy often extended to foreign embassy personnel, so we were put ashore very promptly, wafted through customs, and were soon ensconced in the naval attaché's impressive limousine. I was introduced to Tims the chauffeur, large, stout, and competent, and we were on our way to London. I told Alan I was glad the lodgings had worked out. I had written ahead to a recommended travel agency with the reassuring name of "Why Worry London" and, in addition to living accommodations, asked them to provide a temporary governess for an active American boy of eight.

"They'll probably think he'll wear an Indian suit with feathers in his hair and give war whoops," I said. Anyway they seemed to have done the necessary, as Alan told me a Miss Catherine Robson from New Zealand would call to be approved for the position the day after our arrival. We enjoyed our ride up through the ever-blooming green of the English countryside, stopping for lunch at a roadside inn. This was long before England's high-speed motorways. Narrow roads wound through towns and villages, and the eighty-mile trip took us almost four hours.

Next morning Alan went off to his office at the American Embassy in Grosvenor Square. I did some unpacking in our pleasant rooms in fashionable St. James's Street, then Roger and I walked out into the June sunshine. We were here at last, here in London. At three-thirty our bell rang and I opened the door to confront a tall, strapping young woman whose appearance made it clear this formidable person was truly "Why Worry's" idea of a suitable companion for an active American boy. As we talked I liked her. The accent was pretty terrible, but she had a nice face and looked competent and trustworthy. I explained the position would be a temporary one. I needed someone to be with my son until we were settled in permanent quarters.

Catherine Robson, accent or no, turned out to be a treasure. No question of being temporary, she remained with us until we left England. From the first she and Roger became warm friends, and in the days to come she proved resourceful, a valiant help in good times and also in later times that were dark and anxious.

With Roger happily occupied with Miss Robson, now known as Robbie, I went off with Alan to inspect the Lowndes Square apartment, found it attractively furnished, pleasant sunny rooms, the kitchen modern and well-equipped. We expected to move in the end of the month in order to be in residence before our two girls arrived.

One of my first duties was to leave cards on the American Ambassador and Mrs. Joseph Kennedy, whose twenty-two-year-old son later became President John Kennedy. Within a few days we were invited to a reception at the ambassador's residence, where we met some of Alan's colleagues and a sprinkling of English dignitaries.

As time passed we were kept busy lunching and dining with friends and friends of friends to whom we had been given letters of introduction by our friends. This was a custom of the time and usually resulted in an invitation to lunch or dinner and the possibility of a real friendship, or at least acceptance as a member of "society." It sounds quaint, but it was actually a great help to us.

One noon we attended a large luncheon at the luxurious Claridge's Hotel where the prime minister, Neville Chamberlain, spoke. He was still optimistic about the success of the September 1938 Munich Conference, where he thought he had bought peace with Hitler by agreeing to some of Hitler's demands for territory in Czechoslovakia. Although Hitler's March 1939 takeover of the rest of that country had proved this expectation false, many still hoped that move would satisfy him and avert a terrible war. Chamberlain was one of these, though he must have known there was real danger.

Optimistic Chamberlain might be, but Alan and I were hardly reassured by his speech or his personality, kindly but weak, and we left feeling slightly uneasy. With good reason, for the next day the newspapers published alarming reports of new moves by Hitler. That evening Alan came home looking very grave.

"Too bad," he said. "I am afraid that apartment won't do. There's been disturbing news and I'm convinced war may come sooner or later. I think we would be wise to look for a house in the country, near London of course so I could commute, but if German bombers come over I do not want my family here in the city."

I was appalled. "War. You can't mean it."

"I hope I'm wrong, but better to be safe than sorry."

He took out a map from his briefcase, spread it on the dining table. "If they do come it would probably be in this or that direction, but just here, to the West along the Thames, might be all right. Mind you, I don't think anything will happen immediately, maybe it won't happen at all, but let's not take chances. Hitler's too unpredictable."

Still shaken I asked, "Would you rather we went home? How about the girls?"

"Don't panic. No need for drastic action; time enough should need arise. Let the girls come and enjoy the summer. Nice to get out of the city anyway once the court festivities are over. Then, if everything settles down, we can move back to town for the winter."

I realized Alan must know more than he told me, realized he thought this decision the best for all of us, but I felt quavers and regrets for that charming apartment in Lowndes Square.

We contacted a recommended real estate agent, Mrs. Tufnell, and two days later motored out to Holyport, a village between the towns of Maidenhead and Ascot in Berkshire, about twenty miles west from London, where Mrs. Tufnell had marked a house as especially desirable. We drove into the village, circled the traditional, grassy "Green" in the middle of it, and stopped before a square house, old red brick, probably early-eighteenth-century Queen Anne. It was set behind a white picket fence.

Holyport House—I fell in love with it at first sight. We walked through the gate up a short path, raised the knocker on a paneled door. It was opened by a tall, spare woman, behind her a tweed-jacketed man with grizzled hair and mustache. Both looked at us a little uncertainly; then, as we explained we came from the real estate agent, they invited us to come in. We stood in a small entrance hall, and I glimpsed what seemed to be a dining room on the left, on the right a rather stiff little drawing room out of a Jane Austen novel. The couple introduced themselves as Major and Mrs. Geoffrey Hirst and led us back through the hall down two steps into a comfortable large room with doors opening out on a charming garden and what looked like an orchard beyond.

"But how delightful," I exclaimed.

We talked for some minutes. She explained they were anxious to let the house as they planned a holiday with their son in Scotland.

"But you will want to see the rest of the house." Getting up she opened a green door at the rear of the entrance hall.

"The kitchen, I am afraid, is a little old-fashioned but the stove works well and we have just installed a small fridge. The milkman comes daily, post office and small general store are just across the way. A butcher cart stops twice a week, and there is a laundry pickup."

We went out through the dining room, looked into the drawing room, and then followed her up stairs carpeted in red with gleaming brass rods. There were four good bedrooms plus a small one at the head of the stairs. Above, on the top floor, a storage room and two tiny servants' rooms, bare and dismal. Mrs. Hirst seemed to sense our feelings, for she apologized. "We have not had live-in maids lately but if you are bringing staff the baker across the green has rooms to let."

Alan and I looked at each other. He nodded and I nodded. Alan said, "We both like the house. Would our taking it two weeks from today suit you?"

"That would give us ample time."

"Then," said Alan, "we will let you know our final decision as soon as we have talked with the real estate agent."

This he did next morning. I then called Mrs. Hirst, told her of our decision, and asked her to engage two rooms from the baker for the servants. My next priority was a visit to an employment agency, a task I approached with considerable trepidation. A friend recommended a reliable firm and I made an appointment for the following day.

Walking up a steep flight of stairs, I entered the office to be confronted by a formidable lady in black silk twill who listed my requirements. She consulted her books, then ushered me into a cubicle set with stiff chairs where I waited to interview selected candidates.

The first couple were not too promising, too formally correct for our purposes, but the second seemed possible, a Mr. and Mrs. Chapman, newly arrived in London from Lancashire, the man to be butler, his wife, cook. In addition, they had a young niece willing to act as chambermaid and general help. The wages asked seemed low compared with those at home, but they appeared satisfied and presented convincing references. I explained that rooms in the house were unsuitable and lodgings just across the way would be provided. This was accepted without comment so I engaged them, settled my account with the twill-clad lady, and left instructions for the Chapmans to take the early afternoon train ten days later for Maidenhead, where they would be met.

I felt quite triumphant with my job accomplished. There remained errands to be done and a last round of social engagements before leaving town. On a Thursday of the last week in June we set off for our new home. Mrs. Hirst had left the house clean and polished, and going into the kitchen I discovered there would been no need for provisioning for the evening. The newly employed Chapmans had arrived. They told me the butcher had left a joint of meat, and there was milk, butter, cream, and eggs in the fridge. The baker had asked them to inquire whether we liked our bread hard-crusted or soft and had sent samples for our approval. Mrs. Chapman, black-haired, quite pretty, bustled about the kitchen, and upstairs the little maid Mary had been put to work making beds and laying out towels in the bathrooms. We discussed the menu for dinner and I gave orders for our breakfast next morning.

Roger and his New Zealand governess Robbie meanwhile had gone to explore the garden and tour the village green. They returned with fresh scones, compliments of the baker, for our tea, which Mr. Chapman served with due ceremony in the garden room. Unpacking could wait, we decided, so Alan and I went out after tea to look about.

On the left side of the green there was a large Tudor-style house with extended grounds. Next came the typical village pub with an old gaffer smoking his pipe on a bench outside, then a small cottage, probably lived in by the proverbial lively widow. On the far side were the little shop and post office, the bakery, a couple of tiled cottages, and, on the right, another large house next to a duck pond, obviously the gathering place for the village children. The whole scene, a storybook one, lacked only red-coated hunters and hounds and a stagecoach in front of the pub. We had even that a few months later. All very satisfactory.

England being so far north, June evenings linger on through a long twilight. After dinner we sat on the terrace, then as it grew cool went back into the garden room. Delicious smells drifted in from the garden through the open doors. I looked over at a radio. There should be news at nine o'clock, but who wanted to hear news of Hitler's mad antics? What right did that evil man have to turn the world upside down, threatening the peace of villages like this one? We sat on, then went upstairs, undressed, and sank into a wide, comfortable bed with soft pillows and sheets smelling with lavender. We slept well.

Next morning I walked out our gate to cross the green and give our names to the postmistress. On my way I met a pretty, dark-haired young girl with three small dogs in tow, rust-colored with sharp foxlike faces. We exchanged good mornings and I asked her about the dogs.

"They are corgis," she answered. "My mother raises them. I am Diana Croyesdale. You are Mrs. Kirk, are you not?"

"Yes," I said, realizing the news of the American invasion must have gotten round the village.

We parted and I went on to the little shop, introduced myself to the postmistress who was also the shopkeeper, and asked for needles and a spool of blue thread to mend a torn shirt of Roger's. She looked a bit puzzled about the spool. "You mean a reel, Madam?" I smiled at another of my mistakes. Already I had taught myself to say *cupboard* instead of *closet,* as the latter meant the WC or "water closet" [the bathroom], and *larder* instead of *pantry*. Still much to learn.

On my way back I encountered a short, stout, red-faced gentleman in tweeds who introduced himself as Major Lawrence.

"Welcome to Holyport, Mrs. Kirk. I am a neighbor of yours and once you are settled my wife and I would like to call upon you."

"That is very kind, Major Lawrence. I am sure we will be happy here. The village is charming."

He twirled his stick, walked across the green with me, and left me at our front gate.

Two new acquaintances, I thought—not bad for a morning's work.

As Alan's chauffeur and the official car belonged in London, Alan decided I must have a small car of my own. Telephoning the Ford agency in Maidenhead, we spoke to an eager salesman who volunteered to drive out to Holyport and demonstrate a four-door English model that we might find suitable. He arrived that afternoon in a neat little car, and the family assembled to inspect it. The salesman assured me my U.S. license would be good temporarily and later an English license could be easily obtained at the Maidenhead office.

The car seemed just what we wanted. I got in with the salesman and gave it a try down one road and back. She ran easily, and without undue difficulty I negotiated shifting gears from the driver's seat on the right of the car. If we cared to go back to Maidenhead with him, he said, the car could be ours at once. Alan agreed and we three drove into town and did our business with the agency manager, who then affixed proper plates and handed over the necessary papers. I drove back along the left side of the road as British rules required, skillfully avoiding various obstacles, including a small herd of sheep, and returned triumphant.

I grew very fond of that car. It was the English cousin of one I had in California, a sturdy vehicle in which I had driven the length of the coast from Long Beach to Seattle, Washington. Now with house, servants, and a car, all was in order, and we looked forward to the girls' arrival.

Finally the great day came. We went in Alan's car to Reading, about twenty miles away, to meet the boat train from Southampton. Very exciting it was to see our two pretty daughters standing in the open door as the train came to a stop and the porter deposited a pile of suitcases on the platform. Two or three gentlemen, obviously devoted shipmates, had gathered behind to say goodbye. One tall man bent to kiss Marian's hand, and there were waves as the train pulled out on its way to London.

It was quite apparent the girls had a very fine trip.

Mrs. Tufnell, the real estate lady, telephoned next day to ask us to bring the girls to tea and tennis at Ascot on Sunday, as her son Timothy had friends from Eton, the top British boarding school, for the weekend. Marian and Deborah, rather spoiled by the attention paid them aboard ship, thought Eton boys might prove tame company, especially as a florist delivered a large bouquet of roses without card, Marian's hand-kissing admirer no doubt.

We had a very pleasant afternoon that Sunday, however, and the Eton boys, all of them in their last year, were quite acceptable, Timothy taking a great fancy to Deborah. Marian, aged nineteen, was happy that a couple of Grenadier Guards, a little older than the Eton boys, turned up at teatime. The Grenadier Guards, one of the elite regiments of the British army, was a place for young officers from "good families," and we enjoyed their company. Timothy Tufnell asked me to bring the girls over to his school for tea the following week. I gathered he belonged to a very select group, distinguished, as we learned later, by wearing special waistcoats strung across with gold watch chains.

On the Fourth of July we all drove into London for the annual U.S. national day reception at the Kennedys' residence. Held in the garden, it was crowded with visiting Americans, one of whom held court as she had just flown over on the first of the Pan American Airways clipper flights from America. There was also a group of students from Kent School in Connecticut who had come to row in the annual regatta at Henley-on-Thames, a contest between crews from top schools and universities in the United States and England. We had made plans to go. The girls suggested that we ask the Kent crew to come to lunch the Sunday after the race. They accepted at once.

On Wednesday Marian, Deborah, and I drove over to Eton, located in Windsor, site of the royal family's summer residence. As we entered the town the girls were fascinated to see Eton boys in dusty tail coats, white collars, and string ties, others in flannels and blazers bound for the playing fields, quite different in appearance from the boys they had known from American boarding schools. We reached the old Tudor hall where Timothy had his room, were welcomed by several splendidly dressed young gentlemen, and treated to a sumptuous tea, buns and oozing éclairs, guaranteed I feared to bring out adolescent spots. Two other girls had been invited, both rather plump and shy in badly fitting dresses. Our own girls in their pretty summer frocks shone by comparison, as evidenced by the attention paid them by their hosts.

After thanking our host, we told him he must come to Holyport on Sunday to be initiated into a baseball game the girls planned to hold in the field behind the house when the Kent crew was expected. A day or two later we enjoyed our first social event in the village, a garden party given by Major and Mrs. Lawrence. It was great fun. Their house, a pretty early-nineteenth-century Regency residence, was just round the corner to the left from ours. The major's own flag waved from a pole on the lawn, a flag given him when he was governor of Uganda, then an English colony. The Lawrences presented us to various neighbors who responded with careful cordiality. As strangers and Americans we realized we were subjects of considerable curiosity in so close-knit a community.

As it turned out, our stay in Holyport was a rare experience, for we grew to know something of English country life, so different from the formal diplomatic round we would have encountered in London, and as time went on we managed, with a judicious distribution of simple hospitality and American gin, to loosen old village animosities and bring assorted neighbors together.

On Saturday morning of the regatta we set out for Henley armed with picnic lunches. Alan had obtained cards for one of the boating clubs and reserved canoes from which we could see the races. The first races were school crews, among them our friends from Kent, who won handily, then four-oared boats and sculls and finally the college varsity eights. A fellow embassy officer at the race coached us in the Harvard cheer, and we started in unison when that crew swept down the river, much to the astonishment of the English spectators who made do with a modest "Well rowed." As the victorious Harvard boat crossed the line, the stroke oar looked over in surprise. "Hi, Debby," he shouted, recognizing a friend. The races over, we went back to the clubhouse, drank glasses of sherry or orange squash, a sweet drink similar to our orangeade, congratulated our successful crews, and went home to Holyport.

By one o'clock on Sunday all was in readiness for the arrival of the Kent crew. They turned up in a minibus, one tall boy bearing a bouquet of pink carnations that he handed me with due ceremony. We had planned a buffet lunch on the terrace, and after the last piece of cake had been demolished Roger produced his own baseball bat and ball and we adjourned to the orchard. The game, although slightly hampered by the trees, was great fun, the audience increased by Major and Mrs. Lawrence, who had walked over to watch with another nice couple, the Marsdens, whom we had met at the garden party.

Robbie proved a valiant hitter, and Mr. Marsden took a turn at bat, saying he had played British rounders in his youth and the game was much the same. Everyone enjoyed themselves, and when we went back to the terrace for drinks, Mr. Marsden suggested we might use the village green another Sunday.

"What a fine idea. Would we get permission?" I asked.

"Easy," he replied. "I will speak to the pub owner; he is the village bigwig."

The Kent boys would be gone next week, but Deborah said Timothy Tufnell could bring his friends over. "And those nice grenadiers from Windsor," added Marian.

"Sounds as though you will have two teams," laughed Major Lawrence.

The pub owner agreed we could use the green, invitations were issued, all promised to be on hand, and our Sunday ball games were set up as a regular feature.

The following week held the greatest excitement for us with the long-awaited date for our presentation at court. Rooms at St. James's Street had been engaged. Tims arrived on Monday morning to take us to London. Carefully consulting the printed list of requirements, we set out to do our shopping at Harrod's elegant store: feathers, veils, and long white gloves to be purchased and bouquets to be ordered.

The next afternoon Tims drove us to Ambassador Kennedy's residence for a rehearsal. We were ushered into an upstairs drawing room and greeted by Mrs. Kennedy, a small, very pretty woman who seemed curiously shy. Odd now to think of her poise and gallantry through all the subsequent family tragedies. It was her capable English secretary who marshaled our group together and explained the court procedure.

At eleven the next morning we went to the hairdressers, the usual London hairdressers, rows of shallow booths where elegant young men bent above our heads winding curls and shaking flaxseed lotion into our hair. The hairdresser promised to send someone at five-thirty to comb out our curls and place the feathers. We stopped by a theater to see a newsreel movie. Anything to pass an hour or so, for there was nothing to do at the flat but to thoroughly bite each fingernail. We finally went back to our flat, braving the hazards of the traffic on Piccadilly Circus, had baths, some strong tea, and then checked our clothes item by item. We drank some more tea, very black. Just then the hairdresser came with a bag of tongs and pins and an assistant to hand them to him. He was a cheery little man who left us to go on to do the hair of Mrs. Johnny Dewar of the Dewar Scotch whiskey family. She had a tiara with a piece in front that looked like a bottle, he told us.

We put our dresses on just before he left. He said we must to get the proper effect; besides, the feathers might be loosened if we dressed later. It was just six o'clock and we were not to leave the hotel until eight-fifteen. Very little sitting down during that time. We trailed about feeling like Cinderella's mother and sisters dressed for the ball. The man had curled my hair and set my diamond bracelet into it. I looked like a pseudo-empress Josephine waiting for her husband Napoleon.

The housekeeper arrived to fasten Marian's train. "Sew it on," I said, "with double thread," a good precaution as one poor creature lost hers in front of the queen. The photographers arrived, the *New York Times* with flash bulbs, the Acme Press, Scripps Howard. By eight o'clock we were entirely ready, Alan in uniform, the girls powdered and lipsticked, even our gloves on. Still fifteen minutes. Marian's cheeks grew pinker as the clock went round. We walked downstairs, no room in the lift for so much tulle and feathers. At the door they had laid a red carpet and two or three dozen people stood by to gape. "Gor, ain't she purty." "Nice 'air. . . . " "See the little 'un in white."

Tims drove us down Pall Mall and around to the back of Buckingham Palace. We went up a short flight of stairs, turned right, and walked down long corridors hung with pictures on either side, on through reception rooms until we came to the throne room itself, light and warm, immense, almost empty. As we entered we were greeted by a gentleman usher as friendly and reassuring as a clergyman at a Sunday-school tea. He guided us across the great room and into one end of a wide corridor where we were to wait with other ladies of the diplomatic group.

Someone in a scarlet coat, elderly, important, came through to speak to Mrs. Kennedy, our own ambassadress, who became agitated and began to pull at the diamond bracelets over her gloves. I went up to her. The chamberlain had said she could not wear her blue gloves; someone would find her a pair of white ones from the dressing room. We unclasped diamonds. Minutes were growing short. Miraculously the scarlet gentleman returned with white gloves. They were not long enough. She changed with her daughter Eunice, more clasping and unclasping of diamond bracelets. Meanwhile from beyond the door came the ruffle of drums, surely the same noise they make before executions.

We formed in line, Mrs. Kennedy looking very lovely and quite undisturbed in spite of the contretemps over the gloves. She was only about twelve or fifteen feet ahead of us and quite suddenly I found myself in the doorway, two gentlemen spreading my train behind me. It was a glare of light. I knew the picture was mine, that all this was set and waiting for me alone, and then I had made my curtsy to King George VI and gone on to Queen Elizabeth, who smiled with such amazing charm I could only smile back. Marvelous how she managed that for each one. I stepped to one side as the girls' names echoed out into the room: "Marian and Deborah Kirk" shouted against the walls of Buckingham Palace. My daughters followed me up into the velvet-covered seats against the side wall.

As I turned to look out over the scene I felt overcome by the sheer fairylike beauty of it all, the utterly astonishing color, the pageantry, the ordered, magnificent movement. The king wore a guard's scarlet uniform splashed with medals and the badges of chivalric orders, the queen a state dress of cream satin and gold crossed with the blue ribbon of the Order of the Garter, England's premier aristocratic honor. Her necklaces were diamonds, and the great Kohinoor diamond itself shone from the front of her crown.

Even in movies of coronations I had noticed the blaze of the jewels, so different from the costume-jewelry brilliance to which we are accustomed, and here it seemed the lights sparkled against the facets of the diamonds, against the color of uniforms, the gold, the shining metal of breast plates, helmets, swords, halberds. The queen's train made a little golden pool at her feet. It was a picture, of course, and we have seen many pictures, but this one moved and shone.

The gentlemen of the diplomatic corps followed their ladies. Remarkable uniforms the ambassadors wore, the smaller the country the more gold per square inch. Ambassador Kennedy looked very sober in their midst. He alone of our civilian officers did not wear knee breeches—ambassadorial dispensation no doubt. Alan came after the army attaché. The girls and I admired the crispness of his right face and the precision of his bow.

When the diplomats had all passed, the queen turned, smiled gently at the king, and they both sat down while their attendants spread their robes about them. We sat down as well, and as we did so the first ladies of the nondiplomatic group entered the room. Headed by a duchess, they came in a steady line, hundreds of them, very few pretty women, plump little girls tied in the middle like muslin pudding bags, rangy older women, very tall, very thin, with the distinction of seasoned hunting horses. Finally the last lady made her curtsy, a thin creature in a green dress.

There was a stir. The king and queen rose, faced the diplomats, curtsied and bowed, faced the peeresses, curtsied and bowed. We curtsied and bowed in return, the plumes all going down together, and the royal pair walked out hand in hand, preceded by ushers with rods going backwards before them, while behind came their retinue. We waited for a minute in our places, then, joined by our gentlemen, we walked out two by two.

We went through the long reception rooms and into those set apart for supper. Here we broke up into groups. A knight of the garter handed me a glass of champagne and I ate a foie-gras sandwich next to a lady dripping with jeweled orders and gold sequins. Suddenly I looked down at my glove. Sitting astride one finger was an immense horse fly. Marian said it must have come in with the guardsmen.

It seemed too bad to leave and yet it was time. No use standing wistfully about like children at the end of a school treat. Mrs. Kennedy passed. She had retrieved her blue gloves. We said good night and our escorts' swords clanked down the outside corridor. Out again through the special door and home to more champagne and sandwiches, but with our feathers and trains folded in a neat pile on a bedroom chair. Marian even took down her curls. Perhaps the queen did the same.

On Sunday our baseball players arrived in force, three grenadiers, the Marsdens with two strong-looking daughters and a stalwart son. We played until everyone was a trifle breathless, then adjourned to the house where Mr. Chapman had set out cold drinks on the terrace. The grenadiers left to get back for parade at Windsor and the Marsdens went off, all very pleased when I invited them to return the following Sunday.

Meanwhile the newspapers and radios were full of ominous reports of new German intentions, Hitler renewing his demands for territorial and diplomatic concessions by Poland, threatening armed action against them and the Baltic countries, and talking in more bellicose terms every day. The two Western powers, Britain and France, reaffirmed their guarantees to Poland, and, as the days progressed, war clouds gathered.

Alan's job during this period was to gather as much information as he could about the British assessment of the situation and their preparations for war, should it come to that. As a gregarious man and a real sea dog, he made good contacts, indeed friends, among the British naval officers in England. They still regarded the American navy as a bit of an upstart, but the more intelligent of them realized that they would benefit from a sympathetic United States. Both the British and the Americans were reluctant to pass confidential material to the other, however, and Alan got much of his information during informal talks with friends he had made high up in the Admiralty.

One reason for their confiding in Alan was that many of them thought the American Embassy under Kennedy was a little too impressed by the Germans and in any case firmly wedded to keeping the United States out of involvement in another European quarrel. The British knew that the naval attaché had his own line of communications to Washington and thought that Alan's reports would give a more balanced picture. I gather his reports did, but it was tricky for him, as he had to avoid offending, or seeming to undercut, his ambassador. Alan therefore portrayed his reports as "supplemental military information" and was careful to let his readers at home draw their own conclusions.

Alan also had operational responsibilities. As usual, England and Europe were crowded with vacationing American tourists oblivious of

12. Lydia Kirk with her children, England, 1939. From left, Lydia, Roger (holding the family dog), Deborah, and Marian (in front).

coming danger. Alan told me there might be ten thousand to be evacuated in England alone if need arose. His would be the principal embassy office dealing with this. With this in mind, Ambassador Kennedy asked him in late July to make a survey of the western coast ports, the east coast being too vulnerable to possible attack.

The plan was for us and another member of the embassy staff to set out as ordinary tourists, taking our grown children as if on a sightseeing tour. Off we went in two cars, stopping at each port, where our men got out to inspect the pier accommodations, including shelter and toilets, and estimate how many refugees could be embarked at each place. The British authorities promised rail travel for the refugees provided they had two days before the planned transfer of their own children from the cities into the countryside.

Except for the grim possibilities involved, it was a pleasant trip combined with visits to cathedrals and other points of interest. By the time we returned to Holyport in the middle of August the news had become more and more alarming. In late August Germany signed a nonaggression pact with Russia and in a secret protocol divided Poland and the Baltics into two "spheres of influence," shorthand for occupying them by force. War seemed increasingly likely.

As this would be Marian's last year at Bryn Mawr College in the United States, Alan decided it would be best for her to go home immediately. Deborah would stay for the present. After some discussion we agreed it might also be wise to ship back the few things we had brought over, silver, china, rugs, pictures, etc., still in storage in London, especially as there now seemed little probability of our moving into the city.

We even received a letter from Alan's aunt Bessie Sinclair, the sister of his uncle Caspar Goodrich's wife. From an old Philadelphia family, she had married the British consul general in Philadelphia many years before. Now a widow, she continued to live on his estate in Northern Ireland, at Strabane near Londonderry. She wrote offering us and any others from the embassy a refuge if things got worse.

"No need for that yet," said Alan. "But it is a kind thought and good to know there is an escape hatch."

We saw Marian off on the *America*, packed with a crowd of properly cautious fellow passengers, and settled down to wait on events. To Alan's relief the majority of the ten thousand tourists had heeded warnings and many had found passage back to the United States on Dutch ships as well as on American liners.

6

Wartime England, 1939–1940

In addition to moves against Poland, Belgium's neutrality was now threatened. Alan was spending more nights in town to be in closer touch with the situation. On Friday, September 1, 1939, Hitler invaded Poland. Alan telephoned from London that he would not be down on Saturday, September 2, but would try to be with us late on Sunday in time for dinner. The prime minister, Mr. Chamberlain, was scheduled to speak in Parliament at noon Sunday. No question of our usual baseball game: all of England would be at home listening to their radios, awaiting the results of the speech.

Uneasy, somehow uncomfortable at being alone, Deborah and I walked over to the Lawrences'. We sat in their sunlit drawing room, Addie Lawrence peacefully occupied filling little bags with lavender gathered from the garden. Promptly at noon Chamberlain spoke, recalling the anti-aggression pacts and the promises made to the Allied nations by Hitler. "With the breaking of these pacts we have no choice but to honor our commitments. As of this moment we have declared war against Germany."

Addie went quietly on filling the lavender bags. The rest of us sat silent. Finally the major got up, walked over to the liquor cabinet, and poured out a gin and bitters for each of us. Without speaking we raised our glasses, then, saying nothing, went home.

Alan finally arrived late Sunday to tell us mobilization had been ordered both in England and in France. No commotion in the city, where the news had been expected. The evacuation of city children would start next day, as no one knew if or when German bombing might occur.

Dinner that evening was not too cheerful an affair. Alan was very tired. We went to bed early, only to be wakened by the phone ringing soon after midnight. The only phone in the house was an ancient instrument hanging on the back hall wall. Alan got up and went down to answer a call from the embassy. He came back to tell me the British passenger liner *Athena* had been sunk, possibly torpedoed, off the Irish coast.

"Oh no," I cried. "It has really begun." Horror-stricken, I rocked back and forth in bed.

The phone rang again. This time it was the White House in Washington. President Roosevelt wished Alan to fly to Galway, Ireland, where survivors from the *Athena* would be landed, many Americans among them, and to determine whether the ship had actually been torpedoed.

Alan started to dress. "Wait," I said. "You must go in uniform. If you should fall into the Irish Sea I want everyone to know you are an American naval officer, and the American survivors are more likely to talk freely to a man in an American naval uniform." Grumbling, he assented.

The night wore on. Calls were coming in very fast now, from the embassy, from the British Admiralty saying one of their officers was on his way to make flight arrangements. Our own air attaché phoned that he could come down to join Alan as fast as he could get a uniform back from the tailor's. He had just been promoted and had sent them all to be fitted with his new stripes. He had gotten the tailor out of bed, and he had been promised that a uniform would be delivered in an hour.

An officer from the Admiralty arrived, Commander Dove. With the Chapmans quietly asleep across the green, Roger's governess, the faithful Robbie, already had coffee, eggs, and bacon on the stove. Meanwhile Commander Dove was struggling with the telephone, jiggling the hook up and down, trying to reach Local Air Command.

"Damn it," he shouted to the operator. "Don't you know there's a war on?"

Finally he got through. "Yes, I know Eire is neutral. The plane should be unmarked. You will have to put the crew in civvies. Must be some sort of landing strip in Galway."

Air Command rang back. "All arranged. We are sending a car. The plane will take off from Reading at nine o'clock."

At seven-thirty Slim Hitchcock, the air attaché, arrived, resplendent in his new stripes, and by eight o'clock our men were on their way.

Eight-thirty, a knock on our front door. It was the local warden. "There is a gas alert." Sirens went off. We groped for masks; it seemed impossible to get the things on. Deborah, sensible girl, refused to try and put her head back on the pillow. Sure enough the all-clear sounded. False alarm.

Meanwhile Alan had landed, not on an airstrip near Galway (there was none), but in a cow pasture full of cattle and stone fences. Somehow the pilot managed to put the plane down between them. Alan got out as soldiers of the Irish Republican Army jumped up from behind the fences. He advanced toward them and offered their commander a cigarette. At that time he smoked Philip Morrises, marked "English Blend." One look at the package and the officer marshaled the whole party into a paddy wagon bound for Galway jail, where the doors clanged shut behind than.

Alan protested, demanded to see the prison's governor. "Look," he said, pointing to the star on his sleeve. "I am the American naval attaché, not British, and I am here on orders from my government."

Only half convinced, the governor called Dublin. "There is a fellow here, flown over from England to meet the *Athena* survivors, says he is the American naval attaché. He is in American uniform."

"In an American uniform," replied Dublin. "Get him out quick." The whole lot was released just in time to meet the first boats coming to the pier with the *Athena* survivors. From passengers and the ship's officers Alan was able to verify that the ship had indeed been torpedoed. This news along with a list of the American survivors he took with him to our embassy in Dublin, where he spent the night and phoned his report back to the White House.

"A good thing you wore your uniform," I told him when he returned to Holyport next day.

It was comforting to have him back and get a blow-by-blow account of his adventures, but he soon took off again for London, spending most of the week in town. The village filled up with evacuees. Our gardener insisted on digging up the potatoes from a patch behind the orchard. "Those city folk might steal 'em. Supplies could run short the way they did in the last war. I'll stack 'em up in the shed for Captain and Mrs. Hirst when they come back."

The evacuees caused problems, many of them not too happy with a country diet of eggs, milk, and fresh vegetables. "I would rather have winkles [periwinkles] and vinegar," said one small child to our baker's wife. I heard a mother talking to a friend in the post office, "We're going back, too dull hereabouts."

The news grew worse and finally we decided that Deborah, in spite of her frantic protests, must go back to the United States. Deborah pleaded with us to stay, but there was little for her to do in England. She had passed her college entrance requirements and could enter Vassar even though she would be three weeks late. It was very hard for me to see her go. For Marian it had been different, as this was her graduation year, but Deborah, always a stalwart support, felt she might be of use to us. I knew, however, that our decision was a wise one, and we engaged passage for her on our old friend the *America*.

The Sunday before she left we had a last baseball game. The grenadiers would be leaving for France later in the week. They came in uniform, laid their tunics and ammunition belts aside, and we had a rousing game ended by one of them knocking a home run through the village pub window. We bade them goodbye. "We'll be back," they said, "as soon as we've finished with the Germans."

As we saw Deborah off on the boat train, looking very woebegone, I felt heartsick. So much went with her: the happy winter we had planned in town, the sightseeing we were going to do, the parties we had hoped to give, inviting Timothy and the grenadiers we had grown to know. None of it to happen, all because of the beastly Germans and their beastly war. War, it was with us now. Better, I knew, that she would be safe and away, but I would miss her very much.

Our lease on Holyport House was up the end of September 1939. The large Tudor house on the green, Pebbles Court, was available to

13. *Alan and Lydia Kirk at Pebbles Court, Holyport, England, 1939.*

rent, and two other embassy officers, Theodore Achilles and Vinton Chapin, reluctant to keep their families in town, suggested we pool forces. Joined by a bachelor officer, Rudy Schoenfeld, we settled into Pebbles Court on October 1st, saying goodbye to the Chapmans, who seemed happy to return to Lancashire. Our men came back and forth by train as gasoline was now rationed. We were quite a house party, but there were beds for everyone and to my relief Marian Achilles undertook the job of housekeeping, running the staff, and catering to our various tastes.

14. Governess Catherine Robson, known as Robbie, with Danny, the family dog, Pebbles Court, England, 1939.

One of the first tasks for the women was making blackout curtains for every window and outside door. Not a chink of light allowed after dark. We bought bolts of material in Maidenhead, nasty black cotton, and set to work. As the days grew shorter the curtains had to be drawn at teatime. Happily warm Indian summer does not occur in England, otherwise we would have suffocated behind closed windows and drawn curtains until we were safe in bed with lights out.

We gradually established a routine. Robbie, plus the Achilles's governess and the children, had early supper. Breakfast and lunch we shared with them, but in the evening we waited for our men, drinks laid out in the drawing room, one of us making the run to pick them up at the station. Now and again we visited our friends the Lawrences, walking across the garden and through their back gate with surreptitious use of our flashlights, or they came to us eager to hear any news the men could bring from London. Weekends were pleasant, the October weather still mild. An occasional guest came out from town. We played tennis on our court, held small cocktail parties at noon on the sunny terrace, and discussed the war news, which was desultory, the British crouching behind the defenses of the Maginot Line in eastern France and the Germans ominously quiet behind their own fortified Siegfried Line across the way. The Germans were focused on military operations in the east, occupying their share of Poland and the Baltic states, while England and France built up their sadly neglected war machines in preparation for more intense fighting later.

Alan was busier than ever reporting on the British progress in preparing for war, the possible effects on our shipping, and the situation in the ports. As the war continued, Alan passed on war-fighting techniques developed by the British during the fighting, such as that pilots would eventually crack after weeks of daily combat operations and that ships needed anti-aircraft weapons to counter low-flying aircraft as well as those higher up. These would save our people from having to learn them through bitter experience, all of this helpful in designing our own war plans.

Alan came back to Holyport one evening to say there had been an air raid on the British warships in the Firth of Forth in northeast Scotland. Happily no serious damage, although the Germans claimed on the radio that they had sunk the aircraft carrier *Ark Royal*. The Admiralty promptly denied this, but Alan asked if he might be permitted to go to Scotland, visit the fleet, and send a report back to our Navy Department. The Admiralty, delighted to have the German rumor scotched, said a trip would be arranged for the coming weekend.

Alan took the Saturday night train to Edinburgh and was then flown out to the ships, boarded the *Ark Royal*, and attended divine service. He was given a fine welcome by the ship's officers and was able to cable to Washington that he had been to church aboard her, a significant message as a church service could hardly have been held on a ship sunk beneath the waves. He had enjoyed himself, and afterward one of his precious souvenirs was a cartoon from the German paper *Simplicimuss* (Silliness) showing a blindfolded naval officer standing in the bow of a small boat with the caption, "The American Naval Attaché would not know an aircraft carrier if he saw one."

Life in Holyport went quietly along. Rationing was now in force, but not as yet too severe, and with such a large group in the house our ration coupons were quite adequate. Only butter was in short supply, but we managed to get some sent over from France. Trust the French not to skimp on such a cooking necessity.

Mail to and from the United States had become a problem. If letters caught the occasional clipper plane, well and good, but ship mail took forever, and this made family separation more acute. I missed my girls so very much. If the war came to a quick end they would be back with us for the summer, but that seemed a forlorn hope. I wondered if Roger and I should have gone home, but I knew I might not be able to return to England. I had encouraged Alan to take this job and I felt my place was here with him. Just the same I had many heartsick moments.

As the threat of bombing retreated, one of our families, the Vinton Chapins, decided to return to their London house, and bachelor Rudy Schoenfeld also left us. As Marian Achilles expected another baby in the spring, they planned to leave Pebbles after Christmas for a country house of their own. In spite of the apparent quiet in France, Alan refused to consider our moving into town. "That quiet won't last forever, and it's enough to have one member of the family in the danger zone."

We therefore asked our real estate friend Mrs. Tufnell to look out for a smaller house in the Ascot area. We had heard of an excellent preparatory school nearby for Roger, as Robbie felt he needed regular lessons and the companionship of other boys. At age nine he seemed very young to go as a boarder, but unless we lived in the city there was no alternative. We drove over to Heatherdown School in Ascot, met the headmaster and his wife, and were reassured as the atmosphere seemed happy and relaxed.

We were not as lucky finding a house; none of those offered for rent appealed. In the end we gave up the search and decided to stay on at Pebbles and wait on events. Roger would not go to school until after the holidays. Meanwhile, we prepared to give ourselves as cheerful a Christmas as possible. My own Christmas cards I had confected of black paper, inside a photo of Pebbles Court. On the front I wrote in white ink, "Blacked out for Christmas"; on the back, "The Kirks wish you a Happy New Year." These I got off by early mail to the States.

15. & 16. Outside and inside of Christmas card for 1939 designed by Lydia.

I thought wistfully of Marian and Deborah home from college with Mother, wishing I could see them dressed for holiday parties, longing to share in the fun and gaiety. The separation seemed cruel, though knowing they were safe from war and rumors of worse to come meant much as I talked with friends with sons and husbands at the front and daughters working on the farms, in factories, or in hospitals waiting for the casualties that must come sooner or later.

Alan bought a set of baseball bats, balls, and a rulebook and sent them off to the grenadiers we had known, now stationed on the front, hoping they might initiate their troops into the game. Six months later I was sitting in Washington beside a British officer who said, "Remarkable thing. I have a son in the grenadiers. He told me he and his men had played baseball at the front." I laughed and explained that I knew why.

With bits of colored paper we set about making decorations for a Christmas tree that we planned for the front hall. I found a fine big wreath in Maidenhead for our door, but this was greeted with horror by the butler and staff. "We only use wreaths on graves, Madam," so we solemnly took it across the green and laid it on the village war memorial. With Robbie's help we did trim the house with evergreens and holly; that seemed expected and permissible.

We had friends and neighbors in for drinks before Christmas lunch, then sat down to a splendid feast. Alan sent a bottle of port to the kitchen, as the cook's husband was off to France next day. She had taken him into Maidenhead to be photographed earlier in the week. "You never know, Madam, if I will see him again."

Now we were all wondering how long Neville Chamberlain would last as British prime minister. Before leaving London we had gone to a reception at his residence, and as we went out the front door I spied the umbrella featured in the photo of his arrival from Munich after his "compromise" with Hitler there in 1938. An umbrella is all right for a shower of rain but little protection against a violent thunderstorm, and it seemed characteristic of the feeble resistance to Hitler that he and the French had put up at that meeting.

Winston Churchill, now First Lord of the Admiralty, no longer young but full of vigor and drive, was already talked of as a replacement for Chamberlain as prime minister. Alan had an interview with him before Christmas, scheduled for twenty minutes but lasting nearly an hour. They got on well together, being of similar mind about the Germans and the war, and Alan thought he would do well if chosen.

If we thought the weather was cold before Christmas, it was worse now. How grateful we were for the central heating at Pebbles, far from a universal convenience in England at the time. Everyone, at all times, went encased in wool from head to foot. I met a woman one day who described the costume she had worn at her sister's house, a very cold house, so she had gone prepared. She put on layers of warm underclothing, then a pair of black tights bought for the occasion, two petticoats, a knitted jumper, and on top a velvet dinner suit, jacket, and long skirt, plus a fur coat.

Happily our social life was mainly restricted to a few lunch parties in London hotels that were well heated and teas in front of our neighbors' fires, but evenings spent in fine old ancestral halls must have been glacial.

There were no tears when we left Roger at school in early January. He seemed quite happy, but on our return home there was only our dog to greet us, Robbie having left that morning to visit friends in Ireland. The house seemed very empty, though she promised to return for Roger's Easter holiday. Alan plied me with cocktails and produced a special bottle of wine for dinner, but he was off again in the morning, and I sat at my desk writing to Mother and the girls. How I wished we could all have enjoyed the holidays together, but getting to the States had become more and more difficult. American passenger ships were not coming to Europe any longer, and we were forbidden to travel on ships of the belligerents, so the only possibility lay in crossing over minefields to neutral Italy or Holland and sailing on one of their ships from there—not a comfortable prospect.

Some optimistic souls prophesied that the war would be over by late spring, but that seemed unlikely. Hitler with his craze for power had too much at stake. I wondered, though, what the summer would bring. Our summers in Black Point with their peaceful routine of tennis, bathing, and cocktail parties seemed a distant dream. I was determined that if I ever did get home I would engage in some useful work, for surely America could not stand clear if things really got worse.

I said nothing of this in my letters, only rejoicing that my two girls were safe and enjoying a happy, normal life at home.

The cold weather continued into February, the war news brightened by the heroic resistance of the Finns against the unprovoked onslaught against their country by a Russia seeking to reconquer territory it had lost at the time of the tsarist collapse in 1917. There were collections for warm clothing, and woolens and fur coats were sent off to the Finns that could ill be spared here in England. Everyone knitted madly, and a sewing workshop I had joined switched everything from pajamas for Poles to underclothes for Finns.

Our grenadier friends came home on short leave, telling us what a success baseball had been with their men. We tried to organize a Sunday game for them, but the ground was too frozen in spots and muddy in others. We did, however, have the pleasure of attending a wedding of one of them in Eton Chapel, the bride so pretty and the groom so smart in his regimental uniform.

We had a few more air alerts, and to complicate matters a neighbor's cow produced a noise that resembled the sirens and sent us scurrying to the windows. But still no enemy planes appeared and no bombs dropped. In London barrage balloons were put up over the city—small blimps attached to the ground by strong cables intended to intercept low-flying aircraft. The weather was better now, and by the beginning of March shy crocuses and green bulb shoots appeared in the garden.

In London we now saw not only Canadians, but Australians in wide hats turned up smartly to one side, Sikhs in turbans and beards, and small, dark, fierce-eyed men, Gurkhas from the northern frontier of India. Every other man seemed to be in uniform. Roger was very excited, but it all seemed a prelude to a more serious turn in the war. I knew Alan was increasingly disturbed, and my chances of getting home with Roger for the summer seemed dimmer than ever.

Here I insert some pages written to my mother in the winter of 1939–40, a better description than one I could give today:

> There have been many accounts of London in wartime, of the silver balloons high over the city, of the great houses with sandbagged entrances, of the parks piled with guns, ammunition heaps and trench-digging machines, of the soldiers in the streets, the London Scottish troops, their kilts covered with khaki aprons, the Irish with sprigs of green fastened to their tam-o'-shanters, the Guards proudly stiff but shorn of scarlet coats and tall busbie headgear. There is a quiet about it all, the kind of quiet you feel when men march without a band, a quick, dusty tramp of people going about their business, hurrying along until dusk falls, long queues line up for the busses, and the sudden blackout descends over the city.
>
> At luncheon the restaurants are filled. Not many idle women in town, numbers of them in uniform, the auxiliary territorials from the

colonies of the British Empire, air force clerks, volunteer firewatch, a few WRENS (Women's Royal Emergency Naval Service) in smart blue serge. But there is none of the frantic gaiety of the last war. This is a sober venture. The uniforms themselves have been dulled and made practical. Skirts have been standardized at twelve inches above stout boots and thick cotton stockings. Soldiers, too, are in battle dress, khaki trousers bagged at the bottom like ski suits, short jackets stripped of brass buttons and leather belts.

Cinemas are closed for the most part, and theaters and nightclubs do a furtive business behind thick black curtains. Perhaps there will be more excitement when the men come home on leave or when those who go know their danger to be quick and sudden. Now it is a kind of waiting game and things are at a standstill. The Germans have called it *Der Kalte Krieg* (the cold war). Certainly there is no hysteria, no roses, no glory screaming.

It may be that London in wartime is not actually as significant as England in wartime. The city has been emptied of its scarlet pomp and ceremony, emptied of its traffic, its lights, emptied of the ponderous flow of civil servants in and out of the government offices, emptied of its children. This last was an astonishing exodus, trainload after trainload. Some have returned, but for the most part they are still evacuated. Business concerns have moved into the country, taken over manor houses and hotels, institutions have left, schools, hospitals are deserted and many shops are shuttered and barred. The museums are stripped, only the churches remain open, though there are sandbags around the tombs in Westminster Abbey and the battle flags are gone from its rafters. And yet, for all London's emptiness it is not especially sad, its air is rather one of temporary disuse, a kind of dustsheet appearance. If the war does not last too long it can all come back, the solid astonishing richness of London, its color and its thick, teeming industry.

At night, of course, it is a strange place, blacked out for all social purposes, shutters drawn and closed. Pedestrians wear white armbands, carry checkered canes, the more debonair sport buttonholes touched with luminous paint. Flashlights of certain types are allowed and main cross streets are marked dimly. At night London disappears. Amazing that black paper and blue paint can shutter a city so completely, can close in its life, can even quiet it, for sound has gone along with the lights.

> Only the great railway stations are crowded at all times. There are fewer trains and more people to fill them. Troops on the platforms line up with their equipment. They leave silently, their women already in the country, sent out perhaps with the first evacuations. These men go willingly enough. They will tell you it is a business to be gone through, not doubting the necessity of putting an end to the crises that have threatened their homes, their livelihood, their peace of mind.

In early April the calm was broken by a swift German takeover of Denmark and Norway, accomplished in a single day. In early May, the tenth actually, I went up to town for a luncheon to be given by the Dutch naval attaché. I was met by a sober-faced Alan who told me the Germans had just invaded Holland and Belgium. The luncheon party was a solemn affair. Our host assured us the Dutch would put up stiff resistance, even to opening their dikes. But it was too late. The German army rolled into Holland, a veritable lightning war, a blitzkrieg that conquered all of Holland in five days. The Dutch queen and her government fled to England.

As we returned from lunch Alan said, "You will have a passenger, Bill Mailliard, driving back with you to Holyport. He will be staying at Pebbles. Put him in that room at the head of the stairs along with some packages he will be bringing with him. He must stay in the room with them and he should have some kind of heavy instrument with him at all times."

Bill, blonde and blue-eyed, seemed a very likable young man; poor fellow, I was sorry he had to be shut away with his boxes. He was quite cheerful about it, however, and he and Tims carried them up and stacked them in his room. As for the heavy instrument, I rummaged around in the gardener's shed and could only find an axe, but Bill thought that would answer the purpose.

"I can tell you now, Mrs. Kirk. These are codes and ciphers from the naval attaché's office. If parachutists land here I am supposed to smash them." Parachutists landing in Holyport—it seemed absurd, impossible to believe. Yet I knew this was war, and if a young Yale graduate could foil any parachutist who came down in our tulip beds, so much the better. I arranged to send Bill's meals up to him on a tray, found some books for him to read plus a radio, and telephoned Alan to say we had arrived safely.

Now real spring came in, roses appeared in the garden, and the cuckoos sang louder than ever, although the war news grew worse each day. Home volunteers were mustered and drilled on the village green. Signposts were removed from the roads and cautious automobile owners took the distributors out of their machines each night. Parachutists aside, invasion became a real prospect. Instead of Bill and his boxes plus the axe, I now had a naval lieutenant commander in residence with pistols strapped to his waist.

Events were moving very fast. Chamberlain resigned as prime minister and on May 11 Winston Churchill replaced him, a wise decision welcomed by the country.

The Germans broke through the French army's defense line in Belgium on May 14, threatening to cut off hundreds of thousands of British and French troops to the north. The situation looked very grim. Early on Friday, May 17, Alan rang me from London. "No chance of your getting away by boat. I'm sorry but I think it's time that you and Roger go to stay with Aunt Bessie in Ireland."

I hated the thought of leaving but knew we must go. We were doing no good here and were a nuisance and anxiety for Alan.

"Yes," I answered him, "I'm ready to go, but not to cross the Irish Sea by boat. I would rather stay than face submarines. If we can fly, well and good."

An hour or so later he called back.

"I've got passage for you by plane from Liverpool to Belfast on Monday. I'll get in touch with Aunt Bessie by phone. Better go over and collect Roger at school this afternoon. I'll send the car down for you to come up to London tomorrow, and I'll go back with you to Holyport."

My head reeled and my heart flopped around in my chest. I called the headmaster at Heatherdown to have Roger packed and ready for me, and after a hurried lunch I motored over to the school. Roger told me how worried he was at being summoned to the headmaster's office and his surprise at seeing his trunk in the hallway outside it, packed by school personnel without a word to him. He was, of course, very excited to learn I was taking him out of school and we were going to Ireland three days later. We left school straight from the headmaster's office. Roger was not allowed to say goodbye to his friends. They were told later that he was pulled out for family reasons, not concern over the course of the war. That would have alarmed them, and keeping up the morale of the students and their parents was a prime objective of the school administration.

At Pebbles, Robbie was busy packing things I had laid out on my bed. We could only take suitcases with us; anything else must be sent after. The household had been told the news and was upset, but the cook managed a good dinner, and next day Tims came down and drove me to London. I collected passports, plane tickets, money, and did a last few errands at Harrod's, looking up uncertainly at the great glass roof over their central hall, a nasty target for a bombing raid.

On Sunday, our packing finished, we collected a few neighbors for a goodbye cocktail. Mrs. Marsden pressed a little package into my hand. "Just a remembrance," she said. When I opened it later I found a beautiful crystal pendant with a note. "It belonged to my mother," she wrote, "and I would like you to take something of England away with you." I was deeply touched. Such good, kind people. How fortunate we were to have lived and known all of them, the true fabric of English country life, so different from what we might have found in London.

By nine o'clock next morning Tims was at the door, our luggage packed into the car. When I came out with Roger and looked around the sunlit green it was hard to believe what was happening. The household had assembled, even the old gardener. Robbie stood with our dog Danny in her arms, beside her the dear Lawrences. Alan checked our luggage, gave parting instructions to Tims. Would I ever see my husband again? How could I know? I was determined not to cry. I wanted to show the others how an American woman could behave. Tears seemed foolish, unimportant at such a moment. Good-byes said, one last look back, and we were off.

Happily, Tims had plotted out the roads on a map, as all direction signs had disappeared. We rode through the blossoming countryside, hawthorn hedges in full flower. Never had England seemed more lovely than on that May morning. It took some time and some wrong turns to skirt the Liverpool area, but we somehow managed to reach the airport, arriving just twenty minutes before the plane was to take off.

I had never flown before, and the plane, a small one looking like a shabby old bus, was not a reassuring sight. We got in, however, and groped around for our seats. The lights were dim and the windows blacked out because of flying over military installations on the Isle of Man on our route to Belfast. Just across from us I noticed a priest reading his breviary. A good thing, I thought; he will pray our way over. Nothing about the plane seemed very secure. The shades over the windows rattled and there was an occasional bump and lurch, but better, far better than a too-uncertain sea crossing.

Actually the flight was a short one, and we came safely down on the Belfast airstrip in Northern Ireland. We got out to be greeted at the foot of the ladder by a meek-looking little man, the American consul, who took us in charge. As he went off to collect our luggage Roger whispered to me.

"He looks like Eeyore in *Winnie the Pooh*."

The consul returned followed by a burly porter with our bags. Aunt Bessie lived in Strabane, seventy miles to the northwest of Belfast and very near the Irish border. As the consul guided us to a waiting car, he said, "As there is no train for Strabane until ten tomorrow morning, I have taken the liberty of reserving a room for you at the hotel in town. I hope you and your son will give me the pleasure of dining with me there tonight."

Still a bit shaken and scarcely in the mood for social amenities, I accepted and thanked the man, who then ushered us into his car and had us driven into town. Even on that bright day Belfast looked a gray, gloomy, Victorian city and the hotel a somber pile, but our room seemed comfortable enough. I felt suddenly very tired.

I slept that night from sheer exhaustion, but waking to another bright morning we breakfasted and took a taxi to the station well in time for our train. A porter installed us in a dusty little carriage and we chugged along, stopping at station after station until we reached

Strabane, where the stout, welcome figure of Aunt Bessie stood waiting on the platform.

"No questions now, time for talk later on," she said as she bundled us into her ancient limousine. "You're here. That's the main thing."

At lunch there was much to tell her, but the dear lady insisted that we go up to rest. Lunch had been delicious. No rationing at Aunt Bessie's, where cows, pigs, chickens plus vegetables from the farm provided large, wonderful meals.

Alan called on the telephone that evening and I reported our safe arrival. He said he was working on some way to get us home, but meanwhile we must be content to stay with Aunt Bessie. He knew we would be well taken care of.

I was still very tired but, comforted by his call, I slept well in a great canopied bed, tucked between lavender-scented sheets, the maid coming to light a fire in the early morning, as stone houses can be cold until the sun shines through the windows. Days passed—long, lazy days. Dear Aunt Bessie, I knew, would put us up indefinitely, but I worried about how and when we might get back to America.

We listened to the war news each day. With the French army in retreat, only the British forces lay between the Germans and the channel. One afternoon the radio told of a bloody engagement in which the Grenadier Guards regiments were cut to pieces, those same young men whom we had taught to play baseball, many of them never to return. I thought of the one with a young bride and of the least skillful of our players who had nevertheless knocked the home run through the pub that last Sunday. The position of the British and French forces became untenable, and on May 27 their evacuation by sea to England began. By June 4, some 340,000 men had been ferried across the channel by hundreds of boats, public and private, every yachtsman in the area helping out, but they had to leave all their heavy equipment and most of their arms behind. The situation was truly grim, and England feared early invasion.

Alan telephoned almost every other day. He had left Pebbles, gone to the Connaught Hotel in London—then a relatively modest establishment, not the grand place it has since become, and much patronized by Americans for its location near our embassy. He was of course sending in a stream of reports on the British assessment of the Germans' plans, their navy's ability to intercept a German invasion fleet, and what assets the British had left to defend themselves. He had no need of Robbie, so he arranged transport for her to safety in South Africa. No bombings yet, but the invasion threat still persisted—when and where nobody knew.

Later Alan telephoned to say he had finally been able to arrange for an American ship, one of the "President" liners, to come to Ireland to take off American refugees from the British Isles. We could go with them. The ship was ready to sail from New York and was scheduled to arrive June 5 in Galway on the west coast, about one hundred miles from Strabane. I was to hire a car and drive down the coast, as railways might be too uncertain. We could not have a cabin to ourselves as the ship would probably be crowded. Was there anyone I would be willing to share with? Several embassy wives were on the list. I suggested a good friend, Caroline Brown, the wife of one of the senior embassy officers. Now that we were actually to leave, I felt almost sorry. Here, I was near enough for telephone communication with Alan, but I knew my place was at home.

The days seemed long as we waited for news of the ship's arrival. This finally came through, and on another of those bright, cloudless June mornings Roger and I said goodbye to our dear hostess and set off, crossed the border into Ireland, and started down the coast until we finally came into Galway. I thought of Alan's visit there in September to talk to the *Athena* survivors as we drew up outside a big gray hotel. I thought it probably looked much like the jail he had been taken to. But inside it was pleasant enough, and we were served an excellent tea, interrupted by a visit from the local police chief. He remembered Alan's September trip and had come to pay his respects and assure me his people were ready to help when the American refugees arrived.

I thanked him and said I had heard from my husband of his townspeople's great kindness to the *Athena* survivors.

"No hard feelings then about his arrest?"

"None at all."

We parted the best of friends and he wished us a safe journey home.

The train with the American refugees came in that evening: many friends from the embassy, stranded tourists, and American wives of British husbands, their children still under the care of starched nannies. The nannies were most reluctant to leave their charges to the mothers' inexpert attentions, but they had to, as the ship would take no one but American citizens.

We assembled early next morning to embark on the tender and go to our ship out in the harbor. The ship normally took 250 passengers, but we numbered 750. Beds were made up in the main saloons and stacked away in odd corners. The dining room and a small bar in the bow offered the only places to sit down. There were three sittings for meals and no bugles blown for fear of waking sleeping babies, so many of them, the frantic mothers missing those starched nannies. Seasick pills had not been obtainable in town, but I had provided myself with packets of barley sugar, a good remedy and a happy thought as we had two days of heavy gale, and I could distribute my sugar sticks to suffering friends. Roger proved an excellent sailor and, more by good luck than good management, I did not succumb.

Day after day, night after night, we plowed our way across the Atlantic, our only touch with the outside world the radio blaring out from the bar. We heard the news of the fall of France and the heartening speech by Churchill that the resistance the British would put up would be remembered as "their finest hour." Now and again we passed through large convoys of merchant ships looming out of the mist or darkness shepherded by escorting destroyers. They traveled in groups so a few destroyers could guard them all and went without lights to avoid detection. Our own ship's sides were painted with large American flags, illumined by floodlights at night, to show we belonged to a neutral power. We kept blankets, coats, and life preservers handy, but I was not frightened as I felt the Germans would be loath to attack an American passenger liner, an incident almost sure to precipitate us into war.

Finally the first land came in sight. We packed our belongings and early next morning were ready to disembark. Some hours later we anchored in New York harbor. We were a rather bedraggled company to be met by relatives and friends, plus curious reporters, but there were my two girls, Marian and Deborah, happy and well. It was a joyful reunion. We lost no time clearing customs and going straight to the station to catch a train for Washington, where we would stay with Mother.

PART THREE

The United States, 1940–1946

7

Washington Before Pearl Harbor, 1940–1941

I cabled Alan as soon as we arrived from Ireland, telling him we planned to get off to our summer house at Black Point, Connecticut, as soon as possible, with my mother. Meanwhile, hoping for his eventual return, I would look for a Washington house to rent starting in September and enter Roger in school for the fall. Actually my conscience pricked at the thought of an idle, carefree holiday, and on impulse I called Rear Admiral Walter S. Anderson, the director of naval intelligence, asking if he had any plans for a training program for service wives. "Why?" he answered. "There is small chance of our getting into this war. Time enough should the eventuality arise. Don't worry. Go ahead. Enjoy your summer."

Everywhere I found this same attitude prevailed. Indeed there were those, too many of them, who thought the Germans would win the war, others indifferent, going about their business as usual. "America First" was the cry, with little regard for what happened overseas. Only a few realized, as I did, that sooner or later we must take sides and be in the war ourselves.

Frustrated, I went on with my own plans. I was lucky to find the perfect house on 34th Street in Georgetown. The house would be mine September 1, and I placed an order with the storage company to move our furniture in on that date. I rang the headmaster of the Landon School in the Washington suburbs, where Roger had been before. He was happy to reenter Roger in the autumn. All now in order, Marian, Roger, and I set out by car for Black Point, while Mother went by train.

It was almost a relief to have left Washington's conflicting views and blind misinformation.

In Black Point the sun shone on the water, we bathed, played tennis, picnicked, and held house parties for the girls. My pretty Marian had visiting beaus aplenty, including a young doctor from Philadelphia with a determined look in his eye. Deborah left to pay visits to friends in other seaside resorts, leaving the field clear for her sister. After Deborah's last visit, in late August, she returned with her rumpled summer clothes washed and pressed. "Thanks to a wonderful maid at the Perkins's," she told me. "A pity you didn't take your whole wardrobe," I replied.

It was a happy time except for my gnawing anxiety, as bombs were falling over England. Alan cabled me each Monday. I waited eagerly for the next week's cable and the next. As if to put my doubts of his safety at rest, he wrote in one of his letters, "Don't worry; think of pigeons, how rarely they drop anything on you." I was worried, however, and not only about bombs. Many thought the Germans would invade England immediately after their defeat of France in June. The remnants of the British army evacuated from France, a quarter of a million men, returned with just their rifles and hand-carried ammunition—no artillery, no tanks, trucks, or cars, no gas, no supplies of any kind. Alan wrote on June 28, "Many expect Ireland to be seized by the Germans very soon, probably before this letter arrives. . . . How successful invasion [of England] will prove I am not able to predict, but I would say it has a much better chance now than in Napoleon's time." I was more encouraged by his comment in a letter of July 24, that "a much stouter resistance will be put up now than would have been the case in June," but I still did not like the idea of German troops fighting on English soil.

In Black Point, however, life went on at its usual leisurely pace. Eventually the swallows gathered on the telephone wires to fly south. Deborah packed her clean clothes and went back to Vassar. We put Mother and her retinue on the train for Washington. Marian, Roger, and I closed the house and left to motor back, stopping in Princeton to spend the night with Alan's aunt, Sally Goodrich.

That evening who should arrive after dinner but the determined young doctor, Jack Appel. We left him with Marian while Aunt Sally,

Roger, and I went off to the movies. When we returned it was to find Dr. Appel gone, but a happy, tremulous Marian told me he had proposed and she had accepted him.

Next morning we set out for Washington, Marian in a dream but my mind in a whirl, so much to think about—an engaged daughter, an absent father to be informed, the move into a new house, a maid to be found, so much to be done and done at once.

Happily, the maid problem promised solution. A telegram from Deborah was waiting for me at Mother's. "Remember the maid at the Perkins's? She is free in New York now. Here is her name and address."

I telephoned at once. The terms seemed satisfactory, and I followed the call with a letter enclosing money for railroad fare. Johanna Leichle, born in the German part of Alsace but with a heritage of French charm—cheerful, hardworking, and a staunch prop in the years ahead—arrived in time to help open the house on September 1.

I was very pleased to see how well the furniture fitted into the house, and eventually all was in order. A couple of Marian's summer suitors came to call. Her Yale football captain, hearing of her engagement, was so disconsolate I had to revive him with strong brandy. Another suitor, after bidding her farewell, sent her a gold thimble, a wryly sarcastic symbol of married felicity. Jack Appel came down from Philadelphia to formally present himself to me and ask for my approval. This given, the engagement was officially announced. No date was to be set for the wedding until I heard firm news of Alan's return.

The Germans, having decided against an early invasion of England, now launched intensive air attacks on London designed to break the spirit of the British. Alan's letters were keeping me somewhat informed of what he was going through in London. I knew he downplayed the risks for my sake, but some of his comments were hardly reassuring. I cite a few:

> September 9, 1940
>
> Now the Germans have begun the bombing, apparently in earnest. . . . We generally send the staff into the Anderson shelter then watch the thing from the terrace until we get tired and go to bed.

September 20, 1940

On Monday, the 16th . . . the Germans put on a big show commencing about nine o'clock and finishing at 5:20 the next morning. . . . A large number of fires was started, one of them being the well-known Navy tailoring establishment of Gieves, where a brand new uniform of mine gave an added luster to the flames!

I spent a couple of hours on the roof of the Embassy watching the show. It was a moonlit night with hardly a cloud in the sky. The barrage balloons could be seen, especially those in the path of the moon, but I never caught a glimpse of the attacking planes. The artillery shoots at planes as soon as they start to come into the London area proper, and the horizon is ringed with flashes of light from the discharges of cannon—not unlike what we call "heat lightning" at home in the summer. As the plane or planes work their way into the London area proper, batteries stationed in parks or other open spaces commence firing. . . . The Hyde Park guns are pretty well pointed towards our Embassy at 1 Grosvenor Square and the bang is noisy. When the barrage is working the searchlights are not employed, so the bursts of the projectiles in the air can be plainly seen, like rockets or Roman candles. . . . The question is how long this onslaught can be withstood. Barring unforeseen accidents, it looks to me as if the Germans have found a nut too tough to crack.

"New Pipers," Virginia Water, Surrey, 17 October 1940

Last weekend I moved over here. . . . This permits (gosh—a couple of nasty ones just dropped, over towards Weybridge) us to cook in, I was just going to say, "in peace and quiet!!," but it is such a vast improvement on London there is no comparison.

Alan worked in London, however, and he wrote in late October:

Passed our 260-something-th air raid in London. . . . Four or five a day is routine. In fact we are all growing a little callous. . . . Of course, not infrequently we get a couple of bombs without any warning at all. . . . When I was having lunch at the Connaught Hotel, there was a hell of a bang. The windows shook and rattled and everyone looked a little startled, and immediately thereafter there was a second bang.

In that same letter he said he thought he would be coming home in December for "temporary duty." Finally, in late November, on a red letter Monday, the welcome cable arrived. Alan, his job finished in London, confirmed that he would be home for Christmas. We chose January 4 as the date for Marian's wedding, ordered invitations, made lists, checked and rechecked. From a trunk at Mother's we got out her old wedding dress, made in Vienna in 1894, heavy white satin with train attached. The family lace veil was tenderly washed and pressed by Johanna. Bridesmaids were picked and their dresses selected. I chose a dress for myself I thought suitable, the girls said too suitable, so exchanged it for a dashing gold-colored velveteen to be worn with long brown gloves and a wide-brimmed brown velvet hat.

The invitations were addressed and sent out. Wedding presents began to pour in. At this point, let me warn any parents against holding their daughter's wedding in the midst of the Christmas holidays; it is confusion confounded. Express men and mailmen arrived at the front door every minute, bringing batches of Christmas cards mixed with answers to the wedding reception, plus the usual personal invitations for dinners, dances, teas, as the Washington holiday season was at its height.

Just five days before Christmas I took the morning train to New York, the three children following by plane, a treat for the two girls, Roger a veteran boasting of his flight to Ireland when we refugeed there from England the year before. Alan arrived by Pan American clipper that afternoon, splashing down in the harbor. We met him and it was a splendid reunion, all the family together at last.

We went back by train after Alan had given his ladies champagne cocktails at the hotel across from the station. We were separated at dinner in the dining car, Alan with Marian and me, Deborah with Roger. Wishing to relay the latest news from Washington, Roger's high treble rang out the length of the car.

"Pop, did you hear about Gran's bedbug?" My mother, having developed a mysterious rash, finally diagnosed it when she found a small black insect on the blanket, left when the seamstress brought in a box and unpacked it on her bed.

Harris, the chauffeur-butler, had polished up Mother's old Packard sedan, now mine for the duration, and met us at the station wearing a uniform cap and a gleaming smile. Alan was delighted with the 34th Street house, and when Harris, now the correct butler, brought up a drink tray, he settled back in one of the big armchairs. "You have done a fine job, Lydia, and how good it is to be home!"

Next morning he went off to report to the Navy Department. He was the only officer of rank to have actually seen the war at first hand, and he made the rounds of the Navy Department, telling them of the lessons he had learned from the British. He even had a session with President Roosevelt. A friend of his had told him beforehand that, as the president loved to talk, the entire session would be a presidential monologue unless Alan broke in. In some fear and trepidation, Alan did just that after two or three minutes into the interview, saying, "Sir, I really have some things I want to tell you about."

"Oh," the president said. "Well, go ahead."

Alan spoke about pilot and submarine fatigue, the importance of anti-aircraft weapons to combat low-flying planes, and other matters. Alan told me later, however, that his principal point was to mention the Germans' technical advances and to say that the war had become a test of scientific know-how beyond that available in the military. The government needed to set up a group of scientifically qualified people to work on these problems, a recommendation the president followed to great advantage. Early in the New Year Alan was to address the Navy General Board, consisting of the top naval commanders in Washington, as well as Navy Secretary Frank Knox. Meanwhile we could celebrate Christmas and prepare for the wedding on January 4.

The wedding went off well; our bride looked very lovely as Alan in full naval dress, sword at his side, escorted her up the church aisle. Presents packed up and the wedding excitement over, Alan went down to the Navy Department for his General Board session. Coming back late for lunch a few days later, he asked for a drink. Apparently Secretary Knox, very impressed with his presentation before the General Board, had appointed him director of naval intelligence.

Alan was not pleased. It was a very senior assignment for a captain, but he had wanted badly to go to sea after two years on shore. In addition, intelligence was then considered kind of a backwater, and Alan had just had an intelligence assignment as naval attaché in London. On the other hand, his experience in London and his good connections with the British Navy suited him ideally for his new job, and the American government had desperate need of informed, unemotional intelligence on the course of the war. Alan realized he had no choice, so he took up the job in March with the hope his tour would be short.

Like me, Alan had been dismayed by the general public's feeling that the war did not really concern America, but he was heartened by President Roosevelt's action in giving the British fifty of our older destroyers in exchange for bases in Bermuda and the Caribbean. Many protests had been registered against this in Congress and the papers, but the president stood firm, and it became apparent that his real sympathies lay with helping the British as much as he could.

Soon after Alan took over his new duties, I asked him about the women's training program his predecessor had vetoed. He approved the idea, and I recruited eleven navy officer's wives, plus my friend Kay Bundy, whose husband was special assistant to Mr. Henry Stimson, the secretary of war. After giving the matter due thought, Alan sent us a tweed-coated gentleman with a bulging pistol on his hip who was to instruct our group in codes and ciphers. Week after week we struggled with complex numbers and scrambled alphabets, my feeble mathematical mind strained to its utmost. Some of the ladies, Kay Bundy in particular, proved especially adept, but we all worked hard.

Alan soon received orders to increase his staff substantially, to beef up the naval attaché offices around the world, and to place small offices in each of the major ports in the United States. His office became busier, its work more valued. One major accomplishment of the office, of course unknown to me at the time, was breaking the Japanese naval code, but Alan had a running battle with another office over ownership of the program.

Spring arrived, the dogwoods blossomed, and Georgetown gardens were cheerful with flowers and singing birds. Meanwhile, Alan at the

Navy Department tried vainly to convince those in power of the need for preparedness and the risk from the Japanese to our Pacific fleet at Pearl Harbor. He had learned the hard lesson in England and told them, "Do not put your ships together, do not put your planes together, double your guards on Sundays. The enemy is no respecter of the Sabbath, and, above all, do not trust the Japanese already on a war footing in the East." He also prepared prescient papers warning that the Japanese could invade Burma and take the Malay Peninsula whenever they wished. These views were not popular in the department, and Alan was constantly embroiled in bureaucratic battles that he hated.

Placing Alan's people in American ports proved especially useful a few weeks later. Italy's dictator, Benito Mussolini, deluded by visions of grandeur and the hope of emulating Hitler, had joined the Axis powers in June. On a Saturday evening our telephone rang. It was a call from Alan's people in Baltimore saying the crews of the Italian ships interned in the harbor were damaging their machinery, so the ships would not be useful to us if we joined the war. They might even be preparing to sink them in order to delay shipping to England in and out of those ports by creating underwater hazards to navigation. Alan wanted to alert the authorities in our ports as to what was going on so they could put a stop to it, so reached for his wallet and pulled out a paper. He called his office and asked the startled duty officer, "Have you been to the dog races?"

The young man stuttered. "What did you say, sir?"

"Damn it, look at the paper in your pocket, read the answer." A pause.

"No, but I have seen Vatican City." These were the code signals for an emergency.

"All right, here is what you must do. Call in help if you need it." Telling him briefly what had happened and who should be alerted, he directed him to call back after the messages had been delivered.

"We will go down, use the library phone," Alan said. "When they ring back sit beside me to take notes." Many calls came through, among them a three-way conversation set up among Alan, the Navy Department, and the Treasury office in charge of Coast Guard matters. Alan even asked the Treasury Department to pass the word to the White

House. Finally Alan put down the phone, disappointed at the lethargic response. "Will they never learn?" he said bitterly.

As the months wore on Alan became more and more impatient, and toward the end of the summer an old friend, a little more senior than he and attached to the promotion board, told Alan he would never make admiral until he got to sea again; assignments in intelligence and on shore would not do it. Alan went to work, even approaching then Secretary of the Navy James Forrestal about it. Alan finally got away on October 1, 1941, to take command of a squadron of destroyers protecting convoys crossing the Atlantic with war materiel for England.

The American escorts went as far as Iceland, where they handed the convoys over to the protection of British warships. In spite of the fact we were neutral, Alan's orders were to sink any German submarine he spotted. The convoys had to be protected at all costs, for England desperately needed the supplies they brought, food as well as war materiel. Remembering my travails on ocean liners in the winter Atlantic, I quailed at the thought of Alan tossing about in a small destroyer, especially as their speed had to be adapted to that of the slow merchant ships. The weather was bad and the North Atlantic seas very rough. As captain, indeed squadron commander, he was on call at all times. For many days on end he worked and slept roped into a wadded armchair next to his desk, his food brought him in a mug slipped into a notch by his chair.

In September my dear mother died, her death a great sorrow for me. Though an invalid for several years and bedridden, she had remained her own charming self, beloved by all who knew her: children, grandchildren, and her many friends. She was buried with my father in the old family cemetery in Erie, Pennsylvania. I missed her very much.

With Alan away at sea, Roger, Johanna, and I settled in to keep house together. In November I journeyed to Philadelphia to welcome my first grandchild, Marian's daughter Deborah, named after her aunt and born tactfully on her now Uncle Roger's eleventh birthday. He was proud of his niece and I, a grandmother at forty-four, was very happy.

8

America at War, 1941–1946

Sunday, December 7, 1941. I was lunching with my good friends the Richard H. Wilmers that day, beside me one of the White House officials. I can still see the ice cream melting on my plate as, answering a call from the president's office, he came back to tell us, "The Japanese have just attacked Pearl Harbor!" Across the table on my hostess's right the Dutch ambassador rose from his seat, held up his glass, "I drink to our allies."

America was at war.

That same afternoon I had a call from the Navy Department asking if I would bring my fellow code students to report for duty next morning. Our job was to assemble new codebooks to be issued immediately in case the Japanese might have broken the old cipher. We worked at fever pitch, counting pages and stapling them together. More help was needed, and I enlisted a second batch of volunteers to take over from us in the afternoon. Too soon we discovered that volunteers were resented by the department's chief clerk, and after a few weeks only those of us who had been given official status in connection with our earlier training course were kept on, transferred to cable censorship set up in an office building in Arlington, Virginia.

Our job did not require mathematical analysis, merely divining whether there was a suspicious message hidden in a seemingly innocuous text. I was happy to be released from mathematics and sent to where what was needed was knowledge of the world and feminine intuition.

We were given a supervising officer to whom we took any suspicious cables, among them many from a Greek ship owner named Basil Mavroleon, whose messages repeatedly mentioned girls' names. Our supervisor insisted these were code names for ships engaged in nefarious activities. We privately thought the cables were indeed about the Greek tycoon's girl friends, not ships. I am certain we were right, for years later I came across a picture in *Life* magazine of a fat, mustachioed Basil Mavroleon, one girl on his lap, others just behind him.

"Look," I said to Alan, "Here is Basil Mavroleon with his girls, what our man thought were his ships."

Alan returned from sea duty for a few, very few, days, to celebrate Christmas with us and was gone again before New Year's. A happy feature of his visit, however, was his promotion to rear admiral, celebrated with due ceremony. Now our code group was augmented by more volunteers, several State Department wives and others carefully vouched for. One or two of the more mathematically minded, Kay Bundy among them, left to go to secret installations behind barbed wire, the rest of us moving with the cables to the Archives Building on Pennsylvania Avenue. No more nonsense about objections to volunteers. We were properly sworn in and took solemn oaths of secrecy. Cable traffic increased. The navy censored cables, the army censored letters, and we could request referrals in case any matched up together. We never actually knew the results of our hunches, but we were gratified one morning when a senior officer arrived to congratulate us. "Thanks to you ladies we have just made some valuable discoveries."

One of Alan's letters suggested that our daughter Deborah might want to join a woman's military service corps should one be organized. I was not to oppose her. Small chance of that, for she was determined to enlist in the navy's female auxiliary corps, the WAVES (Women Accepted for Volunteer Emergency Service), in September when the corps would first be ready to receive recruits.

Alan returned to Washington in April with new orders that would take him back to London as chief of staff to Admiral Harold Stark, the commander of the navy's liaison office to the British Admiralty there. We had decided to send Roger to a well-known New England boarding

17. Lydia with her son, Roger, Nonquitt, Massachusetts, 1942.

school in September, and with him gone, Marian married, and Deborah about to join the Waves, Alan thought it best we look for a smaller house. We bought one on 35th Street in Georgetown that had belonged to Mother's old German plumber. It seemed to fit all requirements, with some alterations to be completed by the end of the summer.

Satisfied I could leave my censorship ladies in the good hands of a very competent naval wife, I rented out the house at Black Point and took one in the seaside colony of Nonquitt, Massachusetts, for July and August. There I joined many Washington friends who seemed more aware of the war and sympathetic to my concerns than the residents at Black Point, still primarily concerned with stocks and bonds and ordinary business transactions.

In London Alan was again living in the Connaught Hotel a couple of blocks from our embassy in Grosvenor Square. This staff job was not too much to Alan's liking, but, as we were now in the war beside the British, relations were even closer and confidential information was exchanged more freely. Repeated bombing raids were still reported over the city. I felt very anxious, though Alan made little of them in his letters. The British Air Force was doing a fine job, but listening to the radio and hearing the song about a damaged British plane returning to base with the refrain, "Coming in on a wing and a prayer," I said my own silent prayers.

We returned to Washington in time for me to take Deborah down to be sworn into the Waves. Posters had announced "Join the Waves. Release a man to go to sea." The Wave would fill a navy shore job that a man would otherwise have to do. At that time, no women, except nurses on hospital ships, served on shipboard. Deborah, just twenty and five-foot-two, discovered that the man she released was the runner-up in the Golden Gloves boxing tournament.

I was delighted with my house, so fresh and pretty with late roses still blooming in the old German plumber's garden. I rejoined my censorship group, now busier than ever, catching a bus to work each morning to avoid using any of our small ration of gasoline. Washington social life, formal social life, was at a minimum, with no more balls or large parties, but the town was full of people from all parts of the country: lawyers, bankers, industrialists, and others come to offer their services wherever they might be needed.

Cocktail gatherings were popular, and in Georgetown especially we went back and forth, seeing old friends and making new ones. I recall a little ditty that was making the rounds: "From foxholes in Georgetown/attractively bechintzed/the warriors go forth at dawn/the foe to fight ag'inst."

The winter of 1942–43 settled in, long and cold, but I was comfortable with my gas furnace set at the required sixty-five degrees and better off than many now that heating oil was rationed.

In February I had a letter from Alan saying he had been given a new job, commander of the Atlantic Fleet Amphibious Force, and would be arriving in the United States the following month. He did so, but after a couple of weeks at the Navy Department for consultations he went off to the Norfolk area, where the amphibious force, troops and ships, had assembled. Alan hoisted his admiral's flag on the cruiser *Augusta*. He went about collecting a small staff made up of friends and young men whom he had known and had confidence in. Two or three were sons of his friends, in particular McGeorge Bundy, the son of Assistant Secretary of War Harvey Bundy. (McGeorge Bundy later became national security adviser under President John Kennedy.) Several of these young men were to stay with Alan for two or three years and have since remained friends and admirers.

Alan's job was to supervise training in landing on a hostile beach in preparation for the Allied attack in August on Axis-occupied Sicily. He said it was not easy to persuade old sea dogs to ram their boats onto the beach. After all, they had spent their careers keeping their boats off the shore. He also had to work hard to develop a genuinely collaborative army-navy operation, given the traditional rivalry, even suspicion, between the two services. He said the sailors laughed at the army men practicing going up and down the ships' ladders as the ships rolled back and forth. The soldiers, for their part, sneered at the "soft" life the sailors led compared to the "real war" on the ground. Fortunately Alan's army opposite number was a friend, and they managed to form an effective team once it was sorted out that the naval commander was in charge until the troops hit the beach, when the army commander took over.

I had a brief visit with Alan in Norfolk before his task force left in May for the Mediterranean to take part in the Allied invasion of Sicily. In mid-June Roger came home from school, and by the first of July we had packed up for another Nonquitt summer. There I served as an aircraft spotter, spending some evenings in a tower nearby scanning the skies for German airplanes.

One excitement was word that a German spy had been landed on the coast nearby. One evening shortly afterward a rather seedy-looking man rang the bell at a cottage on the point next to Nonquitt. "I am hungry. Could you give me some bread?" he asked. The cottage owner, a retired marine officer, realized that an American would probably have said, "Could you give me something to eat?" not "Could you give me some bread?" He let the man in, seated him in the kitchen, and called the police from another room. "I think I have the German spy here. I'll hold him but come as quick as you can." The police arrived and the man did in fact turn out to be a German agent.

We waited eagerly for Alan's return in late August, as he wrote he would be coming direct to Nonquitt for a week's leave. On a fine sunny afternoon he flew in to an airport across the bay, then came in a small navy boat. His week's leave was shortened to three days by a summons from Washington, but we had one gala evening when a friend opened her big house for Alan to give an account of the Sicily landing. Someone produced maps, and we all listened with breathless interest.

Alan's task force had landed some twenty-five thousand men and supplies on a beach near Scoglitti, on the central of the three Sicilian beaches assigned to the Americans. Alan told about the strong winds and heavy seas that delayed the landing by an hour, the difficulty of unloading the ships in that weather, and the need to change tactics quickly owing to an uncharted sand bar that blocked access to one area. Nevertheless, he won a bottle of whiskey from Lieutenant General George Patton for completing the job faster than Patton thought possible. As a former gunnery officer, Alan was particularly pleased with the success of naval gunfire against land targets, especially when he brought the ships close to land. With their heavy shells and long range, the ships could hit enemy gun emplacements and armor far to the rear of the beachhead, areas that could not be hit from the beaches themselves.

The very next day Alan headed off to Washington. Johanna, Roger, and I closed the house and followed him a few days later to find he had spent one night there and then gone down to Norfolk to say good-bye to the Amphibious Force. It was a difficult moment, for I knew Alan desperately wanted the command of the U.S. naval forces in the coming invasion of France across the English Channel and was fearful his well-trained Sicily staff would be scattered if the decision were too long delayed. A few days later he received orders to fly to Hawaii to brief our Pacific commanders on details of the Sicily operation.

One evening while he was still away my telephone rang. It was a call from a senior officer just in from England.

"I have a message for Alan. The die has been cast. The job is his. They are waiting for him in London."

I knew Alan would be stopping that night in Coronado, California, on the way home, staying at the Hotel del Coronado, a place I imagined

18. Rear Admiral Alan Kirk, right, with Lieutenant General George Patton, Sicily, 1942. Official U.S. Armed Forces photograph.

riddled with spies. I knew I must get the news to him at once. In our code course we had been taught that a family code was the most difficult to decipher. I tossed round in bed and finally wrote out a telegram. Everyone in Washington was concerned about real estate, finding some place to lay their heads, so the message ran:

"Former quarters entirely renovated according your taste. Advise considering necessary furniture. Occupancy around October fifteenth. Love, kisses."

The telegram went through, was understood, and he and his staff, the furniture referred to, had a big celebration. Triumphant they flew home, stopping in Corpus Christi, Texas, to give a whirl to Deborah, stationed there with the WAVES, then flew back to Washington. Five

19. Rear Admiral Alan Kirk, right, with British General Harold Alexander, left center, and Lieutenant General George S. Patton, Commanding General, Seventh U.S. Army, center, aboard Kirk's flagship, USS Ancon, 23 June 1943. Official U.S. Navy photograph, National Archives.

days later they left for New York to sail for London. I went up to bid my husband farewell on his momentous mission.

General Dwight Eisenhower was in overall command of the Normandy operation, and a British admiral was in charge of the naval side under him. Alan was at the next level, in command of the American naval forces in the operation, with responsibility for landing American troops on two invasion beaches. In all he had two thousand vessels under his command. A British admiral commanded the British naval forces that would land a smaller number of British troops on three other beaches. Each operated fairly independently of the other, and Alan was in effect in sole charge of his share. I was very proud of him.

Meanwhile life in Washington went on its busy way that winter of 1943–44. Roger came home for Christmas and Deborah, on leave from Texas, was soon to be sent to Smith College in Massachusetts for officer training. A nephew of Alan's was a student at the Naval Academy, and he and Deborah went off to a holiday dance in their blue uniforms, Deborah distressed at not wearing a ball gown, frills, and tulle.

"Don't worry," I told her. "If you really want to look sexy, that tight, short skirt of yours does the trick." Quite right. Her cousin reported she was the belle of the ball.

The cable traffic continued to grow through the winter, though our customers had become wary. Aside from a flurry of Swiss watches imported through Mexico with their dials set to different times that might indicate code messages, our work was fairly routine.

My thoughts crossed the Atlantic, wondering when and where the invasion of France would be launched, worrying about the continued bombing of England, applauding the brave men of the British Air Force, now joined by our own aviators, who were in the skies night and day, so many never to return.

I still went down to the office each morning, but no cables gave any hint of the date of the landing, and the very few in Washington who knew never told. I had a call from an operator at NBC. "When and if the invasion takes place we plan to wipe all other news and commercials off the radio. We are asking the wives of our commanders to come down to the studio and broadcast messages to our nation by radio" (television had not yet appeared). "We hope you will join them."

The night of June 5–6 I was awakened by the telephone. An excited voice asked, "Mrs. Kirk, have you got your radio on?" Sleepily, rather crossly, I answered, "What is this, a treasure program?" I had thoughts of toasters, washing machines, a gross of beauty products or other items offered to those listening to a radio "treasure" program at odd hours. "No, no, it's the invasion." I was wide awake now but the voice had gone with "I will ring you again later."

Groping my way down the hall to the maid's room I shook my faithful Johanna. "Admiral Kirk has just invaded Normandy. Put on a pot of coffee and bring me the brandy bottle."

Sure enough, back in my room the radio crackled. "The first gliders are coming in to land. The sea is alive with ships. Big guns from two old warships are firing. We understand they have brought the *Wyoming* and her sister ship out of mothballs to batter the coast defenses." The *Wyoming* had been my father's flagship some thirty years before. I knew her well. "Now the destroyers are going into action and troops from the landing craft are swarming ashore, hundreds of them landing on the beach." And so it went on hour after hour.

Heads of nations spoke: our own President Roosevelt, the king of England, the queen of Holland.

After another hour the radio broke off, difficulty in transmission. At six-thirty the phone rang again. This time I recognized the voice, that of the operator from NBC.

"You will come to the studio after dinner tonight, nine o'clock?"

"I'll be there."

I tossed round in bed, thought of the children—Marian down the street, Deborah in Norfolk, Roger arriving next day from Groton School—tossed round some more, dozed uneasily until Johanna brought me my breakfast. I got up and dressed, started to call Marian at nine when the phone rang again.

"Mrs. Kirk, Mrs. Kirk, where are you? We are going on the air in fifteen minutes."

"You said after dinner."

"No, no, after breakfast."

I grabbed a brooch from my pincushion, dashed out of the house, round the corner to Wisconsin Avenue. A taxi was coming down the street, two women in it. I stepped out, held up my hand. "Stop, Stop! My husband has just invaded Normandy and I have to go to the NBC studio."

"Get in, get in," they said.

I arrived breathless, was led into a room where several cool and collected ladies sat hatted and gloved: Mrs. Dwight Eisenhower; Mrs. Omar Bradley, wife of the American army commander; Mrs. Carl Spaatz, wife of the American air commander; and the rest. Photographers waited outside, twelve of them they told me.

"And I don't even have any earrings on," I wailed.

"Never mind," said Mrs. Spaatz, reaching into her bag. "I always carry an extra pair."

In spite of the earrings I am afraid the pictures in the newspapers showed a rather disheveled admiral's lady.

The day went by in a daze. Marian came over for lunch. I tried to phone Deborah, all lines busy. I remembered I had promised to dine with the Harvey Bundys or the Walter Lippmanns, the columnist, whichever couple would be home on invasion night. The Bundys were free, and motoring back from their house I saw a light in the Lippmanns's so stopped by. Helen Lippmann exclaimed, "Lydia, you look awful."

"With good reason," I told her.

"You had better take a pill tonight."

I had never taken a sleeping pill, but Helen brought me down a little red capsule that I obediently swallowed as I got into bed. Waking eight blessed hours later I reached over, turned on my radio. Fortunately, they announced, "This is a rebroadcast. Admiral Kirk's flagship is now going into action."

Another day to go through before meeting Roger's train in the late afternoon. It was hot in my sunny little garden. I picked flowers and lettuces from the side border, planned dinner for a hungry boy. Friends telephoned, more friends telephoned. After lunch I told Johanna not to disturb me, I was going to rest.

At five o'clock I got into my car and drove to the station only to find the Boston train an hour late. I picked up an afternoon paper and went into the restaurant for a lemonade. As I turned the pages there was a photograph of Alan leaning over the rail of the *Augusta*. "That is, that is my husband," I said to the waitress.

"You must be a very proud lady."

"I am indeed."

The train finally came in with an excited and rather soiled little boy carrying a bulging suitcase.

As soon as I got home I telephoned a young friend in the Navy Department's public relations section. "There's a picture of Admiral Kirk in tonight's *Evening Star*. Could you get me a copy?"

20. Admiral Kirk, June 1944. Official U.S. Armed Forces photograph.

That picture I had to have. My friend rang back. "It's a radio photo but we'll do our best." Today that picture, taken by a sailor the day before the landing, sits in my living room. Reproduced and enlarged, it somehow epitomizes all that the war meant. The prince regent of Belgium, to whom we later gave a copy, called it "Freedom looking at Europe."

Happily, children are resilient. At dinner that night Roger's cheerful chatter about school, studies, and sports was a relief after the hours of strain and tension. I enjoyed having a man in the house again.

No letter from Alan arrived until two weeks after D-Day, but we listened to the radio and read the newspaper accounts. Alan wrote that from the first he had been confident of the landing's success. Everything had gone as planned, though on Omaha Beach where he put some of Lieutenant General Bradley's troops ashore the fighting had been hard. A few days after he wrote, however, a terrible storm blew up, causing great damage and considerable delays. This was serious, as Alan had to keep our men on the beaches supplied with everything they needed to live and to fight. He started a letter on June 21 with the words, "The weather

21. From left, Rear Admiral Alan Kirk, Commander Western Naval Task Force; Lieutenant General Omar Bradley, Commanding General, U.S. First Army; Rear Admiral Arthur D. Struble (with binoculars), Kirk's chief of staff; and Major General Hugh Keen, U.S. Army, off Normandy, June 1944. Official U.S. Navy photograph, National Archives.

has been fearful these last few days. . . . I am concerned." He broke off, and resumed on June 24–25 with the news that "The strain is over and we are getting things going again." Indeed, by July 3 he was able to turn matters over to others and return to England.

With our censorship group at full complement I decided to take six weeks off in July and August. The property at Black Point needed looking after because of a succession of tenants, so we packed up for a summer holiday there. I delayed my departure, sending Roger and Johanna ahead, as Alan wrote he was coming back to report to Washington and would go with me to the Point for a week's leave. He returned in glory, now promoted to vice admiral with a fresh string of decorations on his chest. We flew up to Black Point together by navy plane, landing at the local airfield in great style. Deborah also wangled some leave, and Marian came to join us, so for a precious, all too short time I had my family united once more.

The days passed quickly before Alan went off to France with new orders as Eisenhower's "Commander, U.S. Naval Forces, France," with headquarters in Paris. My brother Selden Chapin, who was in the American diplomatic service, was sent to Algiers to be ready to reopen our Paris embassy as soon as the city was liberated. His wife went over to join him. No wives of high-ranking military men were allowed to go abroad, but that did not apply to diplomatic wives. Privately I decided it was the fault of the generals who did not want their wives. As one of my chief assets was a near-native command of the French language I thought I might be of help. No chance, however.

We climaxed our own summer with a hurricane. The forces of nature unleashed are terrifying, but in spite of warnings from the state police—"Leave the shore. Go to high ground"—we stayed put. I knew the house, very solidly built and on a rise in the ground, had survived the 1938 hurricane and felt sure we could last this one out. We opened spare rooms to friends with less substantial dwellings and battened down for the storm. The winds and rains descended, then that breathless hush when the eye comes and the winds veer, only to start up again. Fortunately the house stood firm with no more damage than shutters torn loose and broken tree branches scattered over the lawn. We mopped up the puddles, picked up the branches, put back the shutters, closed the house, and returned to Washington.

In late summer one of my friends had organized a group of five women to go out under the auspices of the International Red Cross to speak to the relatives of the Americans held as prisoners of war and those listed as missing. One of the women had dropped out, and my friend asked me to take her place. By now cable traffic was strictly routine, so I decided to accept her offer.

I said good-bye to my censorship friends, ordered my Red Cross uniform, studied up on the Geneva Convention governing prisoners of war, and learned the rules and procedures for sending packages to the

22. Lydia in her Red Cross uniform, 1944. Official Red Cross photograph.

prisoners. I submitted my proposed half-hour speech on these matters to our director and received his approval and a notebook listing all the camps. This would be of help in answering questions put to me by the audience. The office in Washington would keep me up to date on conditions within the camps, as these varied enormously.

It seemed a very worthwhile project. My beat would be New York, New Jersey, and Pennsylvania. The schedule made for me kept me busy through most of the winter. I racketed back and forth by train and bus, now and then by plane, making one-night stands. I spoke in mining towns, in steel towns around Pittsburgh, in various county seats, my audience ranging from a hundred or so to a thousand.

On May 8, 1945, in a small hotel in upstate New York, I got the good news of the German surrender and the end of the war in Europe. I went joyfully back to Washington with the hope that, sooner or later, Alan would be coming home.

My hopes were realized when letters arrived saying Alan would be returning with General Eisenhower in late June or early July, returning for good. Finally the date for General Eisenhower's return was set. Accompanied by his staff, a brief stop would be made in Bermuda, then they would fly into Washington on June 18 and proceed next day to New York for a parade and official welcome by that city.

Saks Fifth Avenue telephoned me one morning. In view of the warm weather they were sending tailors to Bermuda to outfit the officers with summer uniforms. Would I please give them Alan's size and send the ribbon bars to be worn on his jacket. I doubted the generosity of the store would run to more than one suit, as the army's olive-drab summer uniform does not soil as quickly as the navy's white one. Johanna and I routed out Alan's white uniforms from the depths of a trunk and sent them to be laundered. A good precaution, as during the celebrations he sometimes wore two a day.

When the great moment arrived, all of us, the whole family, went to the airport and watched as the planes came in, then watched the triumphant cortege from a special grandstand on Pennsylvania Avenue near the White House. As they passed the turn by the Treasury and approached the White House, a navy band, catching sight of Alan's white navy uniform, played "Anchors Aweigh." We felt very proud, and later, in the hotel rooms assigned to us, we held a joyful family reunion. My girls were amused by a phrase in the information brochure. "Hotel accommodations will be provided for family reunions. Bedrooms are included." Sure enough, they claimed to have opened a door and seen a couple taking advantage of the double bed.

Next morning our men flew to New York for another parade. We wives took an early train, as Mrs. Eisenhower disliked flying. We arrived in time for the parade and a splendid lunch given by Mayor Fiorello La Guardia at the Waldorf Astoria Hotel. There Alan and I were put in one of the royal suites and held court for friends and relatives in town.

Deborah had come up so as not to miss the fun, and so had dear Aunt Sally from Princeton. It was all very gala. Two days later Alan and I drove with General Eisenhower's party to West Point where the general asked Alan to take the salute with him, the two standing side by side at the review.

Altogether a very satisfactory homecoming.

With Alan ordered to duty at the Navy Department, it now became necessary to find a proper house, one that could be our permanent home. The one we chose was 3017 N Street in Georgetown. It was a fine old house, large yard in the rear, two magnificent magnolia trees in front. I was uneasy about its size and maintenance, accusing Alan of delusions of grandeur, but he charmed the owner into selling it to us at a reasonable price, and we moved into our mansion in August.

Meanwhile Deborah had become engaged to the most attractive of her many beaus, Peter Solbert, back from his naval service in the Pacific and due to enter Harvard Law School in the fall. Once more Johanna and I got out Mother's wedding dress and veil. Deborah was married on September 8, 1945, at Christ Church down the street, and we held the reception in our garden.

After the wedding Alan and I settled down. The house seemed large and rambling after my 35th Street one, but we reveled in the space and its rather shabby charm. We planned to make changes as we could afford them.

The winter was very gay. We held a dance for young marrieds at Christmas, gave luncheons and dinners, and generally had a good time. We even gave a teenage party for Roger, a little sticky until a round of parlor games broke the ice. We were very happy in what we assumed would be our permanent home.

We should have known better.

PART FOUR

Belgium, 1946–1949

9

A Good Start in Brussels, 1946

Alan's work in the Navy Department in the summer of 1945 proved dull in comparison to the excitement of two invasions, and the top navy brass seemed to pay more attention to those who had been on aircraft carriers in the Pacific theater. In late January of 1946, this became irrelevant, as President Harry Truman asked Alan to go as ambassador to Belgium. Alan had seven more years to serve in the navy before reaching the retirement age of sixty-five, but with the war over in the Pacific he could not look forward to much active duty. He decided to accept the appointment, retiring from the navy with the rank of four-star admiral.

Alan was selected for this diplomatic post because of his abilities, well known to then-Secretary of State Dean Acheson, a good friend since the early 1920s, but also because of his stature as a leading figure in the Normandy landing and then with General Eisenhower in liberated France. This gave him great prestige in Belgium, a country that was well disposed to the Americans in any case because of our role in the war and the good behavior of the American troops quartered there in 1944–45.

Our surroundings would be more cheerful than in much of postwar Europe, as the Belgian economy was much better off than that of its neighbors. Belgium had been the "rear area" of the battle lines for many months, and the Allied armies' expenditures there had given an early boost to its economy. In addition, Belgium had a large dollar reserve in the United States from America's wartime purchases of large amounts of copper, uranium, and other metals from the Congo, then a Belgian colony. The dollars were all in a trust fund in the name of Belgium, and dollars were the thing to have.

Happily for me Belgium was partially a French-speaking country. My French was still fluent, and Alan's Naval Academy French had improved, thanks to lessons taken during his winter in France. But what did I really know of Belgium? Only Bruges, a trading center of the Middle Ages, with its ancient buildings, its canals, the Hans Memling paintings in the museum, and the cloaked women trotting to and fro between their tiny houses in an ancient conventlike compound there.

Some time before leaving Washington, Mrs. Merriweather Post Davies, the cereal family heiress and wife of Joseph Davies, the last prewar American ambassador to Belgium, invited me to tea. She very kindly offered to show me pictures of the embassy residence, the Palais d'Assche, by her description a very handsome house. I was much impressed. It looked very grand. It had been empty for nearly four years, however. It had been sealed up in 1941, when the United States and Germany went to war and all our diplomats had to leave German-occupied Belgium. It was reopened only in 1944, when our forces liberated Brussels. I wondered what it would look like now.

We were asked to dinner by the Belgian ambassador in Washington, who expressed his pleasure at the appointment of so distinguished a war hero as Admiral Kirk. We also went to a dinner in our honor at the Luxembourg legation, as Alan would be minister to tiny, neighboring Luxembourg as well as ambassador to Belgium. In those days the United States gave their head representative to less important countries the title of minister, not ambassador. Alan would only have to visit Luxembourg every two or three months. The rest of the time a middle-grade American diplomat would be in charge.

Masses of new calling cards were ordered and engraved. The stationer also supplied us with invitations, boxes of them, gold-marked place cards, and folded take-in cards to tell the gentlemen what woman to escort from the living room into the dining room, plus a leather table-seating plan with slots for guests' names. All this was packed and sent ahead with a few of our own pictures, books, and mementos.

Passage was engaged for mid-April on the *Queen Mary*. We would land in England and spend a couple of nights with Admiral Sir John and Lady Little, he a wartime colleague of Alan's now with headquarters at Portsmouth on the southern coast. From there we would fly over to Belgium in our embassy's air attaché plane. This plane, in our case a two-engine DC-3, was under the control of the embassy air attaché but would be available for business trips by Alan and other officials.

Upon our ship's arrival in Dover we were met by Admiral Little's car and aide and driven through the green English countryside to Portsmouth, where we were welcomed by our hosts in their fine old house. After drinks and a good dinner of English roast beef we went off to bed, I very thankful to be on land once more.

Next day we were to make an early start. Our suitcases packed, we said goodbye to our kind hosts and drove to the airfield where our plane awaited us, the rest of our luggage, trunks, and boxes roped and lashed in the after cabin. We were off across the channel, a quick flight, and landed at Brussels airport.

At the foot of the ramp the embassy staff, headed by the most senior officer, the counselor, was lined up to greet us. With stiff formality the counselor presented the Belgian chief of protocol, the Comte de Ghellinck, a fussy little man in morning coat and striped trousers (familiarly known, as I learned afterward, as the Count de Gink), then the various staff members and their wives. Compliments exchanged, we got into the embassy limousine. Although the flagship of the transport fleet, it was a truly venerable Cadillac, but the chauffeur, Benoit, drove it with a dash and style that suited Alan very well.

On our way from the airport I remarked to Alan, "That counselor is even more pompous than I expected, and his wife is so painfully correct. Good thing that he's leaving." I knew that the poor gentleman's fate had been sealed when Alan received a letter from him in Washington that read, "You will be happy to know, Mr. Ambassador, that the embassy has a sufficiency of motorized transport."

We drove along cobbled streets, rows of gray stone or stuccoed houses, busy avenues with trams running down the middle, and narrow, crowded sidewalks, until we came into a tree-filled square where we drew near an imposing façade with an American flag hanging from a second-floor balcony. The property of a leading noble family, it was in fact a palace, formerly used for the heir to the throne, and it had all the aspects of one.

We turned into a tunneled entrance and stopped under a central portico beyond which lay a square lawn with stables at the back, now converted into offices and garages. It was apparent there were two sections to the building, as there were steps and a wide doorway on the left, steps and another wide doorway on the right. An elderly guard standing on the right-hand steps advanced to open the car door, showing us into an entrance hall. Large, darkly handsome rooms opened on either side of the hall, offices of the counselor and the next most senior man. Beyond was a grilled elevator and wide, red-carpeted stairs leading to the second floor. We mounted the stairs, before us a long, high-ceilinged room where Mademoiselle Ida Nerincx, secretary and housekeeper for succeeding ambassadresses for twenty-five years, stood to greet us.

Mademoiselle Nerincx was a small, rosy-cheeked woman, pleasant-faced, in a black wool dress touched with jet at the throat. Competent I felt sure, but all doubts were set at rest as she bade us welcome to the Palais d'Assche, obviously relieved we both spoke French. She then presented the household staff to us: Émile the butler; Alphonse the second man; his wife Jeanne, the chambermaid; the chef Merlini; his pink-cheeked assistant, the kitchen boy; the housemaid, frightened and cross-eyed; and another frightened child, the scullery maid. We shook hands and Mademoiselle dismissed them to the outer regions.

We walked on into the room, joined by our counselor and his wife, who drank a glass of ceremonial sherry with us and bowed their way out. Mademoiselle then suggested we look over the house; certain rooms had been prepared for us, but these could be changed if unsuitable.

On the same floor, facing the street and the park square, was the so-called *Chambre Royale* (Royal Bedroom), once used by King Albert and his wife during their residence in the Palais d'Assche before he ascended the throne early in the twentieth century. Alan immediately decided to appropriate this room for his office; the dressing room alongside would do for his secretary, a nice woman whom he had inherited from my State Department brother, Selden.

On the floor above, rows of bedrooms ran down either side of a central hall. Two large ones at the far end had been set aside for our approval. Both looked comfortable, though mine was sparse as to curtains and I was thankful for my foresight in begging a bolt of chintz from the State Department. Bright chintz roses climbing over the windows and furniture in my room would help. From somewhere below decorous brown velvet draperies were resurrected to match upholstered nineteenth-century Empire style furniture for Alan, who would sleep in correct splendor.

Our luncheon that first day was alarmingly good. I was later told that our chef Merlini had the reputation of being one of the best in Brussels. In a city and country where food is taken as a sacred rite we should count ourselves lucky. The first weekly bill, however, was so high Alan asked Mademoiselle to summon the chef. He explained to him that contrary to some of our predecessors we were not millionaires. We appreciated the artistry of his cuisine; we understood too that it would be difficult to adapt his menus to suit our budget, but as he was such an excellent chef we also knew he could make the simplest dishes quite as delicious as any others. If he felt it impossible to remain at the embassy under such restrictions we would be very sorry but would quite understand.

Merlini stayed on, lobster was replaced by humbler fish, and marvelously seasoned meats masked the absence of foie gras. The bills came down and we continued to eat superb food. Alan always liked good wine, and his old friend Raymond Baudouin in Paris, a hero of the French Resistance movement against the German occupiers and a renowned wine merchant, supplied us with a cellar of which even Mademoiselle approved. Wine, I gathered, was even more sacred than food to the Belgians, whose own supplies had been concealed from the German occupiers as carefully as their children or their diamonds. One unfortunate family hid theirs in the pond in front of their chateau. After several months the German officers billeted there noticed interesting labels floating on the surface and dredged up the whole lot.

Our luncheon had been served at a small table at one end of the dining room, overlooking a wide lawn. The main dining area was large with a long, gray, painted table centered under a crystal chandelier, chairs to match lining walls hung with mirrors and flowered eighteenth-century-style tapestries. Mademoiselle reappeared as we sat having coffee in the smoking room. She led us back through the dining room; the table she said could stretch to twenty-four without crowding. We walked on, coming out on a square hall from which a wide wrought-iron-railed stairway, the inevitable *escalier d'honneur* (grand staircase), went down to the state entrance we had seen on the left of the ground-floor portico. The hall opened on two immense salons furnished in the approved palace style with stiff gilt settees and chairs covered in pale brocade, more crystal chandeliers overhead, and a mantelpiece of green malachite, the gift of a Russian grand duke to the d'Assche family. Malachite mantelpieces abound throughout European palaces. Tsars and grand dukes must have packed dozens in their luggage as presents to their hosts.

"Fortunately," Mademoiselle told us, "these rooms were left with the original furniture." There were fringed damask curtains and handsome but worn rugs by Aubusson, the leading French tapestry and rug maker since the sixteenth century. Privately I thought the rooms pretentious. For an embassy residence, however, the building had the advantage of space and considerable prestige as the largest in Brussels. Before we left I grew quite fond of it, knowing the Belgians liked display—a leftover, perhaps, from the tradition of grandeur associated with their fifteenth-century Burgundian rulers, dukes then independent of France and who controlled what are now Belgium, Luxembourg, and part of Holland in addition to Burgundy itself.

Hardly settled and unpacked, Alan received a summons to go to the palace to present his credentials, a letter from our president to the host-country head of state confirming an ambassador's appointment. This presentation marked the formal beginning of Alan's mission, enabling him to be received as ambassador. I say "unpacked," but one trunk was missing, the one containing an all-important costume, the cutaway required for the palace ceremony. There was nothing to do but rent one. The tails came to Alan's heels, but he still looked very smart as he went off with the members of his staff in a cortege of automobiles sent by the palace. In the old days royal coaches were provided but had not been seen since the war. Too bad. I would have loved to see him drive away in gilded splendor.

The Belgians' King Leopold had remained in the country at the time of the German invasion in 1940, saying, "Soldiers, I stay to share your fate." A sorry business, for most of his troops were captured by the Germans while the king, left behind, was a too-willing prisoner of the enemy, living comfortably in his palace. Liberated by the Americans, he went to Switzerland. When the Belgian government-in-exile in England returned to Belgium, they proceeded in a body to ask the king to return. This he refused to do unless granted powers beyond those of the existing constitution, and the question remained unresolved.

Meanwhile Prince Charles, Leopold's younger brother, led the country as prince regent, and it was to him that Alan presented his credentials. Educated in England, briefly an officer in the British Navy, Prince Charles proved a good constitutional ruler. Ably surrounded and seconded by André de Staercke, an extraordinary young man of thirty-two or thirty-three, he presided over the recovery of Belgium, carefully insisting that he was doing so as regent, with no pretensions of usurping his brother's place.

Prince Charles had joined the anti-German underground during the 1941–44 German occupation of Belgium, so there was no question of his patriotism. He had, however, occasionally fallen into the lower depths of society and conduct in his youth. He was an unhappy man, one with a torturing distrust of himself and others, incapable of showing gratitude to those who served him. Yet, if he had so desired, it is quite possible the people would have accepted him as king in lieu of his brother, something that might have been good for Belgium. He steadfastly refused to do so, whether from family loyalty or gnawing suspicion of his own motives.

The most divisive issue in Belgium at the time was whether the king should be invited back or not. The Socialist Party opposed his return, although the conservative Catholic Party favored it. In 1946 the Socialists were the stronger, but by 1950 the Catholics and other supporters of the king were in power. They persuaded the king to reassume his office, and the prince regent quietly stepped aside. Popular indignation at this move soon boiled over, and the king was forced to abdicate in favor of his son in 1951. I sometimes wonder what might have happened if Alan had still been there. All parties respected him—Socialist, Liberal, and Catholic—and the influence of a strong American ambassador might have helped resolve the question more peaceably.

Another, eventually more serious, split was linguistic. The southern half of the country spoke French and looked to France for cultural inspiration, but the northern half spoke Flemish, akin to Dutch, and looked more toward Holland. Feelings on both sides ran high. Later Belgium became even more unhappily divided linguistically. A foolish business in a relatively small nation. In our day, however, the royal question was more important than the linguistic one, and Alan did the best he could to keep it from tearing the country apart, as a peaceful and united Belgium was very much in America's interest.

As Belgium was a member of the United Nations Security Council and the United Nations Trusteeship Council, and both had only a few members, Belgium's vote was important. Part of Alan's job would be to persuade the Belgian government to vote with us. Most important of all, the Belgian government in exile during World War II had secretly agreed that England and America could buy all the uranium produced in the Belgian Congo, then the best and largest source of uranium in the world.[1]

These were the days of the cold war between the United States and the Soviet Union, and Alan's primary job was to do what he could, as the representative of the United States, to keep Belgium united, pro-American, and prosperous so it could make a maximum contribution to the struggle against the Soviets. He had to try to reduce the influence of the local Communist Party and to make sure that uranium, copper, and other raw materials kept flowing to the United States from the Belgian Congo.

1. For a description of this agreement, see the U.S. Department of State, *Foreign Relations of the United States, 1944*, vol. 2, *General: Economic and Social Matters* (Washington, D.C.: United States Government Printing Office, 1944), 1026–30, http://digital.library.wisc.edu/1711.dl/FRUS.FRUS1944v02.

Alan of course had considerable influence as the representative of the United States, but good personal relations would make him much more effective, and he needed to develop a wide circle of friends among leaders in government, business, and intellectual circles.

This is where I thought I could help. A hospitable house, a good table, and a hostess who could converse freely in the local language would make his task much easier. I also fancied that I myself could show that American women could be interesting, interested, and even intelligent, and I was determined to try. That meant keeping a smooth-running household and a busy social schedule, one that sometimes tried my patience as well as my stomach.

Once Alan was duly accredited we were faced with a series of official calls, Alan on certain cabinet ministers and various ambassadors who had arrived before he did, mine on their wives. Happily the number of missions was less than today, but it was still a formidable program. Calls could be timed at thirty minutes apiece, but it was hard to get more than two done in an afternoon. Conversation at first was stilted, but there were compliments for my French, which I discovered was a great deal better than that of some of my colleagues, even better than some of the Belgian ladies I met, whose accents could be as heavy as their figures. For some reason they seemed to be afflicted with very large rears and looked wistfully at mine.

Speaking of rears, a wonderful story current that first year was about an Englishman who came to speak to the Anglo-Belgian Association. All of the members could have understood his address in English, but he chose to speak in French. His opening remarks dealt with his own life, "*Quand je regarde mon derrière je vois que c'est divisé en deux parties égales,*" which translated as "When I look at my past [in French, "my rear"], I see it is divided in two equal parts." The audience was delighted.

I found the British ambassadress, unkindly known as Lady Frigidaire, not as cold as reported, a frail, reserved woman whose only son had been killed in the war. Later we became great friends. There was no Soviet ambassadress. Her husband regretted she was away, but gossip had it he was waiting for a replacement, someone more suitable for the post. He himself left quite soon to be followed by a gentleman with white hair and carefully dyed black whiskers whose wife was reputed to be an expert pistol shot. Whether she practiced in the Lubianka prison cellars in Moscow we never knew. In any event, she was a grim creature of forbidding aspect.

More calls. Tea with the Dutch ambassadress was interrupted by a loud crash in the street outside. My hostess went down to see what had happened, sent up word she was rendering first aid, and came back slightly spattered with blood spots, having helped hoist an injured man into the ambulance. Marietcha van Harinxma was a very large, lusty lady who had served as a nurse and driven ambulances during the war, great fun to be with, if a trifle alarming in her exuberance.

Notable among the other ambassadresses were the Brazilian, small and vivacious, with a husband who invariably went to sleep at dinner parties, and the Cuban, very blonde and handsome in marvelous French dresses, as loaded with diamonds as her husband's fields must have been loaded with sugar cane. Of course this was before Castro came to power in Cuba and nationalized such plantations. Some countries were represented by ministers, and their ladies called first on me, they being of lower diplomatic rank. All these calls had to be returned, floods of tea, polite conversation.

Happily most could speak French, but the visit of the wife of the Czech minister, a stout lady who spoke only Czech and German, was necessarily short as, once I got through *"Haben Sie Kinder? In Brussels nicht Sonnenschein fuer die Kinder"* (Do you have children? In Brussels there is no sunshine for the children), my repertoire of German was exhausted.

Then the Belgian ladies called. Some merely left cards; others, approved by Mademoiselle or recommended by friends, came by appointment. It all made for busy afternoons. This round of calls was standard practice for newly arrived ambassadors and their wives. The object was to introduce the newcomers to their diplomatic colleagues, whom they would be seeing a great deal of, and to local folk whom it was useful for them to meet. It was tiresome, but it did provide a basis for future business and social activities. With so many countries in existence today, calls on all other ambassadors would be an impossible burden, and life in most capitals has become informal enough to make it unnecessary. A simple phone call or a conversation at a reception will often do, but that was not the case in Belgium in 1946.

Quite soon after Alan presented his diplomatic credentials we were asked to lunch at the Royal Palace. Prince Charles entertained rarely, even reluctantly. His secretary indicated we would be alone. I put on my best clothes and best manners, made a kind of bob when introduced. This was my first encounter with royalty except for the grand and distant presentation at court in England in 1939, and a sighting of the king and queen of England at a British Embassy garden party in Washington the month before that.

We were just five at table: the prince, André de Staercke, the prince's military aide Colonel van Nerom, and ourselves. The prince told André afterward he did not think I was always as correct as I appeared. Anyway it was E for effort that first time. Alan got on very well with the prince with the bond of naval service and the war between them, and André, always delightful, helped everything along.

We then settled into our job of making ourselves and our country known and respected in Belgium's leading circles. For me this involved hosting and attending many dinners and lunches, seeking to charm or at least interest my table companions and to give an example of an intelligent, informed American woman, one whose lively curiosity and fluent French would dent the feeling that "Americans have no interest in other countries and know no foreign languages." I also was at Alan's side on official visits to the principal Belgian cities and at various ceremonies, many connected with the war that had ended only the year before. There was tedium, and the weather was foul, but I met interesting people, saw interesting things, and felt I was performing a real service.

One of the best features of Belgian social life lay outside of Brussels: Sunday lunches at chateaus in the country, and in the autumn splendid weekend shooting parties. Besides being pleasant, these visits were part of our outreach to the business community, an important part of an ambassador's job. Too often ambassadors focus only on government officials, forgetting that business people have important influence in their country. The visit I describe here is typical of many that we made during our years in Belgium, visits that cemented real friendships between ourselves and our hosts, some of whom I still see today.

We drove out through the suburbs, pounding along over cobbled streets on into the country, passing the monument at Waterloo commemorating the victory of the British and their allies over Napoleon in 1815, a man-made hill topped by a rather silly-looking lion glaring defiantly toward France. We went through several gray villages, beyond which stretched flat fields planted with sugar beet, a principal Belgian export. Now and again a few picturesque old farmhouses, solid stone-walled structures—too few, for the Belgians prefer comfort to taste, and the newer houses were bright plaster and red brick. We coasted down a hill, crossed a railroad track, up through fields again to the gates of the Château Chenoy.

Prosperity blossomed in Belgium during the late nineteenth century and new money built chateaus, enclosed parks, and set aside wide acres stocked with game, pheasant, and partridge, even deer and wild boar in wooded areas. Chenoy was a large house, very large, and its hostess, Baronne Marthe Boel, matched its size, a tall, older woman of great presence, surrounded by sons and daughters as tall as herself. She greeted us in a wide hall where antlers and stuffed animal heads loomed down from dark paneled walls. Thick oriental carpets covered polished floors, the rooms crowded with heavy furniture, but there were flowers everywhere, great bowls and huge pots of bright color, all brought in from greenhouses we had passed on the way through the chateau's park.

Lunch was served at a long polished oak table, a lunch as long and solid as the table itself—a series of wines, rich dishes, and finally fruits from the hothouses, big and luscious as the vases outside. No wonder Belgians talked of their liver complaints, and periodic cures at local spas were accepted routine.

Belgian society in the 1940s had its definite cliques. These cliques extended so far that even as broad-minded a lady as Baronne Boel never consulted a doctor who did not belong to her party. Schools and universities were sharply divided. There were Catholic and non-Catholic scout troops. Protestants as such were scarce in Belgium, mostly foreigners who attended either of the two English-language churches. Some circles crossed at the edges, especially among younger people. Established wealth was a passport for many, and the great Jewish families moved easily about. Even so, lines were drawn.

A conspicuous figure was the Princess Elizabeth Ruspoli, an exceedingly pretty young woman, a miniature Marlene Dietrich. Born a Belgian, Countess d'Assche, she had married an Italian who was killed early in the war. She returned to Brussels and became the mistress of General Alexander Von Falkenhausen, the German military commander for Belgium. A pocket Venus, blonde, blue-eyed, she was said to have held court to German officers in her bathtub. A storybook adventuress actually playing a double game, from time to time she gave refuge to English aviators in a back room while she entertained the general and his staff at dinner. It was to the Princess Ruspoli that distraught women addressed themselves when husbands or sons were captured, hoping their lives might be saved through her influence with the authorities.

Later in the war, when Von Falkenhausen fell out of favor with Hitler, Elizabeth Ruspoli herself was imprisoned but claimed to have converted her jailer to Catholicism. Back in Brussels she behaved with great discretion and began gradually to move in society along with other, less conspicuous cooperators with the German occupiers who had already been accepted. Finally, after a year or so, the British ambassador invited her to dinner. Alan and I consulted. Now one met her everywhere and, if the British took the lead, who were we to hold out, so we compromised by inviting her to lunch.

An adventuress perhaps, a double agent, but hearing all the tales, how to judge any of these people? How do I know what I would have done faced with torture or death for my nearest and dearest? How do I know what I would have done to preserve my own life, to escape from intolerable pain? Heroics are easy to read about, hard, I am sure, to put into practice.

There were others, brave men and women to whom Alan gave decorations that first summer. After doing so, he often said, "I wish I did not have to give their names. Who knows? We might need them again," meaning of course against the Soviet Union. Happily that has not proved necessary.

One day in early May a nice Middle Western girl, a former Red Cross nurse now doing part-time work with the Red Cross Brussels branch, came to call on me. She asked if I would be willing to go with her and the Red Cross director to visit certain villages in northern Belgium that were anxious to express their thanks for the help given them at the time of the liberation and during the months that followed. There would be meetings arranged in the village halls where perhaps I would say a few words in addition to a short speech by the director. It would mean much to the simple folk who would appreciate the appearance of the new American ambassadress.

I said I would ask my husband but felt sure he would agree. I could even dig out my own Red Cross uniform. Would she like me to wear it?

"That would be wonderful. They are really good people and truly grateful for what we did for them."

It was a lovely May day when we set out, rattling over the cobbled roads, and drew up at the first stop, where the mayor was waiting on the steps of the local town hall. He led our party upstairs to a room full of people, seated us at a table, then pulled out a paper from his pocket and read a speech in Flemish, interpreted by the director who sat beside me. As I got up to speak, the director whispered, "Best speak in English, Madame; your French is too good. They might not believe you were American." I said a few simple words, which some of the audience seemed to understand, while others waited for the mayor to interpret. A tray appeared with the traditional ceremonial glasses of wine, bouquets were presented, and we went on our way to the next village.

Here people were gathered in the street, pressing forward to shake my hand, children offering flowers as we walked along. By the time we got back into the car my Red Cross girl in the rear seat was nearly buried in bouquets.

At another village we stopped at a children's home kept by kind French-speaking nuns who escorted me to the babies' dormitory. Rows of cots were set along the wall, flags pinned to the head of each cot. I paused by one that bore an English flag. The baby was black.

"*Surement, ma soeur,*" I said to the nun beside me. "*C'est un petit américain*" (Surely, sister, that is a little American).

She blushed. "*On n'a pas voulu vous offenser, madame*" (We did not want to offend you, madame).

These babies—English, American, some German perhaps—were clear evidence that occupation brings other problems than ruined crops and shattered homes.

On May 30, our American Memorial Day, Alan chose to visit the American cemetery in Flanders for soldiers killed in the 1914 war, a small cemetery just outside the town where I had gone with my Red Cross lady. Met by the village elders, we got out of our car and walked down a narrow country lane, preceded by a tootling band. A priest standing by the cemetery entrance guided us in among the graves, each decorated by the townspeople with bunches of garden flowers. The little cemetery was well kept, the grass cut, the paths straight and sanded.

Alan laid a wreath on the central memorial and made a short speech of thanks for the care given our American dead in the war we had shared so many years ago. My friend the mayor once more interpreted in Flemish to the assembled crowd, who stood respectfully silent. The priest concluded the ceremony with a prayer. The band dispersed, we shook hands all around, then walked quietly back to our car. I thought how right any relatives had been to leave their men where they had fallen, to leave them in the care of these good, kind people.

A few days later we were invited to pay a formal visit to the city of Liège in the French-speaking area near the forests of the Ardennes, scene of the last desperate German offensive in December 1944. Official visits to towns throughout the country can be trying, but they spread goodwill toward America among local leaders and their people. If these leaders move to the national scene, attention paid to them beforehand is doubly useful. These trips also gave a useful corrective to the special atmosphere of the capital city, and we made many, of which this one was typical.

We drove up through Namur with its seventeenth-century fortress high on a hill and on through villages, their war memorials with names of men executed by the Germans in the two world wars. In the open fields there were still rusted bits of tanks or planes left behind in the final German retreat in World War II. We arrived in Liège in good time for a decoration ceremony in front of the old city hall. Special honors were to be paid to the city's gendarmes, the local police who had joined in a valiant defense of their city. They were lined up in long rows, the first to be decorated. More decorations to city notables and then a large formal lunch in the great hall lasting until four o'clock, after which we went to our hotel and took refuge until dinner. The hotel had served as German headquarters and still bore evidence of the occupiers, scarred walls and broken plumbing, but we were grateful for a few hours' rest.

Our dinner host was head of a large engineering firm. He received us at the door of his house and led us upstairs, where a long table was set for some sixteen or eighteen guests, innumerable wineglasses by each plate. Course after course arrived on steaming platters, each accompanied by the proper wine. In the middle of the dinner a florid lady sitting far down the table got up, followed by a young man, and walked over to a piano just outside the dining room door. Our host explained that a former grand opera star would now entertain us. This was in the nature of *entremets,* a between-course treat. The accompanist sat down and the lady let go with high tremulous notes ending with a crashing finale, all this in spite of having consumed paté, fish, and roast, not to speak of a succession of wines.

Much applause from the guests, who then settled back for ham and salad and a dessert of praline ice cream surmounted by a mountain of meringue washed down with pink champagne. Throughout the meal there was much talk of wines, Alan being teased on his preference for Bordeaux, the Belgians preferring Burgundy because of their historic ties to that region of France. Finally the dinner and the evening came to an end. Almost staggering, we collapsed at the hotel.

As I got into bed I figured we had spent seven hours at table, three at lunch and four at dinner. Breakfast next morning was spartan enough, served by German prisoners very gray and glum, but tea and burnt toast on cracked plates were gratefully received.

Before going to Liège we had made a trip to Luxembourg so Alan could present his credentials as American minister to that country. On the date set we drove up to be met by our chargé d'affaires, Mr. George Platt Waller, a stout, pompous southern gentleman who immediately offered to instruct me on the proper way of curtsying to the grand duchess. I told him I had managed this at the time of my presentation to the king and queen of England and did not think a lesson would be required.

Roger, who accompanied Alan on a trip to Luxembourg a few months later, told me that Mr. Waller informed him that he believed in "government by the wise, the wealthy, and the gentle born." This from the official representative of the United States of America!

Our visit was cheered by a call from the foreign minister, Monsieur Joseph Bech, a truly remarkable man, a great European whose knowledge and salty humor would have graced any major power and who played an important role in European political life for many years. He was a useful source of information for Alan, part of whose job was to report on European developments from the point of view of the smaller countries.

Next day, guided by Monsieur Bech and the ubiquitous Mr. Waller, Alan presented his credentials to the grand duchess, and I joined the party for lunch at the palace. The palace looked exactly like a toy castle from F.A.O. Schwarz toy store, turrets and all. The grand duchess, tall and stately, was very gracious, as was her husband, a typical consort, mustachioed and correct. Mr. Waller, I trust, was satisfied with my curtsies. At lunch conversation was politely sporadic but enlivened by Monsieur Bech, who promised us a meeting on his next visit to Brussels.

With the end of the American school year it was time for Roger to join us. We met him at the airport, looking a bit queasy after a rough trip, the plane having had to fly below ten thousand feet because of mechanical problems. I had found him a bargain dinner jacket in Washington at the Junior League Outgrown Shop, and the three of us went off to several parties. The Belgians mix ages in a pleasant, informal way, and I think Roger, shy at first, enjoyed himself.

In mid-June we three set off on a trip to the French towns of Metz and Strasbourg, now liberated from German occupation. We spent the first night at Metz, then crossed into the French Occupation Zone of Germany, where we were to lunch with General Marie-Pierre Koenig, the French zone commander. Germany at the time was divided into four zones, each occupied by the armies of one of the four major victorious powers: the French, British, Russians, and Americans. This being a military-ruled area, Alan had our chauffeur uncover his four-star admiral's insignia on our official car. As we drew up at the general's headquarters we were greeted by an honor guard of the French Foreign Legion. This was a high point of the trip, only equaled for me when we sailed down the Rhine the following day in a French gunboat, the French flag flying from the stern. We ended the voyage at Worms, where in the sixteenth century Martin Luther had nailed his Protestant manifesto to the church door, then on by car to Strasbourg and home.

That summer of 1946 proved to be a busy one. The word appeared to have gotten around that Brussels was an oasis in the midst of worldwide discomfort, that the Kirks were nice people who lived in a palace, and that they gave good parties. It seemed everyone in Europe and Washington wanted to come—senators and congressmen, distinguished military, occasional friends—and they all had to be introduced to appropriate Belgian officials and business people. As we ran the house with the European minimum of servants and the food carefully budgeted, it was intensive work for everyone but the guests.

Nevertheless we took time out for another trip, this one by embassy plane to Salzburg, at the invitation of General Mark Clark, now U.S. military commander of the American Occupation Zone in Austria. We were put up in a former bishop's palace used by Hitler as a guesthouse for those who could not be accommodated in his nearby mountaintop "Eagles' Nest" at Berchtesgarten. Rumor had it that the Nazis had locked up Admiral Miklos Horthy, the Hungarian ruler, in a dark closet just off my bedroom. Although a fascist who collaborated with the German occupiers of Hungary, Horthy had offended them by offering to surrender the country to the approaching Soviet armies in 1944. Not wanting to encounter his ghost, I hung my clothes elsewhere. Happily, nearby Salzburg had escaped war damage and the city was gay and charming. We poked about the old town, had coffee in the main square, and attended an opera in the royal box, hearing a magnificent performance during which Alan went to sleep.

The culmination of the summer's festivities was a visit from several ships of the American Atlantic fleet, our old friend Admiral Ronald Hewitt in command. With Alan in formal dress, top hat included, we drove to Antwerp where the flagship was anchored alongside the main pier. Alan stood at attention, hat clasped to his breast during the nineteen-gun ambassadorial salute, then advanced to shake hands with Admiral Hewitt. Both men gave each other surreptitious winks as Alan officially stepped aboard a warship in civilian clothes for the first time.

Two nights later we gave a ball at the embassy for the admiral and his officers. They attended in full dress. It was a very grand affair. Mademoiselle had combed her lists for all the pretty girls and young marrieds in town, plus the embassy staff and a select few of our colleagues. A suitable orchestra was provided, and the chef did himself proud with a magnificent buffet. The big drawing rooms were thrown open, and Alan and I stood at the head of the marble staircase to receive the guests. It was a splendid party enjoyed by everyone. Not long afterward we sorrowfully sent Roger back to school in America.

Meanwhile our friend Francis Biddle, one of the two American judges at the Nuremburg trial of top German leaders, had asked us to come to Nuremberg to stay with him and attend a session of the trial. We flew up in the embassy plane, came in low over the bombed-out Old City, and landed on an airstrip outside of town. Francis met us in a military car, complete with armed guard sitting beside the chauffeur, and we drove to his house, requisitioned from a German industrialist now in prison. With a touch of his usual sardonic humor, Francis explained that the man's wife was still in residence, served as housekeeper, and doubled as butler.

We reached the house, a melancholy, dark stone structure surrounded by stunted black trees. The owner's factory, now idle, lay somewhere in the rear. Ushered into the living room we were served tea by the lady Francis had referred to, a grim female, too like a concentration camp matron for comfort. Of course, she did have some reason to be glum; she was now a servant to her country's enemies, who had taken over her own house. Alan and Francis were talking in one corner. I walked about the room, whose walls were hung with a series of colored drawings. On close inspection they all proved to be pornographic.

Dinner that evening was presided over by the owner's wife, standing watching every mouthful that we ate. A most uncomfortable meal only redeemed by some good German wine that helped wash it down before we adjourned to the drawing room. Upstairs Alan and I shared a big bed, but it was a restless night as the quilt was one of those horrid German affairs covering from your feet only up as far as your middle, and if pulled up left your feet in the cold.

Happily next morning, Sunday, we woke to brilliant sunshine and felt quite cheered as Francis announced we were going off for a picnic lunch with one of the British judges at the trial, Sir Norman Birkett, and two of his young assistants. We departed in a cortege, in front a jeep with two British soldiers, tommy guns at the ready, and behind our two cars, another jeep with more armed guards. We drove out through wide meadows, passed farmhouses with flowered balconies, and finally stopped to climb up a grassy rise looking down on a village. We installed ourselves, the soldiers with their tommy guns sitting before and behind us. Below we could see people walking in and out of church, couples strolling arm in arm, and children shooing a string of geese along the road—a peaceful, idyllic scene, quite incongruous as I looked across at our soldiers. Francis explained these were necessary, as the judges were vulnerable targets for any would-be assassins.

As the weather was warmer that night, we were spared the quilt on the bed and slept the better for it, so we were quite rested and ready to start at ten next morning to attend the trial. As spectators, we were ushered to seats in a small upper gallery above the court chamber. As I looked over the railing, down at the criminals in the dock, I thought for a minute I was going to be sick. There the Nazi leaders were, all of them except Hitler, who had died in his bunker in Berlin, and the Nazi propaganda chief Josef Goebbels, who had poisoned himself, his wife, and his children. Only the military prisoners, sitting stiff and straight, had any semblance of dignity. Hitler's deputy, Marshal Hermann Goering, his uniform sagging in folds round his reduced weight, was ogling the crowd with smiling confidence. I guessed then that he would never hang. In fact he did not, as he poisoned himself just before his eventual death sentence was to be carried out. The rest, evil, sadistic men, crouched in their seats, pale and silent.

This morning it was Artur Seyss-Inquart, the German occupation chief of Austria, on the stand. It seemed a perfunctory performance, and my attention centered instead on the judges in their robes and the faces of the men in the dock. The French judges were quick and animated; the British, clear-spoken and coldly incisive. Justice Jackson, the other American judge, shuffled his papers about, now and then interrupting the bullet-headed Russian judge to ask for a repeated translation of his remarks. As for the men in the dock, I wondered, Did they have families? Were they human at all, with wives and children? Did they ever think of the prisoners huddled into cattle cars without food or drink, the prisoners, men and women on their way to labor camps or the gas chambers, the charred bodies left in heaps, the gold extracted from their teeth? And the military with the gray of defeat on their faces, what were their thoughts?

Finally the session was over. We all got up, walked down the stairs and started along the broad, tile-paved hall; just as the defendants were being led under guard from the courtroom, I felt a fatal slip; the button on my panties had given way. Quickly I turned to the wives of two French judges walking beside me. "*Entourez moi, mesdames*" (Surround me, ladies), and with a last look at Goering's back I stepped out of my panties and stuffed them into my bag. Writing of this to my children, their inevitable remark was, "It would only have happened to you, Mother." I was glad neither Goering nor Francis had seen what happened. Both would have enjoyed it. After a quick lunch in the judges' dining room we shook hands all around, said goodbye to our host, and drove out to the airfield for our flight back to Brussels, our summer vacation over.

10

Belgium, the Balkans, and a Royal Visit, 1946–1949

When we returned to Brussels from Nuremberg, we found social activities picking up with the onset of fall. A number of invitations were waiting for us, among them one for dinner at the palace, a dinner to be given in honor of wartime British Prime Minister Winston Churchill and his daughter Mary. They would be staying with the prince regent, and the papers next day suggested a possible engagement between Mary and the prince, a match that would be heartily welcomed by the Belgians. Even if the rumor was true, I guessed the publicity would prevent any engagement owing to the prince's almost pathological dislike of any intrusion into his privacy.

I was right, for on the night of the dinner the prince's manner toward the very attractive young lady was markedly distant. The dinner itself, however, was very pleasant. The prince had enlisted the elderly princess Clementine Bonaparte as his hostess, and she did the honors with dignity and poise. The later Bonapartes had surely acquired refinement quite different from that of their forbears, Napoleon's coarse and rowdy siblings whom he made kings or titled aristocrats. I wore a new dress for the party and enjoyed myself between the prince, always polite to me, and Foreign Minister Paul-Henri Spaak.

"Too bad," I said to Alan as we drove home. "No chance now we will be attending a royal wedding."

Years before Alan had led the naval contingent for the burial of the World War I Unknown Soldier, marching from the capitol to Arlington cemetery. Now he and I were to act as chief mourners for the Unknown Soldier of World War II. The ceremony was to take place in the Belgian port of Antwerp, where the casket would be put aboard an American destroyer to be brought back to the United States and placed in the cenotaph in Arlington.

We drove down from Brussels and took our places in a stand erected in front of the cathedral, facing the main city square lined with troops—American, French, British, and Belgian. There were speeches from various officials, and then the funeral procession entered the square from a side street, the caisson bearing the body, preceded by a Catholic cardinal in red robes. A bell began to toll, the great bell of the cathedral that only sounded in times of alarm or deliverance. We stepped down from the stand and fell in behind the caisson, followed by a group of Americans—parents, widows, children who had come over, hoping perhaps to pay honor to their own loved one. Behind them the city officials and military representatives. The bell still tolled as we walked out of the square along cobbled streets to the pier where the destroyer was anchored, its sides garlanded with flowers.

We stood as the cardinal pronounced a last blessing and the casket, lifted by sailor bearers, was carried aboard. We waited as the ship slowly left its mooring, then turned to go back to our car.

We were creeping into autumn. The leaves in the Forêt de Soigne, the beautiful wood outside Brussels, turned brown; only the beeches showed a glint of gold to remind us of the glory of an American fall. In Europe fall can be a melancholy season, but we had by now made some good friends who invited us for pleasant weekends at their country places. In town we were the American presence at many dinner parties, serious affairs, especially when dignitaries were present. Protocol was always observed to the *n*th degree. Widowed Belgian ambassadresses kept their husbands' rank. Alan found it particularly trying to often be seated next to some half-deaf widow and always pleaded for a pretty girl to look at further down the table at our own parties. We gave many dinners; formal ones were always checked by Mademoiselle to make sure of proper seating.

One evening during that first winter we attended a large dinner given by the Chinese ambassador and his wife, deans of the corps.

Included among the guests was the Papal Nuncio, the title given the pope's ambassadors, a cheery little Italian decked out in scarlet taffeta. I wore a V-necked black velvet dress and my best jewelry with some long costume-jewelry earrings Alan had bought me in London. Just as we were about to leave the table I realized I had lost an earring. Very concerned neighbors looked under the chairs and the table. The procession was forming to go back into the drawing room. "Please don't bother. It is sure to be found," I told them.

I took my place at the arm of my partner just behind the hostess, who was escorting the nuncio, my husband following with one of the stoutest of the elder ladies. Suddenly, raising my hand to the front of my dress, I exclaimed, "*Ah, je l'ai trouvé*" (Ah, I found it).

"*Madame a trouvé son boucle d'oreille?*" asked the nuncio. "*Ou est-ce qu'elle l'a trouvé?*" (Madame found her earring? Where did she find it?).

From behind I heard my wicked husband say, "*Ma femme l'a trouvé par le main de Dieu*" (She found it by the hand of God), but I do not think the nuncio heard him.

Early in November we had the unwelcome news that our government's lease of our residence, the Palais d'Assche, would not be renewed. The American government had rented the house for twenty-five years. Faced with a challenge, Mademoiselle came up with a list of houses to rent to supplement those names supplied by the embassy office. Day by day she and I inspected various offerings. I had always found it distasteful poking into people's private quarters and cupboards. It is a horrid job and quite embarrassing, especially if owners are present.

Several large houses were available but lacked the most ordinary conveniences. All had vast drawing rooms, but bedrooms were small, bathrooms scarce, and servants' rooms were either in unheated attics or dingy basements. Mademoiselle and I came away from our expeditions discouraged. The days were slipping by and so far the only possibility seemed a gloomy mansion on a gray, cobbled street, the interior filled with battered furniture and the walls hung with dusty tapestries and improbable Madonnas.

Happily, a cable from the United States solved our problem. A house belonging to the widowed daughter of our friend James Dunn, the American ambassador to Italy, was available for rent. It seemed an answer to our prayers, even more so on close inspection. On the ground floor were dining room, drawing room, and pleasant sitting room; on the second floor two large master bedrooms with luxurious baths, a charming single room also with bath; and on the floor above two more bedrooms, one to serve as office for Mademoiselle, plus cheerful servants' rooms. In the basement an admirable kitchen, storerooms, and wine cellar. True, the dining room could seat only fourteen, but our stream of official visitors was diminishing and, contrasted with anything else we had seen, it was excellent. Alan decided to close the deal while opening negotiations to purchase property facing the central Park Royale for a new embassy residence and an office building.

We made the most of our last month in the Palais d'Assche, giving several large dinners and a reception for the entire diplomatic corps. Alan distinguished himself on this occasion. Still unaware of some of the niceties of the French language, catching sight of the extravagantly feathered hat of the Chilean ambassadress, he remarked to the wife of the minister of defense, "*Madame, je ne sais pas si je dois crier coq ou poule*" ("I do not know if I should cry cock or hen"—but the French word *poule* also signifies prostitute). Happily that lady had a lusty sense of humor and thoroughly enjoyed his indiscretion.

With the move to our new residence on Avenue Tervueren scheduled for mid-December 1946, we accepted a cordial invitation from Alan's dear Aunt Bessie, to whom Roger and I had refugeed in 1940, to spend Christmas with her in Northern Ireland. This would leave Mademoiselle and the servants free to settle into the new house and have all in order on our return. We sorted out our own belongings—rugs, pictures, linen, and silver—put in requests to Washington for some additional furniture, looked over the house again, and decided where everything was to go.

We sent presents off to the children at home and, our bags packed, left the competent Mademoiselle Nerincx in charge. We set off in the embassy plane, landing at Northern Ireland's Londonderry airport, where Aunt Bessie met us in her venerable automobile. It was good to see her again. Her welcome was a warm one, warmer than her house proved to be, for it lacked central heating, and we huddled gratefully round fires. When I turned a toasted cheek, my breath went steaming out into the room. Dear Aunt Bessie, suffering from chilblains, ate her meals with mitts on her hands, but I piled on woolens, layers of them, and managed to survive.

Christmas was cheerful. Aunt Bessie made us each a stocking, which we opened at breakfast. We went to church in the morning, sat in the great square family pew, happily furnished with a lighted stove. Outside the weather was relatively mild, but stone buildings seem to retain centuries of stored cold. We lunched and dined with neighbors, slept long under piles of blankets, and were almost sorry when our visit ended.

Back in Belgium we settled into the new house. Some extra furniture arrived from the states and a fine set of Louis XVI chairs and sofa was bought for the rather empty drawing room. A dear French friend came to visit and, seeing that room's bare walls, loaned us a beautiful sixteenth-century French tapestry to hang on one of them. The ensemble was very elegant. None of us, including the servants, had any regrets for the palais. Life went along easily and comfortably.

I have said the prince regent rarely entertained, but early in January the Queen of Holland paid a visit to Brussels, and we were invited to a dinner at the palace in her honor. The invitation was an impressive affair. Printed in one corner it read, "*Grand décolleté avec diadem*" (Full décolleté with diadem); in the other, "Decorations." Alan could certainly manage the decorations and I could manage the grand décolleté, but my diamond bracelet seemed inadequate as a diadem. Speaking of this to a Belgian friend, she said, "I will loan you one." "Oh no," I replied, remembering French author Guy de Maupassant's story of the lifelong struggle of a woman to pay for a diamond necklace she had borrowed and lost. "But I have a box full," she protested. "I was lady-in-waiting to Queen Astrid of Belgium, always had to wear them. Mine are costume jewelry. I will send them over for you to choose one to match your dress." My dress was dark red velvet. I picked out a gorgeous tiara of fake rubies and amethysts, tried it on, and even Mademoiselle approved.

The dinner was very grand, the queen appearing upholstered rather than dressed in violet satin hardly becoming to her florid complexion. Her ladies-in-waiting matched her in size and shape, but the Belgians

23. Ambassador Alan and Lydia Kirk in U.S. Embassy residence, Brussels, 1947.

shone by contrast, especially the tall, blonde Princesse de Ligne in white with a matched set of turquoises and diamonds, others in pretty pale colors with family jewels brought out for the occasion.

Two by two, led by the prince with the queen on his arm, we made our way into the dining room. The long banquet table was aglow with silver, crystal, and huge bouquets of flowers. I was glad to find myself seated between André de Staercke and another of the prince's aides, the lively old Baron Georges Holvoet, both entertaining partners. Across the way the prince was making polite conversation with the queen, who seemed mainly interested in her food.

The dinner over, we moved in procession to the anteroom. After a suitable interval the prince and the queen with her suite made ceremonious exits and the guests were then free to leave, trailing down the marble stairway to our waiting cars.

The next great event was the annual trek of the diplomatic corps to attend the birthday celebration of the grand duchess of Luxembourg on January 23. Like Alan, most of the diplomats were accredited to both Belgium and Luxembourg, so we went up en masse. In the hotel, the British and we were favored with two rooms apiece. The Russian ambassador was furious and complained bitterly of favoritism, but the concierge was firm. We were to spend two nights, as there was a special high mass at the cathedral next morning.

That evening we were all dressed in our best. My red velvet complete with diadem went on easily, but to get Alan ready with all his decorations was like trimming a Christmas tree. Arrived at the palace, we were shown into a large room where the chief of protocol lined the ladies along one side, the gentlemen headed by the papal nuncio in his scarlet taffeta on the other. We waited for several minutes, then doors at one end were thrown open and the grand duchess appeared accompanied by her husband and followed by their children in descending ages, seven or eight of them. She spoke to each ambassadress, who in turn presented the ladies of her embassy, the grand duchess's husband greeting the ambassadors and their staffs. My curtsies grew shallower as the children grew younger, finally resolving themselves into handshakes.

In due order of rank, the chief of protocol approached each ambassadorial couple, inviting them to follow him into an anteroom to speak with the grand duchess. When our turn came we found her seated on a sofa to receive us. My brief experience with royalty had taught me they were invariably shy and, as one is not supposed to initiate conversation, the exchange becomes quite labored. But I did my best, and Alan nearby chatted easily with her husband. After our allotted time the chief of protocol appeared at the door, a signal for us to leave. I making my curtsy, Alan bowing, we withdrew.

The rest of the winter passed quickly. The weather was bad at times, floods of rain often freezing to a treacherous skin of thin ice. In spite of the bad weather, social life that winter went on apace. We lunched and dined out, went to innumerable afternoon receptions, gave luncheons and dinners at home. Sometimes I felt like an actress resting alone in her dressing room between acts. We had made many pleasant friends, but at ambassadorial rank intimate relationships were difficult and could cause gossip or jealousy. This I discovered was one of the penalties of rank. I remember my father saying the same thing when he became captain of a ship, leaving the companionship of the wardroom mess. In any event everyone was very cordial and in time I hoped to break down the barriers.

Alan had a bit of a flare-up, however. The Belgian Communist Party got wind of Belgium's secret agreement to sell all the Belgian Congo's uranium production to the United States and Britain. The Communists called it a "sell-out" to the evil United States and raised questions about it in Parliament. Their press trumpeted the "disgrace" every day. To make the whole arrangement look better to Parliament, the Belgian government wanted to publicize parts of the agreement and have a few of their scientists participate in classified nuclear research in the United States. Washington was adamantly opposed, and Alan had many difficult conversations with Foreign Minister Spaak. In the end, Spaak made an anodyne statement to Parliament, assuring the country that the agreement was very profitable to Belgium and a vital part of our joint effort against the Russian menace.[1]

Spring finally was in the air. We had a short domestic crisis when Émile, the butler, went mad and flourished a knife around the kitchen. We replaced him with Alphonse, the assistant butler and husband of the chambermaid. I still hear from that faithful couple, retired now and proud grandparents. The invaluable Mademoiselle, at ninety-three, is resting quietly in a nursing home. During the three years we spent in Brussels we were surely lucky to have such devoted retainers. Those who

1. For details of the discussions on this issue, see the U.S. Department of State, *Foreign Relations of the United States, 1947,* vol. 1, *General: The United Nations* (Washington, D.C.: United States Government Printing Office, 1947), 783–835; http://digital.library.wisc.edu/1711.dl/FRUS.FRUS1947v01.

read my detective story, *The Embassy Madonna,* published by Doubleday in 1971, may recognize my heroine, for it is Mademoiselle, and I dedicated the book to her.

In early June 1947, our son Roger was due to graduate from Groton School in the United States. Alan could not leave but I was determined to go, so took passage on a Dutch liner, the *New Amsterdam,* motoring up to Holland shepherded by one of the young embassy attachés. I enjoyed my first trip on the *New Amsterdam,* and it became one of my favorite ocean-going vessels. We arrived in New York on schedule. I made a round of visits to daughters Marian and Deborah, then went up to Groton for Prize Day and graduation, sitting proudly to watch Roger, at sixteen and number two in his class, walk away with a fine illuminated volume. He and I sailed back on the *America,* landing at Cherbourg, where Alan met us with the car; we stopped off briefly in Paris and then on to Brussels.

On July 4 we hosted the annual U.S. national day reception at our embassy, where one vociferous compatriot appeared in a stars and stripes necktie and held up the receiving line describing his "li'l old ranch in Texas," and two ailing congressmen had to be dosed with paregoric, the diarrhea medicine. Soon afterward Roger and I took off for a two-week holiday in Italy. We spent a couple of days in Rome, then visited Naples and Pompeii and took the boat for Capri. Invited by the wife of the Italian military attaché in Brussels, we stayed in her charming guest apartment looking out over the sea. It was a lazy, delicious life. In two weeks, our holiday ended. We said good-bye to our kind hostess and returned to Brussels, where our life resumed its usual course.

One pleasant occasion was a decoration ceremony to be held in our garden, where our consul general at Antwerp would be awarded the Medal of Freedom for his work during the liberation of that city. At luncheon some days before, I had once again sat next to the prince regent's aide, Baron Georges Holvoet, and I told him of the great service our Mademoiselle Nerincx had been to us in the war years. I added that she had also done quiet work for her own country, carrying papers for the Belgian underground each day in her purse as she took the bus into town. He listened carefully then said, "Perhaps we should do something for Mademoiselle ourselves."

Sure enough, on the appointed day a member of the prince regent's staff appeared to stand by Alan. The consul general was duly decorated, then came the turn of Mademoiselle. By this time she had been warned to expect an award from the Americans, and after Alan pinned the medal on her jacket she moved away. The prince regent's representative asked her to return. Puzzled, somewhat confused, she did so only to hear him make a charming little speech and pin a Belgian decoration alongside the American. By now the tears were in my eyes and there were cheers from the audience assembled. It was a happy moment for all of us and well-deserved recognition for what Mademoiselle had done for her country and for ours.

In late September the shooting season commenced again in full swing and we went the weekend rounds, meeting several new friends. Little by little the barriers were coming down, and I was happy to see we were accepted for ourselves, regardless of rank.

The weeks went by, and late one Saturday afternoon in November of 1947, as I was sitting alone in the house, the embassy telephoned to say an urgent telegram for the ambassador had just come in and they were sending it over by messenger. When it arrived the butler brought it up to me. Worried lest something dreadful might have happened to one of the children, I opened it. The message read, "You have been appointed Chairman, United Nations Special Commission on the Balkans, headquarters Salonika. Pending your acceptance other representatives will join. Department hopes you accept."

The Balkans. The newspapers had been full of troubles on the Greek frontier, savage raids by communist Greeks holed up in the mountains and supplied by the communist Bulgarian and Yugoslav governments across the border, villages looted and burned, children taken hostage, all in an effort to destabilize the noncommunist Greek government. Salonika was the Greek town nearest to the border, but I imagined conditions were pretty rough there so soon after the war, certainly not like Brussels. And there would be danger. I supposed this commission must have international sanction to report what was going on so penalties could be applied against the offending governments, but why choose Alan to head it? Why not somebody else, anybody else? Reading the last sentence in the cable, "Department hopes you accept," I knew Alan would do just that. My thoughts raced back and forth. What would it entail? Would we have to leave Brussels? I was used to sudden, unexplained orders, but somehow I had imagined we had finished with them. How wrong I was.

Hearing the car in the driveway I poured out a drink and went down the stairs, drink in one hand, the telegram in the other. "Drink this," I said, "and then read this."

We went back into the sitting room and sat down. Alan read the telegram over again, took a sip of his drink, then reached for the telephone and called the duty officer at the embassy, dictating his reply to the State Department—one word: "Yes, signed Kirk." Afterwards they told me in Washington they had never received so quick and brief an answer. I said it was a wonder he had not phrased it, "Aye, aye, sir," navy fashion.

The following week all kinds of final arrangements were made, cables and telephones to and fro. Alan's job was to be sure the commission actually did its work, reporting accurately and thoroughly on the many atrocities being committed by the raiding communists, for the latter were denying the whole thing and pouring scorn on the commission's work. Alan's task was complicated by the fact that some of his fellow commissioners had been given this assignment by their governments to get them out of the way of more important things. They had little interest in the issue and did not feel like inconveniencing themselves by hard work. One, a Latin American, summarized his attitude by telling Alan he felt "the night was made for sleep, the day for rest."

To my relief Alan's assignment was to be a temporary one, two months, three at the most, and he would be returning to Brussels when it was finished. Meanwhile his new counselor, Hugh Millard, would carry on in his absence. After discussing the matter we decided I should take this opportunity to go home, visit with the family, and share Roger's Christmas vacation. As the Millards had not yet found a house, we suggested they move into our residence after I left. The servants were informed and Mademoiselle, I knew, would keep watch and ward.

Engaging a passage on the *New Amsterdam,* I saw Alan off for Greece, then early in December sailed for New York. I arranged to stay at the Cosmopolitan Club in New York for a few days' shopping and then go on to Washington. Before leaving New York I had a sudden inspiration. So many people went South after Christmas; why not try to sublet an apartment, a tiny one, for a couple of months? I had never lived in New York. It might be fun to see what it was like. I would be near Alan's Aunt Sally Goodrich and Roger, both in Princeton, and close to my daughter Marian outside of Philadelphia. I remembered a hotel called the Weylin where friends of Mother's once had an apartment. I rang up, giving their name as my reference. "Yes," they said, "something has just fallen vacant," and they could offer me a suite—bedroom, sitting room, and kitchenette, available January 1st. I rushed down on my way to the train, left my taxi waiting, and took a look. The rooms were attractive, the price not too high, and I engaged it immediately, signing a two-month lease.

In Washington also I was lucky. Our friends the Richard Wilmers's old house on 24th Street had been left empty, and they had kindly let me store some of our extra furniture in the basement. Would I like to camp out in the house over the holidays, bring up a couple of beds, a table, sofa, and chairs and a few kitchen utensils? They would gladly loan me enough linen. "Splendid," I said, "but how about heat?" That could be turned on along with the electricity, no trouble. I went over, hired a couple of strong men from a moving company, and routed out all that was necessary. I telephoned Sadie, my old cook, now retired, to come in, clean up, and give us dinners when needed. She was delighted, so all was in order by the time Roger came down for his vacation. We had a gay three weeks, spent Christmas itself with Marian in Philadelphia, and I even gave a cocktail party in my carpetless living room.

Christmas vacation over, Roger and I went off to Princeton together, I to stay with Aunt Sally before taking up residence at the Weylin. I felt very adventurous as I arrived in New York. There had been a big blizzard over the holidays and I waded through slush to lunch and dine with friends. Everyone was very hospitable. I had not realized I knew so many New Yorkers, and others passing through town rang up. In spite of the wet underneath I enjoyed life in the great city. I found it exciting and stimulating. When the streets finally cleared, I welcomed the crisp cold and the blue sky, weather so unlike any found in Europe at this season. I discovered I was growing fond of New York and would be glad to return to it any time.

Letters from Alan came through in slow batches. He had missed us at Christmas, but his deputy, Gerald Drew, had produced a goose for dinner washed down with Greek retsina wine. Alan's multinational team was now very cooperative, but so far there had been little progress in defeating the communists in the hills, and the wretched raids dragged on. Then one morning my *New York Times* spoke of sharp fighting close to Salonika with casualties reported. Alarmed, I rang the department. They assured me Alan was safe but I worried, for he was never one to sit back when action was at hand. It was one thing to face the Germans from the deck of his flagship off Normandy and quite another to encounter screaming mustachioed Bulgarian outlaws.

I waited anxiously, searching the papers for more news, called the State Department again, and received fresh reassurance. Finally a letter came through. Yes, there had been a spot of trouble. He had gone up to the frontier to have a look round, fairly active goings-on, but got safely back to town, thought the worst was over, and hoped I had not worried. I realized he had probably enjoyed the whole business. What a man.

Friends were very kind and, with my mind more or less at rest, I enjoyed myself. However, Alan remained in Greece and I had no idea when or if he would be returning to Belgium. I was growing very impatient. My lease at the Weylin was coming to an end and no word as yet from Alan or the department. Days passed until finally, in mid-March of 1948, a telephone call from the State Department's officer for Belgium settled everything. The prince regent of Belgium would be making a state visit to Washington in early April. As ambassador to Belgium, Alan must be there to receive him. Orders had gone out for his recall from Greece, and he should be arriving in the United States in three weeks' time. At the conclusion of the prince's visit Alan would resume his post in Brussels.

Three weeks. I called the hotel manager's office. Happily I was able to keep the apartment for an extra fortnight, after which I would go to Washington, put up at a hotel, and await Alan's arrival. I rang back the Belgian desk officer, got the date of Alan's return. As yet no definite plan for the prince's visit, but they promised to keep me informed as to the arrangements as soon as the schedule was completed.

A day or two later the desk officer telephoned to say plans were now complete. The prince and his party would arrive in Washington on a Belgian Air Force plane and would be staying with their ambassador at the Belgian Embassy. As there would be no ladies in the party, the White House was arranging a large men's dinner. The Belgian ambassador planned a reception and a formal dinner for President and Mrs. Truman.

I knew Baron Silvercruys, the Belgian ambassador, was a bachelor, and I suspected I might be called upon to act as hostess at his dinner, so I went shopping and treated myself to a wickedly expensive dress, plus two or three spring costumes for lesser occasions. My last two weeks in New York were busy ones, with good-byes to kind friends. Meanwhile, I had tentatively engaged passage for Alan and myself on the *New Amsterdam*, sailing the week following the prince's visit. All being in order, bags packed, I said farewell to New York and boarded the Washington train.

Alan arrived in fine form, having wangled a seat on an Air Force plane that brought him direct to Washington. How glad I was to see my husband again. We had had separations, so many of them before, but I had thought they were finished once he was out of the navy. I blessed the prince regent for putting an end to the Balkan job and hoped the State Department would never think up any more trouble-shooting adventures.

Waking early on the morning the royal party was due to arrive, Alan took a look at the weather and called Ted Achilles, his former deputy in Brussels, who had offered to take him out to the airfield to meet the prince regent.

"Wind is blowing up. That plane may get in ahead of time."

Ted said he would come by after dropping the children at school. "My car is not very stylish, but no one will notice with all the brass on hand." They set off. Just as they approached the airfield, Alan looked up to see a plane circling overhead.

"I told you so."

Ted put on speed and parked his car as the plane, flying the prince's flag, came in to land, a good half-hour ahead of schedule. This was long before the days of great jets that could delay or speed up their flight to arrive precisely on schedule for such a visit. There was no sign of a welcoming committee, no White House cars for the visitors, nor the car of the Belgian ambassador. Alan got out, stood at the foot of the landing ramp. The door of the plane opened and he climbed aboard to greet the prince, shook hands with the rest of the party, made inquiries about the trip, admired the plane—anything to gain time.

"Sorry, we are a bit early," the prince said. "I see there is no one about. If you have a car I will ride into town with you."

Peering out the plane's window, thinking of Ted's shabby car, the back cluttered with children's toys and old galoshes, Alan was relieved to see three White House cars drawing up and Stanley Woodward, the chief of protocol, getting out. Still no sign of the Belgian ambassador.

"Cars have arrived, Sir, if you are ready to go down."

After the formal greetings were over, Alan found a moment to tell the protocol chief he would accompany the prince to the Belgian Embassy in one of the White House cars, as the Belgian ambassador appeared to have been delayed. At the ambassador's residence on Foxhall Road, the two cars drew up at the door of the Belgian Embassy to be received by a startled butler. They entered and sat down while the butler hovered anxiously about. "Would you like something, Sir? A cup of coffee perhaps?" Alan asked.

"A whisky and soda if you will join me," replied the prince.

The butler disappeared, and just at that moment Baron Silvercruys walked into the room, bowed over the prince's hand, welcomed him to Washington, greeted Spaak and Alan with perfect composure. The butler returned with drinks. Alan manfully disposed of his, though he told me it was quite a dose at ten-thirty in the morning. This done, he made his good-byes. When I saw André de Staercke at the ambassador's reception next day he told me the prince had thought the ambassador's slip-up a good joke, so apparently there were no hard feelings.

All of Washington came to the reception. It was a fine, warm April day and the crowd spilled out into the garden, where daffodils and early flowering shrubs put on a good show. The prince bore up nobly. I knew he hated this sort of function, and I hoped one of his aides ministered whisky and sodas to him at crucial intervals. Alan said the bachelor White House dinner the night before had gone off very well, and the prince and the president had taken to each other at once. So far so good. This left only the Belgian Embassy dinner to be faced next night. As I suspected, the ambassador asked me to be his hostess for that occasion, and I was glad I had invested in the so-expensive dress.

According to protocol the embassy dinner guests would arrive a few minutes in advance of President and Mrs. Truman. Alan made sure of proper transportation for us. We found the Belgian ambassador waiting in the drawing room. No question this time of his being late. The prince appeared and other guests streamed in: the chief justice and his wife, various senators, representatives, generals, and admirals, together with their ladies and a number of favored Washington residents. The ambassador went to the front door to meet President and Mrs. Truman, then ushered them into the room where the guests were duly presented to the presidential couple and the prince. Following a short cocktail half-hour, we went along to the dining room where I took my seat at the end of the table. The prince had Mrs. Truman on his right and the wife of the chief justice on his left, two stout but comfortable ladies. I fared very well, seated between the Speaker of the House of Representatives and one of the senior senators.

As the last of the champagne was poured I watched, slightly nervous lest I miss a gesture from the ambassador when the moment came to arise from the table. The attentive butler sensed this and gave me the signal, so I got up at the right time, and we moved back into the drawing room.

According to usual royal custom, the prince seated himself on a sofa with the senior lady present. André de Staercke had given me instructions. I was supposed to edge her politely off the sofa a few minutes later and replace her with another important lady. This I managed to do with his help. Then the process had to be repeated as he came up with the next favored lady. All went well, but it was a somewhat nerve-racking experience and I said afterward to André, "You know, my ancestors crossed the ocean to escape from this kind of thing." Anyway, the evening seemed to have been a great success, and the ambassador thanked me as we left.

I drove down to Annapolis the next day with Alan and the prince, who was in excellent humor, even teasing me about my role as the "Grande Maitresse de la Cour" (Grand Mistress of the Court). On the way back the prince remarked that these formal entertainments were all very well, but almost wistfully he said he wished he could see a typical American house. He would be free the next afternoon if it could be arranged. I thought to myself a typical American house would hardly fit the royal taste. Then I suddenly had an inspiration. I said I would try and would call the embassy to say whether the friends I had in mind would be at home and able to receive him.

As soon as we got back to the hotel I talked the matter over with Alan. "Do you think our friends, the Corrin Strongs, would do it? Their house would be ideal." He advised calling them at once. I did so and got Corrin himself on the phone. He agreed, said they would be delighted, he would speak to his wife Alice. She rang back, frankly appalled at the prospect. I told her it should be no more than an informal cocktail party, mostly younger people. The prince had enough of important elderly folk, especially stout elderly ladies. We would have to think of the prettiest girls we knew. Finally she was persuaded and we made lists. No, that one was too shy, another nice but plain.

I laughed. "We sound like a couple of procuresses." But in the end we came up with enough to satisfy us and, we hoped, the prince.

Messages were dispatched that evening, others next morning, and I sent word to André de Staercke that the party was arranged for six o'clock at the home of Colonel and Mrs. Corrin Strong, the parents of Hank Strong, whom he would remember as Alan's private secretary in Brussels.

Though hardly a typical American house, the Strongs's handsome residence was charmingly set in the midst of Massachusetts Avenue Park, its terrace looking down through trees that bordered a brook below. Alice had exquisite taste, reflected in the colors and arrangement of the furniture. It was a welcoming house where we had many good times and where the Strongs themselves gave a special tone of grace and simplicity.

Everyone invited to the party accepted except those who were sick in bed or away. Alice had filled the house with flowers, and our chosen young ladies were equally decorative. The prince and his aides arrived plus two young bachelors from the embassy. The guest of honor seemed very happy and relaxed, staying on until nearly eight o'clock, when André de Staercke reminded him he was expected for dinner at the Belgian Embassy. He thanked the Strongs, thanked me, said his good-byes, and the rest of the party reluctantly broke up. It had been a great success.

The following afternoon, with the prince leaving for New York in the evening, we were summoned to accompany him to the White House for tea at four-thirty. President and Mrs. Truman were waiting for us in the Red Room along with their daughter Margaret. We chatted pleasantly over the teacups. It was a homey affair. The prince himself was very agreeable, compliments were exchanged, and after an hour the visit was over.

Back at the hotel we put our feet up and congratulated ourselves that everything had gone even better than we expected. Next morning a package was delivered to me, a handsome silver cigarette box adorned with the prince's monogram and his card inscribed "*Pour la Grande Maitresse de la Cour.*" It sits on my coffee table today, a happy reminder of that memorable visit.

Early the following week Alan and I boarded the faithful *New Amsterdam* to return to Belgium. We had a delightful summer with visits from all three children, too soon coming to an end. The fall passed in by now familiar fashion, and we decided to take a Christmas holiday in Washington. We were lucky enough to hear of a house to rent for the period, a house on P Street in Georgetown just across from the first one we had lived in as young marrieds. The deal concluded, we sailed for America in mid-December, this time from Le Havre on the *Liberté*, a sumptuous French vessel. This in spite of my memory of one of our old admirals who said he preferred to travel on a French line, as "There is none of that damn nonsense about women and children first" into the lifeboats.

We found several friends on board, and the sea was smooth. We walked the decks and made up parties for dinner to enjoy the superb cuisine, topping off each meal with mounds of caviar. We arrived safely, though rather bloated, in New York and went straight to Washington. Soon our calendar was full, Roger due shortly from Princeton University, our daughter Deborah and her husband the weekend before Christmas from Boston, where he was attending Harvard Law School, and daughter Marian and her husband coming down from Philadelphia, where he was working. The telephone was busy, Alan lining up appointments at the State Department between calls to and from friends.

New Year's Eve was a festive occasion with dinner at the house of our columnist friend Walter Lippman, an annual event ending up with a rousing Virginia reel late in the evening. The weeks passed quickly, and soon it was time to pack up again and catch the *Liberté* on her return voyage. This time I tried to eat more discreetly, except for the caviar, knowing I had months of Belgian food awaiting me in Brussels.

There we found the servants back from their vacations, the house cleaned and ready for us. Soon the winter shut in very cold, so cold the lake in the park opposite froze over solid, but social affairs went on as usual despite the bad weather. Our British colleague, Sir Knatchbull Hugessen, was replaced as ambassador by a grim Foreign Office–type with a wife whose lack of early dental attention soon earned her the nickname of Lady Toothypicks.

In late March 1949 Alan was called back to Washington for consultation. As his visit would be a short one we decided it best for me to stay in Brussels. Friends were very kind during Alan's absence, but I felt lonely with him on consultation in Washington. I had only expected him to be away for ten days, but time passed and I could only suppose he had stayed on for the signing of the Atlantic Treaty setting up NATO that was taking place in Washington at that time.

Finally I called Alan's deputy, Doug MacArthur, thinking he might have more information, but he was quite noncommittal, and I began to suspect something was afoot.

How right I was.

Soon the news leaked out of Washington that the president had selected Alan as our new ambassador to the Soviet Union.

I was stunned.

"No more than I was," Alan said when he returned. "I knew our time here might be coming to an end and hoped something else might turn up. Nothing happened, and I was about to leave for Brussels when I was called into Ted Achilles's office in the department. 'The secretary of state has a new job for you,' he told me. 'Where?' I asked. Ted took the pipe out of his mouth and answered, 'Moscow.' I saw [Secretary of State] Dean Acheson next day and the president, who said he wanted me in Moscow. It is officially a secret, of course, until the Russians give their formal assent to the appointment. This may take time."

My head was whirling, even more so after Alan poured me a stiff drink. That night I twisted and turned along with my thoughts, proud that my husband should have been selected but fearful of what the assignment to the capital of our archenemy would entail. Just as with the Normandy command, I knew Alan was secretly pleased and looked forward to the challenge. He was as ready to face the Russians as he had been to face the Germans. This being so, who was I, a service woman born and bred, to object, especially as this time I could share the challenge with him. Neither of us would be alone. Reason took hold and, vaguely comforted, I slept.

As Alan's appointment was still not official, we could not comment on it, and it would be embarrassing if the palace or others asked us about it. It would be best if we left Belgium for a bit. Alan suggested we go to Bungundy. That was a good idea. The weather was fine and we enjoyed ourselves, though every now and then we looked at each other wondering what lay ahead.

When we got home we learned that the agreement from Russia had arrived in Washington. The news was out now. The papers were full of it, and the telephone rang constantly. There were congratulations from friends and cables from home. One comfort was that our son Roger, now a sophomore at Princeton, had proposed to his father that he take a year out of college and come to Moscow with us. Alan assented, subject to my views and the consent of the university. I agreed with alacrity, but interrupting college, except for war service, was not as generally accepted as it is now. Alan contacted the university president, who said, after some consultations, that Roger's academic record was good enough to permit a year's absence.

The next two weeks were hectic—lunches and dinners every day, a trial for my digestion as well as my emotions, all our friends so kind. At a given point I succumbed and took to my bed. Mademoiselle insisted on calling the doctor, who examined me and declared, "Madame, you have resisted for three years but finally the liver gives way." I knew full well it was not my liver, rather my stomach and sheer exhaustion, but a rest in bed restored me.

With all the packing and sorting, Mademoiselle and the chambermaid were hard at work and the house was in ferment. Alan said we would take our silver, linen, and various other bits and pieces with us to Moscow, do the thing in style, show the Russians we were not afraid to come with all our belongings and our only son.

Among the many good-bye parties was a magnificent affair given by the Boels, who invited all our special Belgian friends. After an elegant speech by our host we were presented with two handsome silver pheasants, souvenirs of the shooting parties we had enjoyed so much. With them a leather-bound book signed by all the donors. We were very touched.

Other packages arrived at the house, one to my astonishment from the adventuress Princesse Ruspoli containing a beautiful mantilla of Belgian lace with a card inscribed, "To thank you and your husband for what you have done for Belgium." Naturally I could not send it back, so composed a letter of thanks, saying my two daughters were already married but I hoped a granddaughter might some day wear the lace, the gift from a very lovely lady. In fact my granddaughter Alison wore it at her wedding many years later.

The last evening we were to spend in Brussels we dined at the palace quite alone with the prince and André de Staercke. By this time I knew the prince very well and, as a friend and a plain American woman, I felt I could speak, so as we left I turned to him. "Sir," I said, "why not step out on the balcony and be king of the Belgians? You know you could do it, and the people would welcome you."

He demurred, "No, no, my brother."

A pity, I thought, as we walked down the stairs, for he had proved himself to be a good constitutional ruler surrounded by wise counselors, and many of Belgium's ensuing troubles might have been avoided.

We drove the next morning to Rotterdam to embark on the *New Amsterdam*. Our cabin was filled with flowers and messages, and the friendship and affection they represented were very heartwarming. The three years we spent in Belgium would always hold precious memories.

PART FIVE

The Soviet Union, 1949–1951

11

Behind the Dreaded Iron Curtain, 1949

It is hard now to visualize the hostility, contempt, and dread with which Americans looked at Russia in the late 1940s. Americans quailed at the very thought of traveling to, much less living in, Moscow. Going as the chief representative of the Russians' archenemy made the prospect seem even more appalling to ordinary folk and challenging for us.

The Soviet Union—Russia, in popular usage—was considered the mortal enemy of the United States, a powerful and hostile state, one led by a half-mad dictator out to destroy us and conquer the world. Stalin's propaganda talked of inevitable Communist victory in an irreconcilable struggle with capitalism. His actions seemed to confirm this. He had brutally crushed all resistance to his rule in the part of Europe his armies had "liberated" during World War II. He was sponsoring Communist parties everywhere, even in the United States. He had kept his huge wartime army, and he was supporting armed guerrilla movements all over the world.

The cold war was not just a slogan. It was real. To win it, both the United States and Russia were using all the tools they had, except military force, against each other. Indeed the American public and many, even most, government and academic thinkers thought the Russians would attack the United States whenever they thought they could get away with it.

It was not just Russia's rulers that Americans resented. They viewed the Russian people themselves with a mixture of contempt and apprehension, considering them backward, savage, and hostile. I remember an American in Moscow saying, "At least the parents are nice to their children," but then adding, "Of course, animals are, too."

Russian secrecy made it worse. Tales of Siberian death camps and of Russian soldiers' terrible behavior in the places they occupied during the war were all that most people had heard. These tales, exaggerated probably, made ordinary Russians seem brutish and ignorant. There was no way for Americans, or any other foreigners, to get a different impression. Virtually no private citizens, scholars, or even business people were allowed to enter Russia. Those that were admitted, other than convinced Communists, told awful stories of the life there.

We knew that we, as American ambassador and family, would be protected, even isolated, from the seamier sides of Russian life, but we were anxious to find out what our life would be like. Landing in New York to spend a few days before going on to Washington, we were glad to have a chance to dine with Alan's predecessor as ambassador in Moscow, General Walter Bedell Smith. While the men talked, Mrs. Bedell Smith gave me pictures of our new residence, Spaso House, and told me what was needed to make life more comfortable there.

I had already read the State Department's briefing pamphlet for employees assigned to Moscow, but she filled in details, including a description of the existing table in the family dining room, ten feet of fake marble, at the end of which she and the general had to huddle when alone. I determined to ask at once for a replacement. My phone call to FBO, the State Department's Foreign Buildings Office, was so vehement, saying I could hardly accompany my husband to the post unless a suitable replacement was provided, that they promised to ship one over at once.

Alan went down to Washington the next day for his hearing before the Senate Foreign Relations Committee, a prerequisite to the Senate vote on his ambassadorial appointment. I stayed on in New York to finish my shopping and wait for son Roger to join me. I had a lot to buy. There was little in the way of dry goods, toiletries, clothes, or ordinary household items available in Moscow. All these had to be taken along or brought in by one of the quarterly ambassadorial flights from Germany.

On a hot afternoon I embarked for a wholesale grocery establishment near the docks. With their catalogue in hand I gave my name to the office secretary.

"Missionary or diplomatic?" she inquired.

"I may look missionary," I replied, "but it's diplomatic, a shipment to be sent to our embassy in Moscow."

"To Moscow! Do sit down." Now she was all attention, checking over the list with me and making several helpful suggestions. The list was a long one, but she assured me the order would be filled at once and sent on its way.

That done I went about other errands, bought stockings, shoes, snow boots, sweaters, and warm woolens to face the Russian winters. Explaining my needs to the saleslady at the underwear counter in Saks, she remarked, "You are going to Moscow? May the Lord be with you!" We met this reaction everywhere we went.

Roger arrived in New York from Princeton on Friday afternoon. We caught the train for Washington, where we found Alan waiting for us in our rooms at the Wardman Park Hotel. His Senate confirmation successfully over, he had seen the president and had a long talk with Secretary of State Dean Acheson and other government officials. He was to be sworn in on Monday and had asked our friend, Supreme Court Justice Felix Frankfurter, to administer the oath.

Now that Alan's appointment was official, press notices appeared and photographers arrived to take our pictures. Friends called on us and telephoned, wanting us to lunch or dine. Visits to doctors and dentists and opticians were lined up for the following week. Roger and I toured the five-and-ten-cent stores filling our baskets with everything I could think of, thread and needles and pins, pencils, ball-point pens, all kinds of small items, then on to the drugstore for medicines, toothbrushes, soaps, cold cream, shampoos, hand lotions, even chap sticks for winter weather.

It was a busy week. Alan was duly sworn in, and with passports and tickets in hand all was finally in order. He flew off to Paris to attend a conference between the American, British, French, and Russian foreign ministers, and Roger and I followed a week later on the good old *New*

Amsterdam. Our daughters and Alan's Aunt Sally came to see us off. We drank to each other and talked until the bell sounded "Visitors Ashore," then went up on deck. We watched our little group go down the gangplank and waved good-bye as whistles blasted and we were off on our great adventure.[1]

We arrived in Paris after a mercifully smooth trip and spent a busy week seeing old and new friends and purchasing supplies. From time to time our men broke free from their duties at the conference, the latter a frustrating business, with the Russians yielding no ground and reopening issues thought settled the day before.

On June 26, 1949, we drove out to a military plane waiting for us, the crew drawn up in a line by the ladder. The heavy luggage had already been packed into it, and we had to pick our way through boxes and bales, trunks and suitcases. We flew to the American air force base at Wiesbaden, Germany, and went on the next day to Berlin. That trip was carefully scheduled between regular flights of the Berlin airlift, planes flying in every three minutes to supply that city with all the necessities of life, as the Russians had cut off all ground transport routes between the Western occupation zones and Berlin, deep in the Russian zone.

A full honor guard of soldiers was waiting for us in Berlin, two companies with a band drawn up on one side and a group of high-ranking American officers and a big press contingent on the other. I bit my lip hard during "The Star Spangled Banner," for there we were, three Kirks on our way to Stalin's Moscow with the airlift roaring overhead, the music playing, and the American flag streaming out in front of us.

Berlin, in this spring of 1949, I found a horrid sight: no building or house left untouched in the heart of the city, trees cut down, statues mutilated, the empty ruins of government palaces blackened or destroyed, concrete and stone laid as low as the system they were built to glorify.

1. The material that follows in this and the next chapter is drawn from the author's letters, written at the time to her two daughters. Much of this material was included in her book *Postmarked Moscow*, published in 1952 by Charles Scribner's Sons, which Simon and Schuster has graciously permitted me to use for this book—Ed.

The next day we three and one of our Moscow embassy officers come to meet us flew off in a four-engine U.S. Air Force DC-4 amid our boxes and bales and supplies for the embassy, the whole leaving no room in the cabin for anyone but us. Two Russians, a navigator and a radioman, accompanied our crew and routed us around any area that might have been of military interest.

Five and a half hours later we reached the Moscow airport, where our whole embassy staff was out to greet us, together with a Russian protocol officer and Alan's four officially assigned Russian guards. Every time the American ambassador went out of his house they followed immediately behind; if he dined at a restaurant or went to the theater, they sat close by; if he traveled, they went with him. Only in our own and in foreign embassies was he free from direct surveillance, and then his conversations were recorded by hidden microphones.

The embassy staff seemed to be a very good lot. They had to be, for Moscow was not easy. It was the consensus that two years there was about the limit; beyond that one's nerves, health, and outlook grew a bit frayed. A forty-five-minute drive into town brought us to Spaso House, an immense neoclassic palace built in 1913 by a rich businessman and provided as the American ambassador's residence by the Russian government upon the establishment of diplomatic relations in 1933. Its proportions were gigantic, the ceilings some twenty-eight feet high, not to speak of the main hall, eighty-two feet long and two stories high, with an immense crystal chandelier in the middle. Throughout the house the wall paint was light-colored and fresh, however, and I thought it should not be difficult to live with.

Two embassy officers lived with us in the house, one of whom superintended the running of it, so my worries on that score were over. The servant staff of twenty was supervised by two Chinese men, the only ones who spoke English, but they had been there a long time and seemed competent. We had to go through a department of the Russian Foreign Ministry for all our needs, from Christmas cards to a new roof, from servants to tickets for football games and ballets. Like other Russian departments, this one was unfriendly and a mass of red tape and bureaucracy. It managed to make our complicated lives even more so.

Alan presented his credentials to the Russian president a couple of days later, just in time to preside officially at our July 4 national day reception in Spaso that evening. There were about four hundred guests at the reception, mostly diplomats and their wives in white tie and ball gown, plus the five American correspondents who constituted the entire nonofficial American colony in Russia. A Russian orchestra obliged with American dance music, and it was all very gay, many of the guests staying until half-past three in the morning.

Fifty Russians had been invited; about twelve showed up, with Andrei Gromyko, the deputy foreign minister, at their head. I stood with him, reminding him that we had met at a dinner given by our ambassador to the United Nations in New York the year before, and inquiring about his wife, asking to be remembered to her. We spoke of our livers, the strain put on them by diplomatic life. Forty-five minutes went by. As if by signal, the other Russians came up, Gromyko shook hands, they formed in behind him, and out they all went. It was farcical pretending to entertain those people, but we had to continue to play the game while we had diplomatic relations.

As in Belgium, Alan and I had to call on the heads of mission and their wives who had arrived in Moscow before we did, he calling on the men and I on the wives. I found the Polish lady very agreeable, a young, square-faced woman with sad eyes. We spoke French, the usual diplomatic phrases, until she said, in response to my question if she knew Moscow, "Yes, I was here during the war. I came to enlist in the partisan army and fight with my Russian comrades." I had heard the lady was a colonel and had gone with the army from Moscow to Berlin. I asked her a few questions, but she said no more and we fell back again on the weather.

Talking with this woman, I reminded myself that everything was probably recorded, that my hostess herself had to make a report of my behavior and conversation, and that someone else made a report of her behavior and conversation. It was too bad. I had the feeling that the Polish ambassadress would have liked to be friends with me, but, as Poland was under firm Russian control, it would have been damaging or even dangerous for her and her husband. We ourselves even had to be cautious if gestures were made toward us. If the gestures were sincere, those who made them might come to harm; if they were insincere and we responded, we ourselves might fall into a trap. A horrid business.

As for Russians, all foreigners were almost wholly deprived of any chance of "normal" contact with them. The only Westerners allowed to live in Russia were diplomats, half a dozen newspaper correspondents, and unmasked Russian spies who had fled their own countries. Once in Russia, Westerners were watched closely, their living and business quarters bugged, their local servants all informers, and their movements tracked. We could not go more then twenty-five miles from Moscow without special permission from the Foreign Ministry, and even our private cars always had to have Russian chauffeurs who reported on our itinerary and conversation. The only Russians allowed to talk to us were selected Foreign Ministry officials, servants, shopkeepers, and the like, and those conversations had to be strictly business. No social contact was allowed. Violations could mean a one-way trip to Siberia for the Russian.

The security services made sure these rules were enforced. For their first few months in Russia all foreigners were followed whenever they left their quarters, and military or "suspicious" persons were followed throughout their stay. There were guards outside foreigners' residences and offices, and any unusual behavior or dress as they left earned them a police "tail" for the occasion. Russian citizens' knowledge that foreigners were often tailed discouraged them from conversation in the street. Foreigners were truly isolated and felt so.

Perhaps most important, all foreigners knew that they were at the mercy of the Russians whenever they were not actually inside an embassy. They could be drugged and then photographed in compromising situations, harassed by the police, hit "accidentally" by a car, or even jailed, though the latter only briefly for diplomats owing to their diplomatic status. All these things happened. That, plus the everyday hardships of just living in Moscow left everyone on edge. Trips to the ballet and opera were one diversion, but "culture," especially Russian culture, was not everyone's cup of tea, and tickets were expensive and often hard to get. The principal escapes were parties with fellow nationals and other diplomats, and there were many of those.

All this was even more true for Americans, as agents of Russia's "principal enemy." In this atmosphere, one of Alan's main jobs was to maintain the morale of the staff. I hoped I could help with this, as well as show the Russians that I was not afraid of them any more than Alan was.

After I had been in Moscow for two weeks I had talked with no Russians except the servants, the Foreign Office people who came to our Fourth of July reception, and a few men from the Protocol Division, the ones whom I met at all diplomatic functions. There seemed little chance of breaking through the wall—a discouraging business when one thought of living two years in Moscow, one's social contacts being confined to one's diplomatic colleagues. I did not ask to convert anyone, I did not expect to be converted, but, being a friendly soul, I would have liked to talk with these people.

We were also isolated from the outside world. Virtually no Western travelers came to Russia, and most of those who did were Communist-sponsored groups who made no effort to contact us. The only Western businessmen were a few traders who came once a year to buy furs. They seldom came to the embassy, and I never saw them. The newsstands carried no noncommunist papers, international mail was censored and unreliable, and letters and newspapers took weeks to reach us by diplomatic pouch.

The Russian media were no help. The propaganda line, and only the propaganda line, was handed out over and over again, in the newspapers, in the books, on the radio. Shortwave Western broadcasts were our only source of uncensored and up-to-date news. Often, however, when we would turn on the U.S. government's "Voice of America," we heard just the whirring noise of Russian jamming. It was designed to prevent their people from hearing such "subversive" material, but it was maddening for us not to be able hear our own broadcast from our own country. The same thing held true for the British BBC and other Western radios.

As far as other restrictions went, there seemed to be no reason one could not walk freely about town. I promised always to take my identity card with me and had already ventured forth several times in the first few days. It was easy to spot the security men dotted along the route near us that the bigwigs took to their dachas. The cut of their clothes, the very look on their faces was unmistakable. As they saw a foreigner go by, they would often stroll along after, walking down the block until they saw the security man in the next block pick up the trail.

We were in fact constantly spied upon. The household servants, even if not intelligent or highly educated enough to be real spies, had to make reports on us. They were told to notice our habits; what we ate and drank; what medicines we used and how often; when we brushed our teeth and where we put the brushes on the shelf; whether our routine was regular and, if it varied, whether we seemed nervous or upset. Did we quarrel with each other? What was our manner toward our son?—all sorts of small details that, taken together, might make a pattern of our lives. Thus I felt it fortunate that I was accustomed to lead a relatively blameless life.

So far as I knew, I was not followed in the streets at this point. Perhaps it was just that I was unconscious about being followed, for the Russians were devious about this, and instead of men or women tagging behind there was apt to be someone across the way, or even in a car watching. Indeed it is highly likely that I was followed. An American friend whose father was at the embassy at that time told Roger many years later that he and his Russian nanny had always been followed, even though he was then only seven years old.

I was stared at, of course, for no matter how plainly foreigners were dressed, we were still quite different from the Russians, and our shoes especially attracted interest. Theirs were very poor, thin-soled, often made of artificial leather, many of them canvas.

I became a great window-peerer and looked unashamedly into basements and ground floors as I passed on the street. Many of the rooms looked very clean, the walls covered with whitewash or blue water-based paint. Others were very shabby and dirty. Furniture was sometimes covered with white cloths, tables sometimes had hand-knitted dollies on them—that was about the sum total of decoration.

The shops were poor, the goods scarce and ill-made, and the lines long. There were a few "commission shops," sort of state pawnbrokers where one could buy some old Russian silver, but it was expensive, particularly as the ruble was artificially pegged at eight to the dollar, an absurd rate. Our government compensated us by giving us some extra monetary allowances, but life was still very expensive and shopping costly as well as unrewarding.

In late July came word that I was to call on Madame Andrei Vishinsky, the wife of the foreign minister. I was the first Western ambassadress so received that year, so what would be an ordinary occurrence in any other country was a very special favor, not for me but for the United States. I decided to go alone, dressed in my best clothes and my best manner, and I dare say she did the same.

Madame Vishinsky received me in one of the Foreign Ministry's guesthouses, a big, old-fashioned place set in the midst of well-kept grounds protected by high walls. I was met at the bottom of the steps by a footman in livery and a fresh-faced young woman wearing a summer frock and white cotton mesh gloves that she kept on throughout the afternoon. Speaking English, she ushered me into a large drawing room furnished in heavy pieces, all gilt and carvings, with huge vases of fresh flowers set on marble-topped tables. Three ladies rose to greet me—Madame Vishinsky and the wives of two vice ministers. Madame Vishinsky, a slight woman about sixty, looked very worn and sick, but she was beautifully and very quietly dressed, with fine old pearls, no other jewel.

I asked Madame Vishinsky if she spoke French. She said she did and was clearly greatly relieved to find that I did, but the three other women were obviously quite disturbed, especially the interpreter. None of them spoke any French, so from time to time I turned in my most gracious manner, "Madame Vishinsky just said. . . . As I was just saying to Madame Vishinsky. . . . " It was really very comical, and I enjoyed myself immensely.

Actually our conversation was correct in the extreme, the weather, the ballet. It was not quite fair to put any of these people on the spot, for they must have been even more carefully watched and spied upon than were we. However, if I had not realized where I sat and in whose company, I might have felt freer to talk and to ask questions. I could easily imagine Mme. Vishinsky as one of the Russian émigrées one meets in Paris, very ravaged, a little bitter, with many memories of her own. Her looks, her quality of voice and manner, were entirely different from those of the other three, all of them straight Soviet products. When I asked if she had grandchildren, she said, "No, thank God," which I thought very revealing. I really liked her and found her pitiful, lonely, and ill at ease. After about forty-five minutes, I rose and was accompanied to the car by the young interpreter.

A few days later I asked a young Belgian friend of ours, Chantal Goffin, now wife of the Belgian ambassador, to take me to a market. She spoke Russian and, being Belgian, was a good housewife and a canny bargainer. I dressed in my oldest clothes, but she did me one better in a mackintosh with a handkerchief over her head. She said I looked like a capitalist spy. We went to the big central market where collective farm workers were allowed to sell their produce that remained after the state had taken its quota. Not unnaturally they kept the best for this purpose, as they could set their own prices in the market.

The only vegetables—and this in early August, when gardens should have been at their peak—were cucumbers, carrots, cabbages, a few shrunken onions, now and again some small parsnips, and hand-picked mushrooms. These last looked very risky to me—horrid to die of eating Russian mushrooms—but I saw women buying one or two big ones, peering at them, and weighing each one as we might do cantaloupes at home. I saw women buy, not even a half or a quarter of a cabbage, but three or four leaves, two or three carrots, the same with onions. All this went into soup, their main dish, for they had little else.

Housing and office space was also scarce. The government boasted that construction was going on everywhere, and this was certainly true in Moscow, where large construction jobs were mostly done by forced labor. In 1949, though not after, we could see some German prisoners on the construction sites, but mostly the prisoners were Russian. One always knew when forced labor was at work, as there were high board fences around such places, guard towers at each corner, and armed sentries.

People were arrested and shut up on the slightest provocation. We lost many servants out of the embassy in this way. The chauffeur of one of our officers was spirited away on accusation of being too friendly with the Americans. He received ten years in Siberia and permanent banishment from Moscow. The British counselor's wife told me she lost four maids that year, the Luxembourg minister's wife two, and so it went. Any imagined deviation, any small jealousy of one servant for another with consequent tale-telling, were enough to place an individual under suspicion. One day the person was at work, the next day gone.

In early August we made our first expedition outside of Moscow, visiting the Zagorsk monastery, forty-five miles away. As it was beyond the twenty-five-mile limit prescribed by the Russians for foreigners' routine travel, we had to ask the Foreign Ministry's permission at least forty-eight hours in advance, giving the names of the party and how many cars there would be. Word was then passed to the local police, who checked the car at the forty-kilometer mark and looked to see that the proper number of people were inside.

I did not believe this until I saw the security policemen standing in the road. It seemed a foolish gesture in our case, as our car was always driven by a Russian chauffeur and followed by not one, but two cars of Alan's guards on expeditions outside of town. As rain was sprinkling periodically, we ate our picnic alongside the cars, running for shelter when a shower began. Two men from each following car got out to stand guard over us. We offered them some of our sandwiches, but they declined. Alan did not seem to mind their presence, said as an admiral he had grown used to being followed by Marine orderlies, but it gave me an odd feeling to be munching away under the eyes of the Russian security men.

The monastery, founded in the fourteenth century, was a pretty sight as its walls and towers loomed up against the skyline. It was for years the richest in Russia, and before the 1917 revolution over one hundred thousand pilgrims a year had flocked to pray at the miracle-working tomb of St. Sergius. Pilgrims still came, and I saw several kneeling before the saint's elaborate silver-canopied tomb. We were lucky to find a pleasant young woman to guide us about, and she appeared gratified that we were interested in all that she had to show.

It would seem that the Russians allowed religion to be administered as they did certain drugs intended to ease the pain of the old and forlorn.

The Orthodox Church, for its part, made a bargain with the Kremlin and was subservient to its edicts. But the official attitude of the government toward religion had not changed. An article published shortly before our visit in *Komsomolskaya Pravda,* the newspaper of the Komsomol, the Communist youth organization to which most young people belonged, read in part, "Religion is in no way a personal affair for either Komsomol or Communists, and belief in god and participation in church ceremonies, even weddings or christenings, is incompatible with Komsomol membership." Small wonder we saw so few young people in the churches.

In late August Alan received word Stalin would receive him for a courtesy call. Alan seemed quite calm about the whole affair, though I should have been very nervous in his place. His call was scheduled for ten o'clock in the evening, and, at a carefully calculated ten minutes to ten, he, his deputy, and an embassy officer as interpreter set off in the ambassadorial limousine. It was nearly eleven when they returned, looking very pleased with themselves. They had stayed thirty-seven minutes, twelve more than the British, the only other Western ambassador so honored.

Alan reported Stalin, then seventy years old, to be stalwart and strong in appearance, neatly dressed in a well-fitting military uniform without decorations. His voice was strong, his eyes clear, and his whole manner had the simple confidence enjoyed by great and powerful men. The conversation was a bit stiff at first, but cordial enough. The marshal even went so far as to reach for his pipe and light it, a mark of high favor. Alan made brief reference to the question of repayment for the billions of dollars of aid America sent to the USSR during World War II and to the jamming of the Voice of America. When the last was uttered, Stalin turned to Foreign Minister Vishinsky to ask, smiling, "Do they say wicked things about us?" Alan said Vishinsky seemed very nervous, hopping around Stalin like an overzealous young aide whenever the marshal so much as blinked.[2]

2. For details of this conversation, see the U.S. Department of State, *Foreign Relations of the United States, 1949,* vol. 5, *Eastern Europe; the Soviet Union* (Washington, D.C.: United States Government Printing Office, 1949), 646–67, especially 657–64, http://digital.library.wisc.edu/1711.dl/FRUS.FRUS1949v05.

Although Stalin told Alan to ask to see him "without formality" on any occasion in the future when he had an item to discuss, Washington never instructed Alan to do so. Indeed Alan's official contacts were almost exclusively with Foreign Minister Vishinsky and his deputy, Andrei Gromyko. Both men were intelligent, able, and totally bound to the official line. They and Alan traded complaints and requests in firm but diplomatic language. Alan felt his job was not to insult the Russians, but to stand up to them firmly, and he did so. Years of command had made him one not to be pushed around, especially when representing his country.

Alan often went on instructions from Washington to raise problems like Russian repayment for some of the goods we sent them during the war, Russian interference with our planes or ships, their jamming the Voice of America, and limiting the distribution of *Amerika,* a slick magazine about the United States published by our government in Russian, among other languages. He occasionally went in on his own to complain about harassment of our embassy, our personnel, our mail, our goods shipments, and a dozen other things. There was no detail of our life too petty for the Russians to pick at, and we had to show them that we noticed, and that we did not like it.

The Russians, for their part, were always raising alleged American spying, sabotage, and harassment of Soviet diplomats. The outbreak of the Korean War in 1950 brought more tension into the exchanges. On one occasion, when Vishinsky handed Alan a diplomatic note to the U.S. government reporting that we had shot down a Russian plane in Korea, Alan refused to take it, saying it should be addressed to the United Nations Command in Korea, of which American forces were a part. Vishinsky spent the next forty-five minutes trying to make him take the note, but Alan refused.[3] This was the first time any American ambassador, as far as he knew, had violated diplomatic practice in that way. When he informed the State Department, they commended him, but I am sure many there were a bit shocked.

3. The U.S. Department of State, *Foreign Relations of the United States, 1950,* vol. 7, *Korea,* 699–703, http://digital.library.wisc.edu/1711.dl/FRUS.FRUS1950v07.

Alan of course had to supervise the embassy's reporting on developments in Russia and their analyses of Soviet policies. As there was virtually no contact with Russians except Alan's bouts with Vishinsky and Gromyko, the only way the embassy could pick up information was by closely reading the Russian press. There was no question of there being variations in opinion in the press, much less reporting of "leaked" information, as all the papers were tightly controlled by the government. This meant, however, that they spoke for the government, and our people scanned them carefully for any hint of changes in policy or propaganda line.

The embassy staff included an expert on Western Europe and one on China as well as those on Russia, as part of the embassy's job was to send Washington its views on the world situation as seen from the Moscow perspective. Alan paid particular attention to these cables, of course, bringing his own wisdom and global experience to bear on them. His voice was listened to as coming from Moscow and from a man much respected in the State Department.

Alan felt the Russians were confident, feeling their oats, but he did not think they would do anything really rash. He pointed out that Stalin, though very ready to take advantage of others' weakness, was careful not to step over certain lines. He did not want war with the United States, bluster as he would. He had tried to starve us out of Berlin, but he had not interfered with the airlift. He had sent his troops into northern Iran right after the war, but he had withdrawn them when faced with united Western opposition. Alan's job was to make it clear to the Russians that the United States was ready to fight to defend its interests, but was not itself planning to attack.

Alan repeatedly counseled Washington to take the same position, saying firmness, strength, and consistency should be the hallmarks of our policy. He used to say to me that Washington tended to blow hot or cold toward Russia, to lurch from fear to contempt, from conciliation to aggression, and he continually sought to buck Washington up when it was wavering and calm it down when it was on the warpath. He hoped it did some good. I think it did.

Much of Alan's time, however, was occupied with operational questions and staffing. The embassy had a competent administrative section, but details of daily life often became intergovernmental issues that Alan had at least to be familiar with. He saw to it that the embassy followed a very firm but courteous line—as suited the mission of a great power. It took much patience, not naturally Alan's strong suit, but he bit his lip and did his job. Personnel matters were often difficult. Staff were under great strain and sometimes did silly things. Some had to be sent away, more had to be counseled or given a rest. Alan's judgment was needed on all of these cases, as the Russians would exploit any sign of personal weakness to try, through sympathy or blackmail, to recruit an agent. The consequences could be grave, and the responsibility was Alan's.

We both tried to make Moscow life as pleasant as we could for our colleagues and our staff. We held a number of parties for fellow diplomats and for our own people. For the most senior diplomats we occasionally had formal dinners around the large table in the state dining room. That table, a great mahogany affair, was so broad that the houseboy had to climb onto it to arrange the centerpiece. The only way to polish it was for one of the Russian maids to lie on a rag on top of it, arms over her head, and be pushed back and forth by colleagues on either side.

These parties were successful. The cook could give us a good dinner, even if not up to Belgian standard. We had to contrive menus from our deep-freeze and the small things that could be bought in the local market. The house was surprisingly handsome when dressed for a party, and I was only sorry we could not put on the kind of shows our people had arranged pre–cold war, with ballerinas pirouetting under the chandelier in the great hall and Russian scientists muttering in corners. It must have been very picturesque, and certainly much more fun, but the word had gone out from the Russian government that such invitations were not to be accepted by their people or extended by us.

For the younger diplomats and staff and the more spirited and attractive older ones, we arranged Spaso's great hall like a night club, card tables set up around a dance floor under the great chandelier, each table set for four with a bottle of pink champagne in the middle and more available. After a few months we had formed a small band, an assistant air attaché at the piano, an embassy counselor on the trombone, and the Associated Press correspondent on the drums. They made highly acceptable, even if unprofessional, music, and all seemed to enjoy the taste of Western gaiety and informality. I was sorry the Russians could not be there. I think they would have enjoyed it.

I attended a show at the puppet theater early in our stay, an artless little comedy, but the marionettes were beautifully made and manipulated, and there seemed more light-heartedness than one expected of Soviet theater. In front of us sat a row of high-collared generals and their families, both children and their general fathers sitting rapt in delight. These rare aspects of the Russian people were the good ones; we would have liked to think they were truer than some others. If so, it seemed cruel that so much talent, imagination, and creative urge should be channeled into the dull business of communizing society.

I asked for permission to see a Russian hospital, any Russian hospital, but heard nothing from the request. I also put in to see a school, a day nursery, all manner of things, but I never heard anything from any of them. Our own doctor, the American naval physician stationed at our embassy, had no license to practice in Russian hospitals. Any case involving hospitalization had to be sent to the one Russian hospital open to diplomats. There the patient was assigned to a doctor and had no choice about anything from then on. The doctor's technique was often quite good, but hospital equipment was poor and the methods very rough and ready. I could only hope I remained healthy.

We had a remarkable experience at the Bulgarian National Day reception in September 1949. The ambassadress, a grim old party with straight gray hair, a determined mustache, and a hard revolutionary eye, invited us to sit at the head table when we arrived at her huge dinner reception. Down we sat under the amazed eyes of our colleagues, who goggled at us from across the room, as it was unheard of for Americans to be so honored by any of the Russian-dominated countries, of which Bulgaria was one. Beside me I found Deputy Foreign Minister Gromyko, beyond him other high Russian officials, the ambassadress, and Foreign Minister Vishinsky. Opposite us were some nameless East European dignitaries and a famous ballerina, Olga Lepishinskaya. One of the top dancers, thin, quick-moving, as intelligent-looking as a lively bird, she spoke both French and English. I complimented her on her dancing, and we drank a toast together.

It was all that one had expected of Moscow parties: caviar; immense cold salmon; fancy illuminated ices; Soviet ministers in gaudy uniforms; the Bulgarian ambassadress in nondescript black with a red ribbon and star pinned on her bosom; the marshals in bright blue tunics, their chests covered with medals in rows, like cabbages in a garden; the ballerina, badly dressed in wispy chiffon, but with fine diamonds swinging from her ears. It was what we thought such a party would be, but our share in this one was pure luck. Ordinarily we would have been shunted off at a far table, within sight of the Russians, but no more. Alan was delighted and I must say I enjoyed myself.

We had another triumph a few days later: Vishinsky came to lunch, the first time any Russian guest, much less the foreign minister, had taken a meal in the embassy for two years. Alan had sent a personal note inviting Vishinsky to a small lunch with embassy staff before the minister left for the UN General Assembly in New York. Vishinsky was accompanied by the head of the Foreign Ministry American desk and an interpreter, and Alan had four of our embassy officers with him. I gave the gentlemen roast ham, the last string beans out of our garden, and lemon pie. Our Chinese houseboy served with oriental deftness, so all went well. Everyone was greatly pleased, as no other ambassador had done anything like it.

Absurd, was it not, that the foreign minister coming to a quiet lunch with an ambassador accredited to his country should make such news? I laughed, contrasting it with the many times the Belgian foreign minister had come to our house in Brussels and the easy, friendly footing we felt ourselves on with him.

In late September we had our first visit to the Kremlin, an area always closed in those years to all but a few, who had to apply well in advance for permission to visit. As Alan led our small embassy party in his own car, we were allowed to drive through the gates. After our documents were checked twice, we disembarked and were escorted on a three-hour tour of the Kremlin's museums and churches. At the end of the tour, our guide made a little speech: "All of this, once the property of the tsars, now belongs to the people of Russia. The treasure is theirs to guard and enjoy." It was certainly guarded, but hardly enjoyed by the people. We were the only visitors in the museum that day. Probably only fifty people a month ever saw these things, admitted as a privilege rather than a right.

A few days later Roger and I and two or three embassy friends obtained Russian permission to go by car to Yasnaya Polyana, author Leo Tolstoy's country home, now a museum. We were, however, forbidden to stop anywhere en route. We thought this applied only to towns, but not so, for just as we finished our picnic lunch by the wayside, a militiaman popped out from behind a bush, saying, "You cannot stop here, you must pack up and go on. This is a forbidden area."

There was nothing anywhere around us except birch trees and a few cows, and where he had come from we had no idea, but Soviet policemen often sprang from the grass like dandelions. He walked away and we started to pack up our things. He came back to make sure we were leaving and when satisfied hailed a peasant's horse cart, wished us good day, and was off down the road astride a large mattress. We thought some of sitting down again but decided he might have a mate nearby; militiamen often traveled in pairs, like cobras.

The weather was turning colder in the first days of October, and Alan decided it was time for him to take a U.S. Air Force plane to fly to Berlin and come back with a load of supplies for the embassy. He really had to make the trip every three months or so, as that was how our people's shelves were stocked with basic necessities, canned food, and the occasional holiday treat. We decided to use the chance to take a brief holiday in Western Europe as a break from the stresses of Moscow life.

Before I left on this holiday, I dreaded the return to Moscow—fearing it would lack the excitement of the adventure and spirit of dedication when we first came, but as the time came I found myself more reconciled to the months ahead than I had thought possible. Moscow was still difficult, but the sense of adventure and dedication remained, and now it was tempered with the certainty of a comfortable, fairly secure life in palatial Spaso House. We had no personal anxieties, provided our health remained within the bounds our embassy doctor could handle. The servants were good enough and the food sufficient. The embassy staff was good, our son was with us, and the two embassy officers living with us in Spaso were congenial companions.

I was also interested in learning more about Russia and about its people. Even though we had so few contacts with Russians, just being there allowed us to absorb the feel and look of the place. One read in the faces of the people much that could not be put into books or even into the accounts heard outside.

November 7, the Russian National Day, came shortly after our return. We joined the rest of the senior diplomats in a tribune in Red Square to watch the parade. Shoulder to shoulder, security police officers in khaki-colored wool with blue caps stood all around the great empty square.

As the Kremlin clock pealed 10 A.M., the members of the Politburo mounted Lenin's mausoleum, all except for Stalin, who was in the Crimea on holiday, safer for an elderly man than reviewing troops in Red Square on a November day. The massed bands crashed into the national anthem. Every man took off his hat except the Politburo—perhaps the same idea as not drinking your own toast. Then came the parade—large detachments and bands from each service followed by cavalry, artillery, rocket-equipped trucks, and then tanks. The boots worn by all ranks were the only good-looking shoes to be seen in Russia. But the sound of those boots striking the stone pavement was chilling.

The military display lasted an hour and a quarter, and then it was the turn of the civilian organizations, factory unions, sport clubs, school delegations, a march-by that lasted four to five hours. At this point the security police formed lines separating every five columns of marchers, one man facing the columns to the right, the next, shoulder to shoulder with him, facing the columns to the left, so the loyal Russian paraders' every step could be watched. After a half-hour of watching the procession of people go by we walked back to our embassy office building across the neighboring square, Alan's top hat and tail coat causing considerable merriment amongst the marchers, who had only seen such creations in the papers' anticapitalist cartoons.

24. Ambassador Alan and Lydia Kirk with their son, Roger, flanked by two of the Spaso House "boarders," Moscow, 1949.

We now settled in for the long winter. I had provided myself with all manner of footgear for walking in the wet, snow, and cold, but it was not too comfortable even so. Sidewalks were very bad, far too narrow for the most part, and were mostly very broken and badly patched. I purchased a most convincing Russian hat, a round fur turban of sheepskin, sheared to look like beaver. I looked a little like Anna Karenina's mother in Tolstoy's novel, but it was warm and tight against my head, and I was well pleased with it.

The Moscow drama and ballet performances had resumed in the fall after their summer break. Much of it was excellent. It was only a pity that most of the contemporary plays were strictly propaganda and many so violently anti-American that we felt conspicuous in attending them. The ballet was a real treat, and providing tickets was one service the Soviet administration did well for us, perhaps because they wanted to show off their accomplishments. Although the audience was a bit dumpy and smelled of the standard Russian perfume, the theater itself, the prerevolutionary Bolshoi building, glittered with gold. The staging was always opulent, and Galina Ulanova, perhaps the best of all the postwar Soviet ballerinas, was at the peak of her form. One evening five Western ambassadors, including Alan, signed a program with a congratulatory note and asked that it be taken to her. I hope she saw it and that it did her no harm.

Four of Alan's guards always came along with him to the ballet or theater, sometimes displacing a startled Russian member of the audience if the guards' own assigned seats were too far from Alan's. Their enthusiasm for culture was limited, though I imagined they must have welcomed the change from sitting, three of them, in their small car outside our gate while a fourth kept watch on the pavement. They did like the more robust ballets, and the one time Alan went to a soccer game all eight tagged along.

We could also go to the few churches that were open. Attendance at a vespers service in a large church in December impressed me again with the essential religiousness of the Russian people. The church was filled, as were all the services in the few churches remaining open, the people crammed in so tight it was all one could do to find a place to stand. I sensed the government had taken advantage of this deeply rooted characteristic to channel it toward the cult of Lenin, Stalin, and the party.

As Christmas approached, the Moscow shops became bright with trees and tinsel ornaments, all presided over by Grandfather Frost, the Soviet substitute for Santa Claus. It was not Christmas that would be celebrated, but New Year's, for naturally the Soviets abolished Christmas, and the trees were New Year's trees, not Christmas trees.

Just before Christmas we chalked up another personal triumph: Gromyko and his wife came to lunch. I had written a polite note to Mrs. Gromyko, suggesting a choice of dates and saying it would be quite a small party, our own family, two embassy officers, and anyone from the Foreign Ministry the Gromykos chose to bring. After several days the ministry rang to say the Gromykos accepted for the following Sunday.

We received our guests in a small sitting room with a bright fire, where we offered them cocktails, sherry, and tomato juice. One of the Foreign Ministry men took a cautious glass of sherry, but the Gromykos stuck severely to tomato juice. He was in a dark suit, while Madame Gromyko wore a small astrakhan hat and carried a little muff with her dress, which was carefully and expensively made of a style and cut reminiscent of my great-aunt Fanny, who died in 1920 at the age of eighty-seven.

Conversation was a bit strained but very correct in tone and subject. We spoke of Gromyko's son, just Roger's age, who had been with his parents in the United States for several years. I asked his mother if he kept up his English.

"That is very hard for him," answered Madame Gromyko. "Sometimes he locks himself in his room just to talk English to himself. You see he has no one to talk to here."

What a foolish situation. Naturally, one could have said, "But send him here to us. Roger would so like to meet him and talk with him," but that would have been viewed by the Russian authorities as a crude American attempt to subvert the deputy foreign minister's young son. At every turn one had to remember that it was impossible to say or do the natural, normal thing, and that was hard for friendly folk like us.

Two days later there was a reception at the Foreign Ministry guesthouse in honor of Stalin's seventieth birthday. Foreign Minister Vishinsky received with his wife. She wore a dress made from the same cloth as Madame Gromyko's luncheon costume, but she wore a fine string of pearls, a lovely old diamond spray pin, and magnificent earrings. She greeted me most cordially, and I presented the other ladies of our embassy to her. It appeared to be Madame Vishinsky's one outing in high society. She looked as ravaged as ever but seemed to be quite excited and enjoying herself immensely.

All the marshals were trotted out in their blue and gold, and it was altogether quite a glittering affair. The general tone seemed confident and cordial all round. Of course these people felt confident: Things were going well for them; they still expected the West to crumble into economic decay; with the Communist army's final victory in China in October, that country had fallen into their lap; and, with the exception of Yugoslavia, which had broken with the USSR early in the year, the Balkans were under Moscow's control.

It occurred to me what a skillful substitution the Soviet rulers had made of one birthday for another, Stalin for the Christ child, and I wondered if the man was really born on December 21. Anyway, his picture and acres and acres of red bunting vied with the "New Year's" trees in the shop windows, and high over the Kremlin floated his portrait suspended from blimps, a Soviet version of the Star of Bethlehem.

We had a supper party for 108 on Christmas Eve—all the Americans in the embassy, the five American correspondents and their wives, one lonely American fur buyer and his wife, and two visiting American lady chess champions; in other words, the current American colony in Moscow. It was a great success. One of the young air force attachés played carols on our piano, and we all sang for an hour or so. I wore a new red skirt, strung Christmas balls into a necklace, and put tinsel stars in my ears. The boys thought I was wonderful. Everyone had a good time and for a few hours stopped feeling lonely and forgotten.

After it was all over we went to work clearing the room and switching the chairs about to prepare for church service at 11 A.M. the next day. It looked swept and decorous when we came down in the morning to dress the altar with our silver candlesticks and my best tea cloth. The congregation arrived promptly, 125 of them, all nationalities. Our young carol-playing friend, who was also to play the hymns, overslept, so the Dutch ambassadress obliged at the piano and the British counselor's wife led the singing. The clergyman, an earnest young man down from Helsinki, Finland, where he was chaplain of the Anglican church, gave a good simple sermon, and Alan read the lesson. Altogether it was a dignified and pleasant service. Afterwards we offered sherry to the reverend and the distinguished guests, and they all left in quite a glow. Our embassy-officer boarders and we opened our presents after Christmas lunch, and very nice they were.

It was a good Christmas, though we missed home and family and hoped to be in the United States on Christmas leave the next year. The following day we held a children's party for sixty, including our six embassy children, those from other missions, and the children of the Spaso servants. We pieced together a movie program of animated cartoons followed by ice cream and cake. I had not worked so hard or given out so many presents since my Red Cross years during the war. But it was all worthwhile.

We held a ball New Year's Eve, one like many New Year's balls, but with an added Moscow feeling. It was very, very gay. The ballroom was decorated with swags of colored streamers and a huge revolving glass ball in the middle of the ceiling. The punch, brewed weeks before, was excellent and effective. The women wore their gayest frocks. We managed to forget how far away from home we all were until we opened the windows at midnight to let the New Year in, and no sound came through—no bells, no singing, no whistles, only a draft of chill Moscow air. It seemed an augury for the next year.

12

Making It Work in Moscow, 1950–1951

We decided to start the new year with a trip to Leningrad, some four hundred miles north on the Baltic Sea, a city filled with imperial palaces, museums, and handsome churches. It had been the capital of Russia under the name of St. Petersburg for two hundred years until the Communists took over in 1917 and renamed it Leningrad [renamed St. Petersburg in 1991]. I was glad at the prospect, for packing and going off somewhere gave us a real holiday feeling. Even though the weather turned bitter cold, we set off by night train as planned.

In Leningrad we were given a government travel agency guide and a most impressive, atrociously decorated suite at the Astoria hotel, a very grand establishment on the main street, one of the two top hotels in tsarist times. Now the hotel was kept at sixty-three degrees, and in the cold bathroom only one hot-water faucet worked, the one in the tub, and that gave out a brown trickle. Alan's guards had a room next to ours, and one of them kept watch outside our door day and night. In the train as well, one remained on watch in the corridor, usually the same one, the junior of the lot, whom the others made do the dullest work.

We did some walking but not much, as the temperature hovered between fifteen and twenty-five degrees below zero Fahrenheit, and one could stay out only fifteen or twenty minutes without freezing toes or fingers. We did attend the ballet and a play, went to restaurants, and made more than one visit to the Hermitage art museum, seeing everything except their fine collection of French impressionists, bought before 1913 by two Russian sugar barons and confiscated by the Communist government after the 1917 revolution. I asked our guide about them and she answered vaguely:

"Those rooms are closed off. They are under repair. I do not know where the pictures are stored."

The Soviets had declared them decadent, unfit to be seen, just as they had a similar group of impressionist paintings in Moscow, the other half of the sugar barons' collection.

I found Leningrad a handsome city. I wished I might have seen it before the revolution, when it was the national capital and residence of the ruling aristocratic class. Now it was a ghost city, cold and deserted. The great churches were empty and shut, the palaces vacant, the government offices closed. It was a dream frozen in space and, like dreams, a little blurred around the edges, but with now and then a gilt spire rising distinct and bright against the sky.

Shortly after our return from Leningrad, when an embassy wife and I were out walking, a pleasant-faced woman came up to us and said, "Do you think there would be any possibility of getting streptomycin? I have a brother dying of tuberculosis. The doctors think he might be saved if we could give him the drug." Streptomycin was then a relatively new antibiotic, unavailable in Russia to all but the most privileged. We said we were sorry, we wished there were something we could do, but surely her doctor must have his own supplies.

"I understand," said the woman. "It does not matter. Perhaps some day better times will come."

It was all very tragic. It was highly unusual for a Russian to come up to us in the street, and we had no means of knowing whether the woman was sincere or a police plant. We could not have done anything for her in any case, for that would have been too dangerous both for her and for us. We were probably followed, and certainly were being watched by the police on the street, and the woman took a real risk in even speaking to us. She must have been truly desperate to do so if she were not a plant, which she might well have been.

One technique the police used on foreigners was to offer them something on the street and, if they took it, claim they were trying to acquire "secrets" or "national art treasures." A variation was for the Russian to ask for something and, if it was given or promised, the authorities would claim the foreigner was trying to "subvert" or even "recruit" a loyal Soviet citizen. The foreigner would be embarrassed, perhaps thrown out of the country. If the foreigner were anxious that the transaction not be revealed, the Soviets could threaten to reveal it as blackmail. The Russian, if not a police plant, would probably end up in a Siberian prison camp. That was life in Russia.

In time the weather warmed up a little, to about twenty degrees above zero, and the snow turned black and mushy. My walks grew a little longer. I found it interesting to check the housing in the city by counting the names listed over the doors. I passed a one-story house, eight windows across and five windows deep. There were thirty-two names on the board tacked over the front door; farther along a smaller house of the same character, only five windows across and three deep, had twenty names. These were old houses and obviously no money had been spent on them since the 1917 revolution, so plumbing must have been rudimentary—probably not more then one bathroom, at the most two, for the whole lot—and, of course, only one kitchen.

Housing was in fact a terrible problem for our staff. We depended on the Russian government for it, and they gave us very little. Newly arrived singles or couples had to live weeks or even months in one hotel room. They cooked on a hot plate and did their wash in the bathtub to avoid high-priced, greasy restaurants and laundries that sent clothes back ruined or as dirty as they left, if they came back at all. The quarters available, some in our chancery building, a few elsewhere, were shoddy and cramped.

There were only two American Embassy families with children in Moscow. One's experience was typical. They lived in the last single-family dwelling the embassy was able to rent, a bit out of town. They met with disaster after disaster, ending with a fire from an overheated stove, the insulation of which they discovered to have been sawdust! The father finally decided, with Alan's encouragement, to have his wife and children go home. He moved into Spaso with us, as one of our officer boarders was leaving.

The housing shortage meant that all the wives except for me had to work at the embassy. In one sense this was good, as it took minds off the difficulties of life and built a real sense of partnership, but it was hard on some.

My last venture before we left in February for a holiday in the Mediterranean was a trip on the subway in the company of one of the embassy wives. The Russians boasted loudly about it, and I had to agree that it was most impressive—clean, fast, grandiose. It was an excellent psychological investment on the part of the Russian government, a promise of things to come in the brave new Communist world, besides being an excellent air raid shelter because it was so deep.

In late February of 1950, Alan, Roger and I set off for our holiday trip. The first stop was Rome, where Alan attended a conference of American ambassadors to the major European powers, together with the directors of our postwar aid program, the Marshall Plan, in those countries. They were a remarkable group of men, with great power as representatives of the victorious United States and the then-almighty dollar. I felt as if I were at a meeting of Roman proconsuls at the height of the empire. Many were good friends of ours. A number of the wives were there. Rome was a wonderful change from Moscow, and I had a very good time.

Our embassy would have had a two-engine military DC 3 attached to it in Moscow if the Russians would have permitted such a thing, but imagine the chances of their allowing an American military plane to fly about their country with an embassy pilot! As a result our air attaché needed to get flying hours to keep up his proficiency. Alan and he conceived the idea of doing his hours flying a DC-3 about the Mediterranean with us and a few other embassy people. The U.S. Air Force, probably bearing in mind the rigors of Moscow life, made a DC-3 available for the trip.

First stop was Cairo, where we stayed at the Mena House Hotel near the Pyramids, Alan and Roger playing tennis with a guard (Egyptian this time) sitting at the end of the court. We toured the sights, dined more than once with our nice ambassador to Egypt, and went with some well-to-do Egyptian Christians on an elegant picnic in the desert, lunch served on fine china in tents laid with oriental rugs. Alan said that was the kind of picnic he enjoyed.

The only problem was being sure that King Farouk, then the ruler of Egypt, would not be at any restaurant where we went with our attaché's wife. She was a striking redhead, and if the king caught sight of her he might send his guards over to take her away for his pleasure. Judicious advance telephoning to restaurants avoided this problem, and we flew safely away to the island of Cyprus. Here we had a lovely two days in the British governor's mansion in what was then a peaceful British colony.

Our next destination was Istanbul, where we took a boat up to the submarine net laid at the entrance of the Black Sea to prevent Russian submarines from sneaking out. We reflected on the odd world beyond the net that we had come to know, so different from the "normal" world we were used to. On to Athens, where we lunched with the king and queen of Greece, no doubt partly owing to Alan's yeoman service on the Yugoslav frontier. Afterward the queen, an intelligent and energetic, too energetic, woman who was considered to interfere too much in Greek politics, escorted us around the Parthenon. Though Egypt was interesting, I much preferred Greece, the cult of the living being more to my taste than the cult of the dead.

We ended up in Paris. Alan and Roger flew back to Moscow, and I returned to the United States to attend the arrival of two new grandchildren and have a good break before the next phase of my Moscow sojourn. Once my two daughters had their babies, just a week apart, I returned to Europe by boat, then a journey by train from Paris to Helsinki, where Roger met me, and two nights more by Russian train to Leningrad and on to Moscow, arriving in late May, almost three months since we all left for our European trip.

At Leningrad the travel agency people were so blatantly rude and the charges for accommodations so monstrous, it was maddening. The hotel room was dirty, of course, and there was no hot water, but the attitude of the people at the desk would lead you to believe the Waldorf Astoria in New York was a roadside inn compared with their magnificent establishment. I got into the train for Moscow and went to sleep exhausted by sheer rage. In fact, my overall feeling in coming back to Russia was one of violent indignation, though I was heart-warmed by my cordial welcome at Spaso, not only from my husband and our embassy boarders but from all the household staff lined up to greet me in the front hall.

In Moscow things had changed very little, though the house had been cleaned from top to bottom—perhaps not to the very bottom. No matter how thoroughly the basement was scrubbed and whitewashed, the insects managed to hide out, and they and the mice returned the next day. In New York, I had telephoned my personal shopper at Bloomingdale's and asked:

"Do you carry mousetraps?"

"I will find out," she answered. "How many would you need, four or five?"

"Oh, no," I replied. "Let me have three dozen."

She was horrified but produced them, and they met me at the ship along with elegant presents from kind friends, orchids and baskets of fruit.

With the coming of spring and the planting season, the Russian and East European press carried stories that the Americans had scattered Colorado potato beetles all over East Germany to destroy the crops there. As our statistics showed that the beetles were prevalent in Poland all during the year before, it was an unlikely tale, but the Russians played it up full blast. They even put out matchboxes with pictures of the beetles on them, warning people of the danger and of what the wicked Americans had done. Meanwhile, our houseboy was delighted with the mousetraps. He put a bunch of tempting cheese sandwiches into them—result, eight mice in the traps next morning. He was triumphant.

Spring brought rain, and rain seemed wetter in Moscow than any place else. Gutters were almost nonexistent, and there were floods at every street crossing. The side streets had a mass of mud holes, and rusted, broken drain pipes spilled water onto the sidewalks, so I needed rubber boots for my morning walk. The Moscow winter is hard, and snow and ice leave damage behind, but the Russians just slapped on a little plaster and whitewash and splattered some watery paint on the walls. A month later, it looked as bad as before. With all this, the Russian newspapers carried long articles on the sad conditions of Western slums, on buildings in America where hundreds of people lived on top of each other without light or air, the streets dark caverns below where the sun never shone.

In late June Alan, Roger, and an embassy officer set off for a two-week trip to Siberia. Roger had told his father he desperately wanted to see Siberia before he left in August to return to Princeton, and Alan said he would like to go also. I must admit I hated to see them go so far into the interior of that vast land and would be glad when they came safely home again. It was an uncomfortable feeling, seeing my husband and son off for Siberia under the care of the Soviet police; certainly it was not a sensation I had ever thought to experience. Gromyko had asked Alan why he wanted to go to Lake Baikal. Alan explained that he had always had a curiosity about that body of water, the deepest on the earth's surface, and that the lake was as far to the east as the Russians permitted foreigners to travel.

As our men were not allowed to stop in any major town near Baikal, their actual destination was a village on the shores of the lake. The tickets arrived only an hour and a half before departure, the usual thing. It always made one feel a bit uncertain, as one never knew if in fact they would arrive, trips sometimes being denied simply by nondelivery of tickets from the government tourist agency, the only source of tickets or hotel reservations for foreigners. At the station I shook hands with Alan's head guard and asked him, through an interpreter, to take good care of the ambassador. He gave me what was meant to be a reassuring smile and a hard, horny hand.

On the day before our men's return we received word that North Korea had invaded South Korea. Alan heard nothing of the attack en route, so was greeted with the news on his arrival at dawn the next day after a fourteen-hour flight from Novosibirsk, a city two days' rail journey back from Baikal. This was the first city on their route where they were allowed, as foreign diplomats, to get off their train and transfer to a plane. After a few hours' sleep Alan rushed to the office, while Roger spent the day turning the crank on the embassy incinerator to speed the burning of the secret papers.

That evening we were invited to a minor diplomatic reception. Alan said we must all go and stay a good while to show we were not unduly worried. Nevertheless, I was concerned. I hated the thought that my family and our colleagues were living in the center of what would be the American bombers' target number one in case of war. Alan spent much time at the office that week and, as if the Korean situation were not enough, the Russians lodged another formal protest on the Colorado beetle. It would have been ludicrous if they were not presenting it in such a serious way.

Soviet tempers seemed to grow worse with the passing days. They were now accusing us of sending in all sorts of harmful germs and insects hidden in the huge amount of supplies we sent them under our Lend-Lease program during World War II. To hear what the Russian dailies and magazines contained, it was a wonder we were not stoned in the streets, for we must all have appeared to the Russians as devils with horns.

The excitement and the increased apprehension among our own staff made it, we felt, all the more important to keep up our usual diplomatic life as a sign to all that we, at least, were not panicked. To bolster morale and provide a diversion from gloomy thoughts, we gave parties and went ahead with our usual Fourth of July ball, to which we invited 350 people. The American flag flying on our office building right across from the Kremlin that day was a welcome sight. It seemed just the day to wave the flag, for Gromyko gave a speech that morning that was anything but cordial, we thought timed as a Fourth of July greeting to us all.

It was a job to put on a big party such as our ball, for one had to contrive and improvise what would be easy to arrange in more civilized spots. All in all, however, it was a good party. Toward 2:30 A.M. the light began to come in through the open terrace door and the big skylight above, but the dancing went on. We finished off toward 4:30 A.M. with a spirited Russian folk dance.

About seven or eight Russians came to the party, all minor officials; they stayed half an hour, took nothing to drink, and went off after stiff handshakes. They were a scruffy lot, definitely the second team, so it was almost more insulting to have them come than none at all. The real mark of Russian displeasure was the withdrawal of Alan's right to turn left in the Moscow traffic, a privilege of high rank that he and the British ambassador, alone among the diplomats, had enjoyed heretofore, and which the British ambassador retained. In addition, the guards at our gate and the policemen on duty outside the chancery stopped saluting as Alan passed through in his car, though only for twenty-four hours.

I must say that listening to the Western broadcasts and reading the Western papers made me very uneasy, as it sounded as though the tempo was speeding up, the symphony of the spheres growing faster and faster, until one day all would dissolve into nothingness, a chaos of destruction. I only hoped that, if it did come, it would be general and not leave a few of us to drag about a ruined earth. News from Korea grew worse as July wore on, and I did not sleep too soundly. It was hot and the sun streamed in from 3 A.M. on, and once awake there was much to think about that was not sleep-making. I took a half-day job at the embassy library, as sitting at home was tiresome and social life at a minimum during the servants' summer vacations.

In mid-August we bid farewell to Roger, who was returning to Princeton after thirteen months in Moscow. We topped off his stay with a gay buffet for sixty at Spaso. Our band made good music at the party, we sang raucous songs, and I was told there were sore throats and heavy heads at the chancery the next morning.

Later that month Alan and I flew out to Germany in the usual DC-4 to replenish supplies. This time I wished we might be going for good, but we returned immediately, as it did not seem the time to be away for long. Even our two days in Germany did us much good. One thing that gave me new courage and strengthened my wobbling resolution was the confidence people showed in the job we were doing and their genuine sympathy and understanding of our many problems and difficulties. Of course Germany was also under the gun, as it bordered on the Russian sphere, but our people there lived in a very American world, and the atmosphere was gay and free compared to anything behind the Iron Curtain.

Not everyone could take the strain of Moscow, and the Russians preyed on human weakness, fear, and insecurity. That was why we had a policy that any officer or clerk could be instantly detached and sent home, either at their own or the embassy's request. The year before, one young man, after he had been in Moscow two months, came to our doctor and said he could not take it. The doctor reported the matter to Alan's number two, and the man left within the week with Alan's commendation for his courage in admitting his difficulties. Another newly arrived officer was so affected he could not walk down the ladder of the plane bringing him in. He left on the next flight. Moscow was no place for scratchy nerves or hidden complexes. It was not because any of us were in physical danger, for we were not; it was the indefinable pressure that lessened, only to increase, and the knowledge that the Russians were ready to exploit any weakness or transgression for blackmail purposes.

A couple of weeks after our return the Russians told the French priest whom they had allowed to live in Moscow to administer to the foreign colony that he had to leave and that no successor would be accepted. Our embassy went to his final mass sixty strong, Alan in the lead, most of us not Catholic but wanting to show support. The priest was visibly affected as he celebrated the mass while Alan's four guards stood glumly in the back. When later we had the priest to lunch he seemed truly grateful for the support given him, realizing that we had done so to show solidarity against one more example of unreasoning harassment of the foreign colony.

With the progress of autumn it was growing steadily colder, but we had no heat in the house, as the cleaning of boiler, fuel tank, and radiators by the diplomatic service bureau had gone slowly and the last details remained to be done. The Russians never quite did a job right, never seemed to finish it. When Alan would get angry about it all, I would remind him it was hopeful for our cause, so he should not complain. Finally our embassy engineer decided to go ahead and start the system anyway. Fortunately it worked.

We set off to view the November 7 parade from the diplomatic tribune in Red Square in rain and fog. I bundled up in a borrowed overcoat that, unlike my more elegant affairs, had a hood. I wore knee boots. Alan said afterward I could have joined the Russian people parading by after the military finished, as I looked just like them. After two hours of standing in the rain, we returned to our office building a little ways away, a large American flag waving convincingly from it in the face of the paraders as they assembled for their march through the square. That flag is a good one, and it looked especially fine in that place on that day.

Our house manager told me the Spaso staff had asked for their bread ration in flour for the holiday. They would have liked it in flour every day, but that was not possible, as their own government allowed them to buy flour only twice a year and, if we gave it out daily, they would be tempted to sell it on the black market. We made our own bread in the house out of the flour we brought in from Germany or Finland, and each employee—house servant, yardman, and chauffeur—got a loaf a day. While the bread in the Russian stores, both the light and the dark, was excellent, our own was good and cost only a tenth as much.

November 7, however, was one of the two occasions on which the Russian people might purchase flour, about five pounds a person. Not to be outdone by Father Stalin, we supplemented his generosity with that of Uncle Sam, and each employee received five pounds without having to wait in the long queues we saw on every street corner.

That evening I went to the Foreign Ministry's diplomatic reception in my best clothes. When we arrived half an hour late, the reception line had broken up and already the hordes had fallen on the supper tables, so the big ballroom looked like an overdressed version of a fast food restaurant. I took off my diamond earrings and put them in my bag—no use losing anything in that mob—held the skirts of my best dress tight in one hand lest something be spilled on me, and made my way to as clear a corner as I could find.

There was a tap on my shoulder and there was Madame Gromyko, grown fatter than the year before and dressed in pale green so she looked like a round, soft caterpillar. But she was a kind, rather frightened woman, and the brief encounters we had before were pleasant. I corralled my ladies and introduced them to her, asked about her children and her health. She said she had a rather uncertain gall bladder, which could not have been improved by the food she was eating that evening. Alan had told us we were all to leave after forty-five minutes, the same length of time the Russian officials stayed at our Fourth of July reception. We felt like a pack of Cinderellas, but watches were synchronized and out we went when he gave the signal. I hoped the Russians noticed it—our colleagues did—but the Russian heads were pretty well down in the troughs. Poor Madame Gromyko must have felt very tired indeed the next morning.

We took a month's Christmas holiday in the United States, caught up with the children and friends, and refurbished our supplies and clothes. It seemed harder than ever to return to Moscow. It was always something of a shock after a glimpse of the outside world. Once away, Russia seemed all a dream; coming back, it became reality again. As one of our officers remarked to me, it was not only the people's sodden misery, but their acceptance of it and the fear one read in their faces that most shocked Westerners.

A big boost, however, was the embassy delegation out to meet our plane. We were really pleased to see them. I kissed many people I had not expected to, my hat fell off, and I dropped bundles, but it was all very gratifying. Everyone seemed glad to have us back. This was natural. There was a kind of team loyalty that kept us all together as if we were serving in the same front-line regiment or tossing about the ocean on a large raft. We shared each other's joys and sorrows, and later, when we met in the outside world, we were very glad to see each other, for we had truly been comrades-in-arms. That was what made coming back possible, though I had regrets. It was hard leaving my family; my month at home had made me realize how much I had missed them.

I did notice that the Moscow people were far better dressed than the year before, and they looked better fed as well. The clothes were not stylish by our standards, but the coats were warm and shoes more plentiful, though of poor quality. The favored form of winter footgear was high felt boots, and the sound of their shuffle along the streets was one not to be forgotten. The people themselves looked better in winter, with more color, even a little red in their cheeks, but they still seemed consistently sallow, their skin, their hair, their eyes all of a dun color.

They had plenty of reason to be, and it was no wonder they liked the brilliance and gaudy show in their churches and theaters.

These, too, were filled with propaganda. One evening we attended a contemporary Ukrainian production, a straight propaganda affair about life on a collective farm. The most impassioned scene took place in a wheat field. The curtain went up to show the heroine laid out on the top of a haystack. At last, we thought, a little bit of sex, but as the hero drew near he plucked a paper from his bosom and burst into song—not a love song but a detailed exposition of the new dam and power plant to be built, the sluice gates, the gushing water, the mighty creative power of the Russian people.

I went to several Moscow department stores to check the progress that had been made over the past year. With some difficulty I forced my way up the stairs at the leading store. I was greatly interested in the infants' and children's departments, as I wanted to see exactly what Russian children wore. Nowhere did I see any woolen underwear—no strips of flannel, even. There were no knit shirts, no dresses or nightgowns. I gathered the infants were simply wrapped in a square of cloth, anything the mother might have, and the same must have been true of diapers. Nor was there visible any woolen underwear for older children. There were cotton shirts and bloomers and drawers made of knit rayon and cotton. As no one could afford to buy very many, it was understandable they had to be of a dark and serviceable color. Dresses were of poor quality, boys' suits a little better. Children's coats were of thick stuff, often lined and padded, but again very expensive.

I had thought Moscow and the Kremlin might defeat spring, but somehow, in some way, in April it crept in, the air grew balmy, and every household wife up and down the street started window washing. Alan's guards sported new hats—green plush—and smart lightweight overcoats. A young, black-eyed guard had become quite friendly, smiling as I went out the gate. He was the one we called Long Knife because he carried a wicked blade that reached almost from his armpit to his waist.

The big excitement in the Diplomatic Corps the month of April was a costume ball that we gave for 225 guests, buffet supper at nine followed by dancing on into the night. We ourselves rented costumes from the Bolshoi, where one could have satisfied any fancy one might have and come as Peter the Great or the Black Swan from the "Swan Lake" ballet. We had quite a time providing supper for all those people—hot dishes, cold meats, masses of salads without a lettuce leaf to go with them. The guests came in varied and decorative costumes. Alan had the orchestra play "Good Night, Ladies" at 4 A.M., otherwise the guests might have stayed on until the last drops of punch and champagne were gone.

We might have waited to hold the ball until Roger arrived—he was due in June—but there is a time for everything, and the end of the season, with our colleagues' faces, conversation, and clothes a bit tired and spotted, seemed the perfect moment for a boost. We enjoyed it ourselves. Everyone did, and we realized again how important such things were to keep spirits up.

After the last revelers left, Alan ordered up some reserve bottles, marshaled the staff from pantry, telephone, and kitchen, made them a speech of thanks for their hard work, and drank to their health. The men bowed; Frieda, the cook, wept; the younger men tossed their drink down fast; and dear little Stepan, the pantry man, made a long sentimental speech in response, saying that never before had there been such happiness in Spaso, they loved us both and were glad to do what they could. It was all very touching. We left three or four of our young officers behind, and through the doors, which we carefully closed, we could hear the sound of music, singing, and Russian gaiety.

Our next project was a trip to Tbilisi, capital of the Georgian Republic in the Caucasus. We spent a memorable ten days, six of them and six nights aboard trains in tsarist-time sleeping cars, each one forty to fifty years old, but even so more comfortable than the modern ones. We went with three couples from the American embassy plus the Belgian ambassador and his wife, whom we had known in Brussels, and of course Alan's guards. The Russians gave us an entire car to ourselves going down, a comparatively comfortable one with compartments for two and wash basins in each. Our car was at the rear of the train, quarantined behind the diner, with a guard at each end. One of our officers said we also had six unofficial guards scattered elsewhere in the train. He pointed three of them out to me, and they did have a look that was unmistakable.

We had a fine time in Tbilisi, savoring the local atmosphere, quite different from Moscow, visiting some truly ancient Christian churches and savoring Georgian wine, the best in the Soviet Union. Our train back to Moscow was an uncomfortable and rattling affair. The diner looked like a low-class bar in a mining town. There was only one waitress, very dirty and very drunk, even in the morning. Fortunately we took most of our food with us and cooked cans of hash in the lavatory basin. Our party all laughed at me when I donned white gloves for our arrival in Moscow. I might have deceived the friends who came to meet us, but my traveling companions knew how dirty I was underneath.

Tbilisi and the Caucasus were worth the visit, however. I was glad we went and delighted we chose May 1st, the annual workers' holiday, to be away, as it poured rain for the parade in Moscow, and the official speech on the occasion was reported as more insulting than usual to Americans.

We gave our annual Armed Forces Day reception shortly after we returned to Moscow. Five Russians, headed by an air force colonel, attended. They marched in together without their wives, shook hands, passed on into the ballroom, where each took one small drink, then out they marched again. The affair was quite splendid, however, as we hung the ballroom with navy signal flags, all the military attended in their best uniforms, and we lined up our senior attachés and their wives to receive the guests. With Alan's four-star admiral's flag and our army attaché's brigadier general's flag behind us, we looked like a recruiting poster, but it was annoying that so few of the locals came.

Our head gardener had disappeared a few weeks before, supposedly arrested after a drunken brawl in a café where he was said to have hit a one-armed man. His wife Frieda, our head cook, had gone to one prison, then another, but could not get any news of him. She had concluded she would never see him again, but she had accepted the possibility with frightening resignation, and his disappearance seemed to make little stir in the household.

Now, however, Frieda received some good news. Her husband had been let off with one year's imprisonment instead of five. The Soviet system was clever. He had been given five years, but a kind, considerate government reduced it to one! He would not be allowed to live in Moscow after his release, but this did not bother Frieda too much, as her son would be in the same case when he returned from his prison in Siberia. Frieda was allowed to visit her husband in prison occasionally. She was not allowed to take food and medicine to him, but she was permitted to give him personal necessities, and she would go from one end of town to the other, shopping for little things and standing in queues, first to buy and later to wait for busses and streetcars. This took a lot of time.

Indeed it took much of a Russian's time just to live. Many trades and industries required their workers to spend twenty-four hours straight on the job, then allowed them two days off. Much of the two free days was spent searching for food, clothes, and household items, as these would appear and disappear from various stores on a day-to-day basis.

Thus Moscow streets were full of people at any hour, and of course the housing conditions were so bad that people would rather roam the streets than stay home. They seemed content even just to ride to and fro in busses, and they crowded into the parks even on cold, wet days. There was little recreation offered, even simple recreation. It was all mixed with lectures and propaganda, and much of it cost money, so the average citizen also went out into the streets and shops just to amuse himself.

By this time we had been in Moscow nearly two years. That was about enough, I thought. I now could see that I was followed in the street. Perhaps I was before also, but now I noticed a young man in a gray suit and cap who popped up here and there, sometimes in front, sometimes behind me as I walked along. At the theater, even when I was without Alan, I had often seen one or more of his guards hovering about, and one of our assistant military attachés riding with me on the metro said he noticed his regular followers joined by two or three others who must have belonged to me. It could not have been a very profitable occupation for them, as I did nothing subversive. It did not really bother me, but it was an odd sensation.

The national day season was now upon us. We, along with our principal allies, had decided to make our national day receptions brief, late afternoon affairs instead of fancy supper parties. So few Russians came that it hardly seemed worthwhile to put on a big "do" to entertain them. Nevertheless our 6 P.M. reception was graced by a higher Soviet group than the year before. We fetched the secretary general of the Foreign Ministry, the highest-ranking officer of the ministry after the minister and deputy ministers. I had a pleasant conversation with him in French. Altogether, I found him very agreeable. He even cracked a joke. Much to our astonishment, two East European ambassadors came, the first time in six months that one of their representatives had accepted an invitation to Spaso. We speculated that it must have been because of the beginning of peace talks on the war in Korea.

What an aggravating system the Soviets had that forbade our knowing people like the secretary general, indeed cut off any contact and separated us into hostile camps even on social occasions. It was hard for anyone not there to visualize the situation, to believe that tiny incidents such as those that Fourth of July were significant, but it was exciting to us as they reflected Soviet government policy. It was the government that determined whether the secretary general was willing or not willing to make a joke, whether the sentry at the door might or might not salute, whether we received theater tickets or not, and if servants stayed or left. All this was dependent on the word that came down from above. Nothing was too small for the regime to think of, no detail too obscure. On that Fourth of July permission was given for polite speech; the next day that permission might be reversed or we might be invited to dine off gold plates. One never knew.

It was now the time for summer rotations, and we lost many good friends on the embassy staff, including Wally Barbour, our wonderful number two, and Dick Service, one of our Spaso boarders after his wife and children had left a year before. We replaced Dick in the "Spaso collective" with Bob Blake, a fine young man and an inveterate sightseer who I knew would take me traipsing about the town once the unusually hot weather passed by and Roger returned from Princeton for the summer. Our existence was full of those comings and goings, one's heart pulled in and out like an accordion, the music sweet or sour.

Sure enough, shortly after Bob's arrival in Spaso, he and Roger persuaded me to visit the remains of the Donskoi monastery, one of a ring of fortified places in a semicircle around Moscow, protecting its vulnerable side. They said an added attraction was the city crematorium, just next to the monastery. Somewhat dubious about the crematorium, I agreed to the expedition. The monastery, dilapidated and neglected, had the remains of grandeur. The same could not be said for the crematorium, a big gray building with four chimneys, one on each corner, unpleasantly reminiscent of similar installations in the German concentration camps. It is true that the building was set in a kind of garden cemetery, but it was neither neat nor pretty, the whole place fairly lugubrious. I did not go too close.

A few days later we dined one with the Burmese ambassador on the Moscow Hotel roof, ourselves and the Italian and French ambassadors and wives. The restaurant was crowded with men with shaven, polished heads, dirty white blouses open at the neck or sweat-stained blue jerseys; soldiers in crumpled khaki; thick-necked women in sleazy prints, some still wearing their winter best—bottle-green crepe or wine-red, trimmed with bands of satin or velvet—their hair frizzed in thick bunches or braided around their heads. They normally sat at table for hours, the men often drinking until they literally could not get up, their heads going down on the table, as happened to one man near us. The waiters wore loose white blouses and carried soiled napkins over their arms. They, too, had shaved heads, a fortunate precaution, as I found a very long black hair in my salad. Our table was covered with dishes of all sorts. It was poor food, all of it, and hideously expensive. I hated to think what it must have cost.

One ambition of mine was fulfilled a few weeks later. Ever since my arrival in Spaso, I had dreamed of holding a wedding in the Great Hall, and in September the pretty secretary of Alan's deputy was to marry one of our assistant naval attachés. Holding a wedding seemed a simple enough idea, but it was not so easy. The bride and groom thought they could have a very quiet affair with a few intimate friends, but they soon realized how disappointed all the rest of the embassy would be, so they ended up with a hundred and fifty guests, including four ambassadors.

The logistics were formidable, though typical of how one operated in our Moscow community. We rented an altar from the Bolshoi theater, bought quantities of lovely white flowers in the market (this being the one time of year when they were available), and fixed up two trash cans as pedestals for the vases. For the bride's dress, one of our ladies contributed a white organdy number that she had ordered by mail and, after wearing it once, had found it too bridal for ordinary use. The air attaché's wife made the bride's veil out of a summer evening skirt belonging to the sister of the Australian chargé. The British ambassadress contributed some Belgian lace. The prayer book was supplied by the bride's roommate and sent to Helsinki to be covered in white silk, and other friends loaned two crinoline petticoats.

The dress for the maid of honor, Alan's secretary, was ordered from Stockholm but did not arrive until the afternoon before the wedding. It turned out to be a droopy model of cream net with purple velvet bows—consternation in Alan's outer office. I rushed down bearing my ice-blue satin skirt over one arm. We ripped the bows off the imported dress and put the skirt on top of it. With the cream net blouse it looked quite fine; someone else produced a straw hat exactly the color of the skirt, and the costume was complete.

Although bride and groom were both Protestants, the American Catholic priest searched his records and his conscience and found both permitted him to perform the ceremony. At the appointed moment I entered in style as mother of the bride, the British Embassy officer serving as organist struck up the wedding march, and Alan, in his admiral's uniform for the occasion, brought the bride down the aisle. The priest conducted the service very nicely, gave the couple his benediction, the organist played the Mendelssohn march, and back down the aisle went the newlyweds. It was all done with great style, and even the chief of protocol, the lone Russian who attended, was visibly impressed.

The reception was very gay, lots of champagne, the cake cut with a scimitar loaned by the Turkish naval attaché. Below stairs the servants carried on with wine supplied for the occasion. They must have done well. Toward midnight the yardman was found asleep in the middle of the entrance driveway and the yardwoman in a back hall, but otherwise no casualties. I was now quite satisfied. We had our wedding at Spaso.

It was a good thing, for a month later, October 6, 1951, we were due to leave. We packed our trunks and emptied our cupboards, made our rounds of good-byes, received presents, and wept a few tears, for I was sorry to see the last of our own embassy people and friends in the diplomatic colony. We had grown close to one another, almost interdependent. The servants in the house went about with red eyes. Poor things, they had so little security and could not know if their government would have them stay for the next ambassador or send them out into the cold. I had a last look at Red Square and the Kremlin by moonlight and, followed by a dingy little man in a gray coat, a last walk down the crowded Arbat Street near our house.

Our plane came in on October 4. Our Polish overflight clearances were in order, our permits received, but I bit my nails lest there be a hitch, some document incorrect, some new regulation dreamed up, until we took off the morning of the sixth, our staff waving as we left. I relaxed even more once we had gone beyond the borders of Stalin's empire. Later that day we were in Paris, Moscow a dream behind us, a dream that would be a conscious memory, a part of ourselves.

Russia one never forgets.

PART SIX

The Republic of China, 1962–1963

13

A Flattering but Unwelcome Assignment, 1962

After a brief stay in Washington, Alan and I moved in early 1952 to New York, where he served as head of the board governing Radio Liberation and Radio Free Europe, CIA-financed radio stations broadcasting, respectively, to the Soviet Union and Eastern Europe. Later that year we returned to Washington, as Alan had been asked to head the Psychological Strategy Board, a body under the National Security Council.

Very little had been written about postwar Russia, and I thought the public should know what Moscow was like. I wrote three or four articles for the *Ladies Home Journal* and lectured to a few women's groups. I worked on a book, drawing from my letters to the family from Moscow. *Postmarked Moscow* was published by Scribner's in 1952 and remained on the *New York Times* bestseller list for several weeks.

A little later, thinking Americans would be interested in what kind of clothes the Russians were wearing, I arranged to bring a selection of them to the United States. Saks displayed them in their New York department store windows. They were quite a hit and even toured around the country for several months.

Upon the change of administration in 1953, Alan retired. Always a man of action, he found enforced idleness tedious. After a few months an American admirer offered him a job in New York as CEO of a small corporation. Although the firm was not a major one, he accepted. Both he and I had enjoyed our earlier times in New York and had made a number of friends there. And, as Alan said, "In New York, a former admiral and ambassador is special. In Washington, they are all over the place." A cousin of mine was the administrator of a prestigious old apartment house in New York, the Dakota, at 1 West 72nd Street, and he arranged for us to rent an apartment there. It was a fine apartment, truly ambassadorial in style—high ceilings, large dining room, and magnificent living room with tall windows looking out on Central Park. It was affordable, however, as the building's owner had no real need for funds.

We soon had a busy social life in the city, but Alan's job was not very challenging, and the people he had to deal with were not quite up to the level he was used to. He read much and slept frequently, while I busied myself with friends, cultural activities, and keeping him amused. A great joy was the frequent presence of my daughter Deborah and her husband Peter Solbert. They lived on Long Island but were often in town, where Peter was a senior partner at the law firm of Davis, Polk.

Alan left his corporate position after a few years, but we lived at the Dakota for several more, nearly ten in total. As always Alan smoked too much, sat up too late reading, but compensated by late breakfasts. "I've seen too many sunrises in the navy," he said. The smoking gave him occasional spells of emphysema; otherwise he seemed in good health for his age. He became interested in various civic activities and had a marvelous time reading through Homer's *Iliad* and *Odyssey* with an old friend, Ernest Angell. "You can best understand Homer at my age," Alan said.

By May of 1962 Alan was seventy-four years old, his mind still alert and keen. Lunching out one day and stopping to do various errands, I had walked home across the park to find Alan having a cup of tea in the library. I poured one for myself, started to tell him about the luncheon party when something about his expression made me stop.

"What's happened?" I asked.

He smiled. "You'll be amused. The telephone has been ringing all afternoon, the press asking if it's true that I'm to be the next ambassador to the Republic of China government on Taiwan."

When the Chinese Communist forces drove Chiang Kai-shek out of the Chinese mainland in 1949, he went with the remnant of his army and government to the island of Taiwan, some one hundred miles off the Chinese coast. Although Taiwan was virtually the only territory he controlled, the United States refused to recognize the Communist government in Beijing and treated Chiang's government as the government of all of China. The American ambassador on Taiwan was officially the ambassador to the Republic of China, and that is what Alan was talking about.

"I'm not amused at all," I answered. "It's ridiculous."

"I told them so, said I knew nothing of it."

"Why Taipei, of all places?"

"There's been trouble out there. The Chinese Communists have bombed Quemoy and Matsu [two small islands just off the mainland China coast but under Taiwan's control]. We have a treaty with President Chiang. He's an odd sort of fellow, a nuisance to us, and he's making noises about invading the mainland. He can't do it without our support, of course, and we're not about to give it. Anyway, it's not my affair, so don't worry."

I did worry though. By dinnertime Alan seemed to have dismissed the afternoon's rumors from his mind, but my thoughts dwelt on them all evening. I slept uneasily that night, waking early next morning. I finished my breakfast, waited until a little after nine, then called our friend Averell Harriman, now assistant secretary of state for the Far East. He came on the line at once.

"Averell," I asked, "what about these rumors of Alan's going to Taipei?"

"No rumors. We need him there, need him badly. I was just going to call him."

"He's asleep."

"Lucky man. Give him a good breakfast and I will ring back in an hour."

My head whirled. Why, why should it be Alan at his age? Surely he had done enough for his country to deserve a quiet, peaceful retirement. Worst of all, I knew that if they felt he was really needed he would accept. I did not like what I had seen of Taipei when we had gone in 1960 to present formal letters of invitation to the 1964 New York World's Fair to the government there. Taipei was a grubby place and Chiang and his wife a formidable couple. Alan must go to Washington, tell them to find someone else for the job. I got up, went to his door.

Alan was already awake, a bad sign. There was a light in his eye. My heart sank. The phone rang. It was Averell and from Alan's side of the conversation I knew the die was cast. He laid down the phone. Feebly I started to argue. He countered:

"The president wants to see me. There's a conference this afternoon so I'll have to go down to Washington this morning. I'll listen to what he has to say, but I promise not to agree unless he makes a pretty good case."

Nothing more to be said. There it was, a small consolation, but Alan breakfasted quite cheerfully, packed a bag and was off. I felt very uneasy, proud of course that Alan should be thought of again but hoping against hope that providence would intervene.

Providence did not intervene, nor did my protestations have much effect when Alan returned. President John Kennedy had told him that an older man, a man with diplomatic experience and a military background, was required to face up to Chiang. Alan's qualifications were exactly those needed for the job. Chiang was desperate to attack the mainland, with or without our agreement. This could pose a real and serious threat to our national security. There would be pressure in Congress and elsewhere for us to support him. But this could involve us in actual war with Communist China. That must be avoided.

Alan told me he had no choice but to accept the assignment. The president asked if we could be ready to leave for Taipei in late June, about six weeks hence. He hoped Mrs. Kirk planned to accompany her husband. Alan assured the president she would certainly do so.

"You were right there," I said. "I wouldn't let you go alone to be vamped by Madame Chiang!"

Madame Chiang was a highly attractive and intelligent woman, a political power in her own right. She had managed to charm any number of American congressmen and ambassadors over the years and was indeed responsible for much of the esteem that the Chiang regime enjoyed in the United States. She did what she could to put pressure

25. Photograph of President John Kennedy with inscription to Ambassador Kirk, 1961. Library of Congress.

on successive American administrations to fulfill her husband's wild dream that the United States would help him invade the mainland and rule China again. This had been resisted, but president after president had to cope with the public and congressional pressure resulting from her efforts.

Alan continued, "If I can do anything to prevent war, even the threat of war, I must go." I had to admit the arguments presented by the president could hardly be resisted. Alan, laughing as I shook my head, said, "I'm afraid we're for it. If we have to leave in six weeks we'd better start making plans."

The Taiwanese agreement to Alan's appointment came through almost immediately, and a few days later he and I were on our way to Washington where he would appear before the Senate for a confirmation hearing and I would do odd errands and confer with the Foreign Building officials. In the past I had not found them very cooperative, but this time the lady in charge was prepared to be amiable. She showed me photographs of the house, hardly an inspiring structure. It was a small concrete building in midtown, apparently set back by a short drive from the main street.

"The walls are probably bare now. I am sure you will have to repaint," I told the lady. She agreed, said she would cable instructions immediately.

"Don't worry about colors," I said. "Tell them to use off-white throughout. That's always safe. And what about some bolts of material to take along and chintz for the bedrooms?"

"Our supplies are rather short just now," she replied, "but the embassy plane makes frequent trips to Hong Kong and, once you see the house, you may want to choose things there. We can make any reasonable sums available."

I still wished I could have something in hand but I suddenly remembered that Dorothy Draper, the capable and friendly decorator who helped me fix up the Dakota apartment, had a charming young Chinese assistant, now returned to Taipei with her husband. I mentioned her and it was agreed she could be employed if needed. My next stop was at Copenhaver's, the stationers on Connecticut Avenue, where I was cordially welcomed by the manager, whom I had known as a young clerk, now solemnly gray-haired. I explained I needed calling cards, new calling cards. "Not again" was his comment, a comment I privately echoed. He got out his files—Lieutenant Commander Kirk, Captain Kirk, Admiral Kirk, Ambassador and Mrs. Kirk, etc. All my life seemed to be spread out on the counter.

Shaking his head he wrote down the order.

Next day we were photographed, new passports were issued, and we visited the dispensary of the State Department for a series of shots—cholera, yellow fever, typhoid. Alan stayed on in Washington for briefing sessions, but right after Alan's swearing-in ceremony I went back to New York rubbing my sore arms, for there was still much to do in the apartment.

Alan returned, trunks and boxes went off air freight, their packing finished. It was arranged that our maid Sally would clean up after us, then fly to visit her sister in Scotland, promising any job she took on her return to New York would be temporary so as to be ready to come back to us at any time.

Our last evening in the Dakota, June 28, 1962. Our suitcases, packed, quite a lot of them, stood in a row in the hall. Alan had papers to look over and I walked through the rooms, the shelves and walls now empty. I thought of the nine and a half good years we had spent there, the parties, the quiet evenings in front of the library fire. Another chapter was closing. There seemed to have been so many chapters in my book, Washington, California, England, Belgium, Russia, so many comings and goings. The one ahead was not of my choosing, but who was I to expect anything but the unexpected. Alan had a job to do, a job that I could share, and that was that.

In the morning we flew to San Francisco, spent the night there, and went on next day to Hawaii, where Alan met with Admiral Harold Felt, the commander in chief for the Pacific, and I had a nice luncheon with Margaret Sullivan, Alan's secretary when he was in Moscow. We left the next morning for Tokyo, where we were to spend two nights with our ambassador and his wife, the Edwin Reischauers. We were met by a solicitous young embassy officer and driven to the embassy, where Mrs. Reischauer was waiting to receive us. A tall, American-born Japanese woman, she apologized for her husband, who had to go to a men's banquet and asked if we had had dinner.

"Yes, too much of it on the plane," I replied.

"Perhaps you would like to go straight up to your rooms. You must be very tired." I agreed. We talked for a few minutes, then she led the way upstairs and ushered us into a very handsome guest suite, telling us to ring for our breakfasts whenever we would like. What a nice woman. I liked her at once.

We slept well. Alan was off in the morning with the ambassador, and later Mrs. Reischauer and I set out for some last-minute shopping. We reached the main department store and made our way through the crowded aisles to the china counters, where I bought four gaily flowered breakfast sets and several lacquer trays. For some curious reason the State Department must think breakfast in bedrooms is immoral, but who wants to disturb embassy servants cleaning up downstairs? Official U.S. Embassy china is quite handsome, white, gold rimmed, with the State Department seal embossed on each piece, but I did not want to face the official china at that hour, with the gilded American eagle leering up from my morning tea cup.

We enjoyed being alone with the Reischauers at dinner that evening, the ambassador a most interesting, knowledgeable man, very ready to talk of current affairs and sympathetic with Alan's mission and the problems of the two Chinas, the Communists' and Chiang's.

I had a dream that night concerning my first official interview with Madame Chiang. I had said to her, "Madame, I know you are one of the great women of our world and highly intelligent. I, of course, am nothing like that but I am not all that stupid and you know you cannot go back to the mainland. So why don't we two women agree on it?"

I told Alan of my dream as we drove to the airport. He laughed, "Watch yourself," he said. "She's a real charmer."

At the airport a special Taiwan government plane was waiting for us, highly decorated inside in red and gold with an attentive costumed stewardess in attendance. The flight was a short one and we arrived ready for the official welcome, Alan in a thin dark suit, I hatted and gloved in a pretty blue and white cotton outfit. A small group from our embassy and the Chinese Foreign Office met us, along with the inevitable photographers. After shaking hands all around we were driven off in the embassy limousine accompanied by Alan's deputy, Ralph Clough, and his wife—nice, unpretentious people. As it had been arranged for Alan to have lunch with the men at the embassy, Mrs. Clough asked me, if I was not too tired, to come to an informal lunch to meet a few of the embassy wives after a brief stop at our residence.

The residence was much as I remembered it, a very ordinary, square stucco structure on the city's main street, a far cry from the glories of Spaso House, our residence in Moscow, or the Palais d'Assche, our first residence in Brussels. The Taiwan assignment, while important, did not compare in elegance to our previous job in Belgium or the prestige of being accredited to the Soviet Union, and the size and decor of the residence reflected the fact. The Cloughs left, I promising to be at their house at one. Two servants, number-one and number-two boys, met us respectfully at the door and ushered us into the house. The ground-floor rooms looked bare and gloomy.

We followed the servants and our bags upstairs to the living quarters, which were happily lighter and more cheerful in aspect. Air conditioners appeared to be installed throughout the house, a good thing, as the weather outside was hot, very hot, and sticky. I inspected the master bedroom, comfortable enough, with good cupboards in a bathroom and dressing room alongside. I shed hat and stockings, washed my face and hands, and was ready to start for the luncheon party, my one concession to protocol being a pair of clean gloves.

After leaving Alan at the embassy office, his chauffeur took me to the Cloughs' house on the edge of town. A number of correctly dressed ladies were already assembled, the wives of senior embassy personnel and of the navy admiral and the army and air force generals, and an attractive younger woman whose husband I gathered was chief intelligence officer. All wore hats and stockings.

I apologized for my informality.

"Don't," they said, almost in chorus. "The previous ambassadress insisted we dress this way." I assured them I had no such ideas. "It's no hats and stockings until the weather turns cold!" Hats came off immediately. A good beginning, I hoped.

The three military ladies in particular were very agreeable and full of information. The American forces on the island numbered ten thousand, including dependents. There were schools, clubs, a large commissary, a medical clinic, and all the facilities of a big military establishment. They agreed the climate was bad but told me there was a small house in the cooler hills outside town for the ambassador's use. We chatted over lunch. They were eager to hear news from home. Then, feeling I must get back and sort things out at the residence, I left.

Back at the house I rang for Chao, the number-one boy, and asked him to tell me about the working of the house and its domestic arrangements. I told him we had two good Chinese boys in our embassy in Moscow. "I know you will take care of us just as they did."

After giving him instructions I went back into our bedroom, opened the suitcases, hung our clothes in the closets, and laid the thin blankets I had brought with me out on our beds, long travel experience having taught me only thick ones were usually provided in hotels and embassies. I suffered one summer in an Italian hotel and had vowed I would never be caught again without light cotton ones for warm weather.

This done I walked down the hall to inspect the small bedroom on the front, very sparsely furnished, but there was another, larger, with twin beds and bath that would answer as a guest room. I determined I would ask Alan to beg the loan of a typewriter from the embassy for me, and I would set the smaller bedroom up as a kind of office. It had a bath that I could use if we were both dressing at the same time. All this done I sat down to take stock of our rather Spartan quarters. Alan and I had not shared a room for some years. He was an owl and I was a lark. He liked to sleep late and I wakened early, but in this strange, alien place it would seem more comfortable to be together.

Some little while later he came back from his luncheon and a visit to the office. Word had come for him to present his credentials to President Chiang two days later, no cutaway but white suits to be worn. A tailor had been summoned and would make one for him overnight and fit it in the morning.

I showed Alan around the upstairs and was happy he agreed to our new sleeping arrangements. A most understanding man. He planned to get to his office at ten, just as he did in Moscow, giving time for the staff to settle down before the ambassador's arrival. When Chao brought our tea I told him the ambassador would breakfast at nine. If I woke earlier I would ring for mine.

I poured our tea. We looked at each other and laughed at the turn of events that had brought us to this odd, unfamiliar place and to this house, so removed from the friendly splendor of the Dakota and the magnificence of Spaso in Moscow. The job, too, might prove an ungrateful one, for the Chinese on Taiwan would hardly relish discouragement of their forlorn hope of returning to the mainland.

Pulling a note from his pocket, Alan said, "You're to call on Madame Chiang Friday afternoon at four o'clock. Word just came down from the palace. That's the day after I present my credentials to the president."

After a quiet dinner, deftly served, we settled down, Alan to read the papers he had brought home and I to look over the list of American personnel, trying to match the names of the ladies I had met at lunch with those of their husbands, then glanced at the diplomatic list.

Next morning Chao presented me with a list of items for me to purchase at the commissary, and after the car returned from taking Alan to the office I set forth, having first called Sue Wang, Mrs. Draper's assistant, asking her if convenient to come by the house after lunch.

The commissary, resembling a stateside supermarket, was lodged in the big army compound on the edge of town. It was already crowded with eager shoppers, but the chauffeur and I made our way down the aisles as I bought needed items.

Mrs. Draper's decorator assistant appeared promptly after lunch armed with tape measure and notebook. "It's hardly the Dakota," I said, "but we'll have to make the best of it." We went all over the house, Mrs. Wang writing all our needs in her notebook. Once completed, she shook her head. "There's not much available here, nothing good enough for much of what you need, I'm afraid." I told her the department suggested I go to Hong Kong on one of the periodic embassy flights. Her eyes brightened. "You will surely find what you want there. I will look up addresses for you."

That same day Alan had been summoned to the palace for a meeting with Chiang before presenting his credentials. This was unusual, but Chiang was going into the hospital a few days later and clearly wanted to have a good look at this new ambassador early on. In this session, and in a brief meeting following Alan's formal presentation of credentials the next day, Chiang told Alan he would launch no unilateral attack on the mainland, but he stressed the importance of doing something soon to maintain the morale of his people and his armed forces. Alan in turn assured Chiang of our continued defensive support of Taiwan but reminded Chiang that our treaty with him required joint agreement on any action against the mainland.[1]

Next morning the tailor delivered the white linen suit, which Alan put on, and we went down to the drawing room to meet the staff, all similarly attired.

I laughed. "Gentlemen," I said, "you look like a group of Good Humor vendors." This they took in good humor, and after Chao brought coffee they were off to the palace.

Later when they came back Alan told me the ceremony had been a short affair, strictly formal, no chance for more than an interchange of cool greetings. He said little about his meeting with Chiang after the ceremony, as both he and I knew there were probably microphones about, whether Chiang's, the mainland's, or someone else's.

Next day, Friday, I was received by Madame Chiang. Fortunately I had dressed early, as word came from protocol that I must be there ten minutes before the hour. The president's country residence was on Grass Mountain, thirty minutes from town. One merit to traveling in air-conditioned automobiles, you arrived unspotted and unblown. I stopped to pick up Mrs. Clough. We checked watches and went up the mountain into the grounds of the president's house and drew up before the door at exactly ten minutes to five. An aide met us and ushered us into a large room, dark and made darker by heavy hangings and heavy, highly polished wooden furniture. Mrs. Tan Shan Chen, the foreign minister's wife, was there and we stood chatting for a few minutes before Mme. Chiang came in.

Quick, graceful, she greeted us and motioned me to sit next to her at a hideous table, an immense rectangular block sliced from some native tree. I was on her left facing the light, an old diplomatic trick, the other two women six feet away across the polished wood.

1. For details of this conversation, see the U.S. Department of State, *Foreign Relations of the United States, 1961–63*, vol. 22, *Northeast Asia*, item 139 (Washington, D.C.: United States Government Printing Office, 1996), 285–89.

A servant immediately brought her a package of cigarettes from which she took one that he lighted, whereupon I took one from my own bag, lighted it myself. Mme. Chiang wore a charming, well-cut Chinese dress of small patterned flowered chiffon, the high collar closed with a large pearl and diamond pin, her hair done simply, close to her head. She had very lovely hands, which she used to advantage, handling a six-inch-long cigarette holder, flicking ashes into a large open-mouthed cut-glass ball set directly in front of her. She sat very straight, her figure in shadow against the light. The conversation was contrived at first, the weather too hot, an unusual summer but cooler here on the mountain where she hoped we would enjoy our cottage.

Then the president's health, from which she plunged into a lively talk about a benefit to be given for Hong Kong refugees. One could not say Mme. Chiang prattled, but I had the impression she was making conversation about things that really did not interest her—the prizes to be raffled, she named each one, the picnic she had arranged for her four nephews, the food she ordered, she named each cake, talked of a new recipe for the butterscotch sauce they liked on their ice cream. I could not help sensing this woman is obviously bored and the chatter comes out turned by a tap. She must have filled her days and thoughts with inconsequential detail, filled them to overcome intense boredom and deep frustration—"the Woman of the Ages," trapped in minor good works and children's birthday parties.

I spoke of our life in Russia, of the coming elections at home. The tap was turned off, her face changed with the questions she asked. We talked of personalities. She mentioned Mikhail Borodin, the Russian Communist leader associated with the early days of the Kuomintang party, which was now headed by her husband. We went on to recent happenings in South America, to the dangerous potential there. She told of her stay in Brazil and of her impressions.

A different woman now, relaxed, she settled back in her chair, an intelligent, well-informed, highly sophisticated observer whom it was a pleasure to be with. Her English was impeccable, her voice lovely with a kind of smooth viola quality. A very fascinating woman, she was not so much unhappy as deeply anxious as she felt her beauty and her

26. Lydia Kirk with Mme. Chiang Kai-shek, 1962. Official Republic of China photograph.

power—and the years—slipping away. She must have struggled with herself to keep hope alive, but surely she was intelligent enough to realize the hope was a vain one, and the agony of this must have been excruciating. One might have felt sorry for her if pity did not seem unworthy of so skillful, so adroit and experienced a human being.

Apparently she had become interested as she discovered she was talking to someone quite different than she expected. I sensed I should not go too far. Any kind of intimacy of feeling should be avoided, for the charm was there and I had no intention of succumbing to it. She was too clever not to realize my instinctive withdrawal, but we parted with apparent cordiality after a photographer had appeared to take our pictures, of which she promised me a copy. I have it here today on a shelf in my living room. I smile every time I look at it, for it certainly represents two cats on a back fence.

This was the first of several calls I made during the course of our stay. Now and again I had to accompany visiting American ladies quivering with excitement at being received by so distinguished a personality. I particularly remember four senators' wives. Madame Chiang had sent rolls of Taiwanese silk and her tailor to them the day before, and the unfortunate women wore the Chinese outfits he had made for them overnight. As they were all on the stout side the results were not happy, but they seemed very pleased with themselves.

"Oh, Madame Chiang," one remarked, "ah never thought ah would have the great privilege of meeting youoo." All this in a breathless southern drawl.

I could tell that Madame took malicious pleasure in the performance, but I sat straight-faced and she knew that I knew.

I saw Madame Chiang many times afterward, but always in groups, where our conversations were brief and inconsequential. It would have been interesting to know her better, to exchange views and serious thoughts, but that would not have fitted into Alan's mission to restrain her husband.

14

A Mission and a Life Cut Short, 1962–1963

The week after I called on Madame Chiang I made calls on the wives of various officials and ambassadors. We met the rest of our diplomatic colleagues at the July 14 French National Day reception a few days later. Alan felt they were not an inspiring lot, but perhaps everyone looked a little damp in the hot weather.

I was sure that once we met more Chinese we would find some likely friends. It was hard to decide among those we met, however, for they were all past masters at ingratiating themselves, outdoing each other in polite speeches, subtle flattery. I did miss the atmosphere of close relationship with staff that we had in Moscow, relationships with fellow warriors in the trenches whom one was happy to see, and certainly I missed the fun of the houseful of attentive gentlemen I had there!

Soon after we arrived, we attended a dinner given by the foreign minister and his wife. Chiang insisted upon austerity, pretending his government was only temporarily resident in Taiwan pending the triumphant return to the mainland. Faithful to the regulations, the minister's house was small, simply furnished. The party included two or three officials with their rather silent wives, some single men, and the visiting ambassador from the Ivory Coast. His wife, a handsome woman, wore a dress that had certainly come from Paris, fine pleated chiffon in shades of tan deepening to dark brown.

Minute cups of wine were served in lieu of aperitifs. I was glad Alan had fortified me with a real cocktail before leaving. Then we were led into the dining room and seated at a round table for twelve with a large revolving tray in the middle leaving just room for our plates. One platter with the first course was put on the tray in front of the host, another in front of the hostess. Both took chopsticks and helped the honored guests to their right and left, after which the tray was turned and the rest reached in to help themselves. It was a rather messy proceeding. Courses followed in succession, many of them, all presented in the same manner, fish, meats surrounded by hot spiced vegetables, the latter very handy to conceal unwanted bits of meat on my plate. The parade of dishes seemed interminable but finally ended with a mound of what my host called "eight precious rice"—rice stuffed with sweetened condiments and dotted with specks of gold foil.

Our hosts rose and we got up and went back to the outer room, where coffee was served in lacquer cups, after which it was apparent the party was over, quite a gastronomic ordeal. The same format was used at all the Chinese dinners we attended. As we left I noticed several grease spots on the Ivory Coast lady's beautiful dress and shuddered to think what skillful cleaning would be involved.

A day or two later there was a drop in temperature of one degree, ninety-seven instead of ninety-eight, perhaps two degrees less of humidity. This being so, I drove out with the wife of our retiring U.S. Information Service officer, an intrepid young woman, large, very large, with child, to visit two artists' studios. She called for me in her small Hillman sedan and tooled us very expertly through the traffic—bicycles and pedicabs, a few trucks, fewer cars and busses, but the whole crisscrossed and right angled so progress was slow. Our own chauffeur always crawled along; a gentle soul, he must have had a Buddhist's reluctance to crush ants. Alan had nostalgic regrets for the dashing speed of his chauffeur in Brussels and even for his Moscow chauffeur, who drove with the conscious authority of a security service colonel.

The first young artist lived down a small side street, up a narrow stair to a second-floor flat—a bedroom, studio, kitchenette, and bath. Shiiy de Jinn was thirty-eight, looked younger, and affected a modest beatnik appearance. But he was a gay, voluble fellow, his pictures popular with our junior service people. The oils I did not care for too much, but the watercolors, street scenes, sketches of fishing villages and boats, were bright and fresh, great fun. He was a graduate of a good mainland art school, and his drawing was exact. Even in some of the abstracts there was a sense of design, of brush stroke, almost of calligraphy.

From Jinn's studio we drove to his friend's, a batik designer. This man lived in a cottage on the edge of town. Jinn came with us, keeping up a cheerful chatter all the way. The batik artist, very small, very thin, with a large head, almost a caricature, ushered us into his house. There was a front room, quite clean, whitewashed, three chairs, a bedroom behind in which his wife lay ill, a workroom, and, surprisingly, an indoor bath. I bought a batik square and hoped the few dollars might help.

My companion told me there was a large group of struggling young artists and writers on Taiwan, but struggling was the right word, as they were resented and criticized by the older intelligentsia, all bred in age-old mainland traditions. I confess the old scroll, the disciplined calligraphy, the classic pottery, were more appealing to me than what seemed adolescent, explosive disorder. But I could understand the young's feeling of revolt, for Chiang and his Chinese mainland comrades had total control of the government and severely restricted political activity by the population, mainly ethnic Taiwanese.

Word soon came that the embassy plane would be going to Hong Kong and I was included in the passenger list. We arrived in late morning. After a quick lunch in the coffee room of the hotel, fresh air seemed to be in order, so I went out and walked along the main street, buying a few useful items on the way. Then I went back to the hotel and joined some of our ladies having tea in the long balcony overlooking the harbor. My shopping next day was not as successful as I had hoped, but I did manage to find upholstery material for the dining room and guestrooms.

When I got back to Taipei my desk was packed with messages. Would I speak to the American Women's Club, would I speak to the Enlisted Wives' Club, an invitation to visit a school and lunch with the director, a couple more dinners to be accepted, and a luncheon to be given for former Secretary of Defense and Mrs. Neil McElroy due in Taipei the next week.

We went to dine with Vice President and Mme. Chen at the palace. President Chiang still convalescing from an operation a couple of months earlier, there was no formal entertainment at the palace. We were invited for seven thirty, dress informal. As usual, the Chinese officials wore uniforms or business suits, their ladies traditional Chinese dress, short in the daytime, ankle length for afternoon or evening wear. Very few jewels, a finger ring, sometimes a pin fastening their high, stiff collar. Slit skirts of officials' wives were discreet; younger Chinese women cut them high in the summer weather.

The vice president was a cocky, red-faced little man, a long-time associate of the president's, his wife a frail, exquisite little lady whose father was briefly president of China in the early days. She came from one of the great Chinese families, the Tangs. One saw this at once, for she looked as though she might have stepped out of an ancient palace screen painting. She was not young, older perhaps than her husband who was in his mid-sixties, but I found her very charming, thin black hair drawn into a tight knot so much more becoming to Chinese features than the modern bouffant style the younger women affected. Her dress, dark blue overlaid with fine black lace, a jade brooch at the throat, a superb diamond on her left hand, a great jade ring on her right. She spoke gentle, correct English and was altogether most appealing.

The foreign minister's wife was round-faced, rather silly, her main interests clothes and the making of dolls, not Chinese dolls but French affairs, the kind that used to be put over telephones in old Hollywood movies. She was exceptional, for many of the women I met had long strings of academic degrees in art, medicine, even science, and once you could get them to talk were most interesting.

I found the foreign minister, who sat next to me, a voluble, facile-speaking gentleman, younger than many of the Cabinet ministers, how profound I have no idea. The vice president was a strong character, certainly a man to be reckoned with, and many of the other men were impressive in their own right, a cultivated group.

A few days later I had one of my most interesting mornings. It was at the Academia Sinica, the intellectual arbiter of the country. Chiang had brought some of China's most important ancient artifacts to Taiwan when he fled there in 1949. I saw two small museums with their most precious early objects, quite remarkable. The second museum was presided over by an utterly fascinating woman, small, thin as a twig and brown as an old leaf, beautiful violet-blue eyes. Late sixties I thought, an Austrian lady who ran away with her German dentist, left the latter to live twenty years in obscure regions of Southern China, then came to Taiwan with Chiang's government. An anthropologist of note, she had spent months on various islands, living on nuts and locusts with the natives, still in all very much the great lady of aristocratic lineage—a strange version of Margaret Mead, our American anthropologist.

As time went on I was struck more and more that all these people, the government, the educators, even some of the military, were old, certainly leading me to question whether their hope of return to the mainland, to power, could ever be realized. They existed in semi-isolation and knew so little of the pace and speed of the modern world. It is true they made the island a show place, a show place for the Orient—in terms of literacy, health, and so on—but it was hard to know what the ethnic Taiwanese themselves thought about it, how happy they were living under the dictation of a small group of mainland Chinese. Except for our two gardeners I had virtually no contact with other than ethnic Chinese, extraordinary when there were only two million Chinese, but ten million Taiwanese on the island. We had put much money into that Taiwan experiment; I wondered to what avail.

I love to walk, and I found the streets picturesque, though hot and humid. They were always crowded with bicycles and pedicabs, women strolling about holding bright umbrellas but otherwise looking quite cool and fresh, children rolling happily down the sidewalks, a great many children. Men ran up and down the bamboo scaffoldings of new buildings, very insecure, both the scaffoldings and the buildings. Small boys led ox carts across the street. Sidewalk stands offered soft drinks, bright colored; trays of pastries, fly covered; bottles of sweets; fruits—bananas, pineapples, small green melons, and large green watermelons from the nearby island of Quemoy.

One morning I was awakened by band music alternating with wailing as if from bagpipes. At breakfast I asked Chao what was happening.

A funeral, he said, the proprietor of a big shop at the corner died two days ago, a very rich woman, very old; there would be many relatives and friends. Already the street was crowded, and as I looked they were lowering the coffin from the second-story window. It was too large to come down the stairs.

It was a very hot morning, scorching sunshine. I put on a large straw hat and walked out to our front gate to see the excitement. Huge tables on sawhorses were laid end-to-end on the sidewalk in front of the shop. These were laden with food; they were literally groaning boards. Between the dishes of food were piles of colored tinsel and false paper money for the deceased's use in the next world.

The coffin, a huge, bright red, highly decorated affair crowned with a gigantic lotus flower, stood at the far end of the row of tables. At the other was a kind of altar in front of which a group of priests, dressed in white robes and high, pleated hats banded with red, knelt and swayed back and forth chanting prayers. An older man, perhaps the husband of the deceased or the nearest male relative, stood near them directing the proceedings. The mourners, men and women, wore different colored hoods and cloaks over white gowns.

I called to Chao to come out and explain. The nearest relatives—sisters, brothers, sons, daughters wore burlap hoods; nephews and nieces wore blue ones; cousins and young children yellow. One by one they took incense sticks handed them by the old man and joined in the prayers. All the while the band kept playing, though groups of two or three of them would drift away briefly to the soft-drink sellers on the corner. All that tootling must have been thirsty work.

Toward noon men began loading the food onto carts. The women gathered up the tinsel streamers and fake paper money, which they piled in a heap and burned, this to ascend heavenward with the deceased as journey money. An hour later the procession started down the street, flower-draped trucks, cars and buses for the mourners, strings of pedicabs, bicycle-type vehicles propelled by coolies, each cab bearing a huge white wreath, a second and louder band, more wreaths, then another string of pedicabs with four-foot-high colored pictures propped on the seats, scenes depicting the life story of the departed, finally the truck bearing the coffin and a last band to send the lady on her way.

As I drove out to pay a call at four o'clock I noticed the unfinished building down the block had been taken over for the funeral feast. Inside I could see rows of tables, some on the ground floor, some on the second. The mourners were busily consuming the baked meats, and baked they must have been after sitting for five hours in the hot sun.

In early September we had a visit by General Maxwell Taylor, the next chairman of the U.S. Joint Chiefs of Staff. Alan arranged to call on President Chiang just before the visit. Chiang had a way of summoning important visitors and discussing vital questions of which the ambassador was not apprised until later. It was not that he meant to be discourteous, but he was a canny bird, liked to get in his word before the ambassador could tell the visitor what to expect. Now he realized he had another canny bird to deal with.

I learned later that Alan's conversation with Chiang had been a very tough one. Chiang had complained about United States opposition to his making a landing on the mainland. He said he did not know how long he could resist the pressure from his army and people to do so. Alan reminded him that his 1954 treaty with the United States required that both sides agree on any such step. The conversation grew quite testy, but Alan held his ground. Chiang, being used to more pliant American ambassadors, did not like Alan's message or his firmness. Relations between the two men, already a bit difficult, became more distant.[1]

We made our Friday night dinner for General Maxwell Taylor black tie, and high time for I was getting very tired of Alan's blue serge suits and decided that from then on dinner jackets would be the order of the day. General Taylor, a handsome man, spoke some words of Chinese to the generals and their wives, excellent German to the minister of defense, a graduate of the German General Staff College, made a joke in French to one of his own officers, and in English charmed all the rest of us.

1. See the U.S. Department of State, *Foreign Relations of the United States, 1961–63*, vol. 22, *Northeast Asia*, item 151 (Washington, D.C.: United States Government Printing Office, 1996), 306–12.

General Taylor sat on my left, and on my right General Chiang Ching-kuo, the eldest son of the president. Ching-kuo was then a man in his early fifties, short, stocky, physically very unlike his father. He occupied himself with security matters on the highest level and was an important figure on his own account. We did not know then whether he expected or aspired to succeed his father, but he did so on Chiang's death in 1975.

The Chinese ladies had a deplorable habit of huddling together before and after dinner like frightened hens; it was very hard to break them up, so I often found myself alone with the gents. At a dinner we held a few nights later, the ladies were curious about our new furniture, wanted to see and touch everything, so I took them on the Grand Tour, feeling like Jackie Kennedy in the White House. Their own houses were pretty sad, reflecting the austerity approach; many had owned beautiful things that had been lost or abandoned in their flight from the mainland, so they loved and admired fine textures, furniture, and carpets.

October 10, China's National Day, came soon afterward. We diplomatic ladies, some from the business community, and a few of our husbands were marshaled up to go en masse the day before to distribute gift packages to veterans' hospitals. We asked Mme. Chiang to let the gift money be used to buy one substantial present for each hospital, such as a record player or movie projector, but she said no, the personal approach was preferred.

Therefore the morning of October 9, we ladies, hatted and gloved, assembled at what was known as the Anti-Aggression League. The hundred-odd foreign women were matched in number by Chinese, members in good standing of the league. A high-ranking gentleman had been assigned to sponsor each group, and there was Alan, looking quite rebellious at 8:15 A.M. We filed into the league building's main hall where we were greeted by Madame Chiang, looking very lovely in clinging chiffon and diamonds. The thermometer by this time stood at ninety-five, with humidity to match.

The hospital assigned to our group was a small one, happily close to town, in the valley at the foot of nearby Grass Mountain, the presidential retreat. We were welcomed at the gate by a very impressive officer, the assistant chief of the Intelligence Service; the hospital, we discovered, cared for the officers and men of that service and their dependents. Our group leader handed each lady two bright red plastic envelopes such as you get on airplanes; we were twenty and there were forty patients. Each envelope contained a pack of American cigarettes, chewing gum, candy, a package of local dried beef (nasty stuff much esteemed by the locals), and a very attractive little brochure entitled "Seeing the World." This we had substituted for the missionary tract distributed in former years. The patients seemed pleased with our gift, and the Chinese ladies followed with their own comfort kits: a washcloth, a pair of socks, and some money in an envelope.

We played the Lady Bountiful, shook hands all around, and smiled at the wounded paratroopers, men being trained to drop down into China but who had been injured falling into their own paddy fields. Then we adjourned to a room tastefully decorated along the wall with jars containing bits and pieces of former patients. The general made an address about his brave men, Alan responded, we drank healths in warm tea, then bowed right and left and drove home.

Next day we rose a bit less early, dressed in ultra-formal attire, and set off for the presidential reception. The president's office was in a huge old building constructed by the Japanese, who occupied Taiwan from 1895 to 1945. It was a relic of Japanese-empire dreams, red brick and stone, with high echoing halls and large rooms hung with crystal chandeliers and frowning official portraits, a building duplicated in every world capital, Paris, Berlin, Buenos Aires.

We were ushered into the Chiangs' presence in order of protocol—in our case, directly behind the Jordanian ambassador and directly in front of the Argentine. The President and Mme. Chiang stood to receive us, Sun Yat Sen bestowing his blessing above their heads. Sun, a leader in the overthrow of the Chinese imperial regime in 1911, was founder of the Chiangs' party, the Kuomintang, and had allied it with the Communists at one point. Odd to realize that Mme. Chiang's oldest sister, Sun Yat Sen's widow, was highly revered by the Communist party on the mainland. A talented family, theirs.

The president looked well and Madame Chiang superb in a glittering frock, rows of medals this time instead of jewels. One almost felt required to back out the door and sidle away. Sad, when you think how much this pair would have enjoyed holding their reception in the Temple of Heaven in Beijing instead of in this abandoned Japanese railway station.

The following week Alan and I flew to Hong Kong for a brief visit. That place I find pure enchantment, the color, movement, physical layout. On that visit we dined one night at the residence of the British governor, white gloves and trailing chiffon. We were put through a drill unequaled, I am sure, at London's Buckingham Palace, but the governor and his wife were friendly and even asked us to come and stay next time we were in Hong Kong! After dinner, as the ladies sat on the lawn, lovely spot looking out over the city and harbor, an aide, stiffly handsome, approached every other one and moved her to another seat to make room for the gentlemen who joined us in dignified procession. Then a few minutes later the aide whispered to me, "You will make the first move, Mrs. Kirk, and leave about ten minutes after the second drink has been served." Just as those drinks went round, no one taking them, I rose to my feet, unable to sit out those last ten minutes!

We lunched the next day in a lovely house on the Peak, high above the city, with the lord chief justice and his wife, both extremely nice. Another time we lunched with the Belgian consul general and his very beautiful Chinese wife. Several Chinese were there, all very rich and very remote from the problems on Taiwan, even though they lived on the threshold of Communist China.

On October 23, back in Taipei, we were wakened at 6:30 A.M. by the embassy duty officer. An urgent message was on its way to be signed by the ambassador. This message must reach the Chinese Foreign Office before 7 A.M. At 7 A.M. our time, 6 P.M. October 22 Washington time, President Kennedy would broadcast to the nation, and our allies were to receive an advance copy of the speech. We shook ourselves out of bed. I asked Alan what the speech was about. Cuba, the duty officer had told him, and that day President Kennedy told the nation about the presence of Soviet missiles on the island. We worried through the next several days, as did the whole world, and were vastly relieved when the crisis was resolved October 28. I am sure my earnest prayers and everyone else's, plus President Kennedy's strong stand, did the trick.

We celebrated Alan's birthday on October 30 with special gusto. He had three cakes, one at the house at lunchtime, one at the office, and one at a dinner given by the Cloughs that night. Presents poured in all day, especially as the fact Alan's birthday was the same day as Chiang's caught everyone's imagination.

The finale of it all was the Cloughs' party. They had a gay, not too official group, mainly Chinese. Everyone brought amusing presents and read poems. The presents ranged from a straw farmer's cape and hat, a Chinese cap with queue attached, and mechanical jokes, to the most amazing ancestor portrait of Alan done in the old Chinese manner. He was pictured as a high government official in a wonderful blue robe, sable collar, and cap with button showing his exalted rank, really superb. It was very touching to see the real affection that went into all of this, heartwarming to be held in such high esteem in such a short time. Even the Marine Guards came up with a gift for his desk.

The weekend before Christmas we were favored by a visit from Francis Cardinal Spellman of New York. As Vicar of the Armed Forces he spent Christmas with the troops each year, and this was the turn of the Far East. He was an old friend of President and Madame Chiang's, old friend to the extent of donating ten thousand dollars a year to Mme. Chiang's good works, so he was put up at the palace guesthouse. The poor gentleman looked much older than when we had seen him on our return from Moscow in 1952, but, a politician par excellence, he visited Mme. Chiang's orphanage, received some four hundred well-wishers later in the afternoon, said mass at 8:30 the next morning, shook hands with every member of the congregation, and then attended a breakfast at the Officers' Club to which we were invited. He rose and saluted Alan as "Mr. Ambassador, Mr. Admiral, Mr. Friend"—the royal touch. After breakfast he took off for Vietnam, having already visited Korea, Japan, and Okinawa.

On Christmas Day we breakfasted early and then went downstairs at 9:30 A.M., where the household staff, plus two chauffeurs, two gardeners, and eighteen children were assembled. We distributed presents and boxes of candy for each child, with Chao, the number-one boy, conducting the proceedings.

We went to church at the Navy Chapel and were duly escorted to the front pew, where we sat with the U.S. Navy chief on Taiwan. The service was so strictly nonsectarian it did not seem to bear much resemblance to a Christmas celebration beyond a lusty rendition of the carol "Come All Ye Faithful," but there was a large congregation, all of whom looked quite satisfied, so perhaps they enjoyed sanitized religion.

We went back to the house to open our other presents, all very well meant. It was fortunate that no one sent anything really valuable, as such presents, by American government regulation, must be returned. Altogether it was a pleasant day and so very unlike any normal Christmas it was easier to get through it without too many wistful thoughts.

This really ended our time in Taiwan, for Alan fell ill shortly afterward, and in mid-January we left hurriedly with the well-wishes of all ringing in our ears. There were no formal farewells, as all thought we would return, though I myself had doubts. But for Alan's illness, I would not have been sorry to leave, as I never felt really at home in the place, and I sensed Alan had put things on the right track in the embassy and with the Chinese. In both cases he had clearly established that the ambassador was in charge, and U.S. policy was against getting mixed up in an attack on the mainland. Heaven knows there were many problems with Chiang after that, and Madame Chiang continued to win over gullible folk, but a standard had been set that others could try to follow. My one regret, other than Alan's illness, was that I would have liked time to say a proper good-bye to our embassy people, our few Chinese friends, and our faithful household staff.

We flew to Tokyo, where competent doctors said Alan could go on to New York after a brief rest, but that further tests and care would be needed in the United States. We left a few days later and returned to our grand apartment at the Dakota, but Alan was not well. Shortly after we returned, doctors discovered an aneurysm that needed urgent attention. We flew to Houston, where the famous cardiovascular surgeon, Dr. Michael De Bakey, operated successfully.

I had not looked forward to two anxious weeks in an unfamiliar city, so I fortified myself with letters from friends to people in Houston. I had nice visits with several of them once Alan was out of danger, and my two girls each came down for a few days to keep me company. In all I had as pleasant a time as possible in the circumstances. Dr. De Bakey, an immensely capable and interesting man, got along well with Alan. He never sent a bill, saying the operation was his gift to a man who had served his country so well.

Once Alan was strong enough, we went back to New York. There we lived quietly, attended by our faithful Sally, true to her promise to come back to us once we returned from Taipei. In August we rented a house in Cold Spring Harbor on Long Island, not far from daughter Deborah Solbert. Alan stayed very quiet but liked to sit out on the grassy terrace in front of the house, monitoring the sea and the boat life of the harbor below. He faithfully watered a young sycamore tree that, to this day, shows his care. He read a great deal, going right through a complete set of Rudyard Kipling's works that he discovered in a back bookcase.

I spent my time looking after Alan's needs, doing the marketing, talking with friends on the telephone, and of course reading, always a favorite occupation. High points were daily visits from various members of the Solbert family, visits we kept short so as not to tire Alan.

Meanwhile we started the process of selling the Dakota apartment, and on our return from Long Island in late August we selected a smaller one on the East Side, at 3rd Avenue and 62nd Street. In September I left Alan long enough to launch the Solberts in Washington, where Deborah's husband Peter had been assigned to an important job at the Pentagon, deputy assistant secretary of defense for international security affairs. I hosted a cocktail party for them at the well-known Sulgrave Club, receiving friends and well-wishers at the head of the stairs, flanked by Deborah, Peter, and their daughter Leslie. I was very proud of Peter, going to such an important job, and my daughter and granddaughter were truly charming.

Not long after my return to New York Alan's heart weakened to the point where he had to go into the hospital. There he grew steadily worse, so much worse that in early October I telegraphed Roger, who had joined the U.S. diplomatic service and was serving in the U.S. Embassy in Moscow, to come and say farewell. He arrived within two days, and Alan picked up enough at the sight of him to sit up and converse with us for the week Roger was there. That was Alan's final effort, however. Within a week after Roger left, Alan's heart had grown so bad it simply was not strong enough to clear the fluid from his lungs. My daughter Marian and I were at his bedside when he died on October 15, 1963.

The funeral was in Washington at St. John's Church on Lafayette Square, where Marian had been married. It was filled with friends and admirers, and several of Alan's young aides, now in prominent government positions, served as pallbearers. From his post at the Pentagon Peter Solbert had arranged for a fine spot in Arlington National Cemetery for the grave, and Alan was buried with due military honors on a glorious fall day. My daughters by my side, I received the many guests at Deborah's house in Washington. Roger had said he would come home again for the funeral, but his work in Moscow was pressing and I knew Alan would want him to attend to it. I told him to stay in Moscow, much as I would have loved his support. Tributes to Alan and condolence letters came from President Kennedy on down, and the *New York Times* carried a laudatory editorial. It was a magnificent send-off, but I would miss my husband very much.

PART SEVEN

Postscript, 1963–1984

15

The Final Years

ROGER KIRK

Mother wrote nothing about the next twenty years of her life, so I have added this postscript, drawing on my own memory and that of my two sisters.

Shortly after the funeral the Dakota apartment was sold, and Mother moved into the one she and my father had selected, a two-bedroom, big-living-room affair that suited her nicely. She called once more on her decorator friend, Dorothy Draper, who gave good advice about what furniture would fit in and how to arrange it.

Mother was just settling in with the help of her Sally when three blows came in quick succession. The first was the assassination of President Kennedy on November 22, 1963, some five weeks after my father's death. Mother, a confirmed Democrat and great admirer of Kennedy, was terribly shocked. Then came Kennedy's Arlington funeral, so reminiscent of the one she had just gone through for my father. Finally, driving with some friends along a country road, there was a head-on collision, and Mother, in the right front seat, suffered several broken ribs and badly bruised hip and legs. She spent several days in hospital before she could return to New York to limp about her apartment.

Never one to complain, Mother gritted her teeth and got through it all, answered the many condolence letters that had poured in, and set out to build a widow's life in New York. She missed my father dreadfully, told me she greeted his picture every morning, but the earlier separations had prepared her for life on her own, and she soon set up a good routine.

She waited for breakfast until eight o'clock, never earlier no matter when she awoke, as she said she was not going to be one of those old people who breakfasted at six, lunched at eleven, and dined at five. She made her own breakfast of tea, toast, and orange juice and took it on a proper breakfast tray back to her bed, where she enjoyed it and the *New York Times* in ladylike style. Sally came in a bit later to clean and prepare lunch for Mother and perhaps a guest or two. Mornings were the time for errands. Mother was delighted to find most things were available in the neighborhood, but she almost always took a good walk or made an excursion to a museum, exhibit, or park.

Afternoons usually included a nap and, of course, tea about five. Friends young and old might drop in for a cup or a drink. Sally would stay in the evening for parties but otherwise left supper for Mother to warm up. Mother became quite good at that, though she never got into serious cooking. She would settle on a favorite couch, pour herself one drink, usually a short bourbon and water, watch the evening news, and then have her supper.

Mother would often go to the Cosmopolitan Club, a select but unpretentious women's club on 66th Street between Park and Lexington avenues, for lunch or a lecture. She invariably walked there, rain or shine, and often continued on to the New York Society Library, where she was a steady customer. In fact she walked most places, unless they were really too far. Then she took buses, not taxis, if possible. She used to laugh about standing at a bus stop in the rain with some other nicely dressed older women and hearing a passing taxi driver shout, "Take a taxi, ladies! Let your heirs walk!" She told this in jest, but she was very conscious of saving as much as possible for her three children and twelve grandchildren.

Mother often lunched and sometimes dined with friends, local or visiting, went occasionally to the theater or a concert, and kept up an active correspondence around the world. She maintained her interest in foreign and domestic affairs, read widely in English and French, and was a leading light in a very select women's policy-discussion group. She was one of the founding members of the still extremely popular "Off the Record Lunches" held on Wednesdays during the winter.

Distinguished pundits and statesmen, usually friends of group board members, were persuaded to come and lecture to an increasingly eager audience. She was also a twenty-year board member of Community Service Society, a New York charity that did all kinds of work to help the poor and lonely.

A great blessing was the presence and loving attention of her daughter Deborah and husband Peter, as well as occasional visits by Marian from Philadelphia and myself from Washington or overseas. Mother adored her grandchildren and became a good friend and role model for several of them. She never hesitated to give them her opinion of their dress or hairstyle, and they respected her for it. They also knew that if they were ever in trouble or distress, she would be right there to help them. She used to say, for example, "As a family, we do not believe in divorce," and indeed there had been none, but when one grandchild divorced, Mother immediately reached out to console and sympathize.

Always a good lecturer, and with considerable experience from her Red Cross–speaking days in the Second World War, she let herself be persuaded to go on the circuit again a year or two after my father's death. This time she spoke mainly to ladies' clubs on the East Coast, and once in Chicago, about her life as the wife of an American naval officer and ambassador. As she did in her conversation, she enlivened these lectures by anecdotes of embassy life and personal observations about the appearance, customs, and idiosyncrasies of the countries she knew. The audiences enjoyed it, and I think she did too, though after a year or so she tired of the one-night stands and gave it up.

Mother had enjoyed detective stories, and in the late 1960s she decided that she could write one herself. By this time she was in her seventies, but she turned to it with energy and determination. With occasional help on plot from Bob Blake, one of her Spaso House boarders in Moscow, and Deborah's husband Peter, she wrote and published three mysteries, each inspired by a personal experience.

Peter was chosen in 1965 to be U.S. ambassador to Singapore, but he declined for health and salary reasons. During discussions with Peter and Deborah about their prospective life in Singapore, Mother said to Deborah, "You could write a mystery story about the area." When

27. Lydia in New York, 1970.

Deborah said, "I could not possibly," Mother countered, "Well, I will." Peter and Deborah, who had collected material about Singapore to help decide whether to accept his appointment, gave Mother a *National Geographic* magazine with wonderful pictures of Singapore, as well as pamphlets from the State and Defense departments on living conditions, on the economy and geography, and on the life and customs of the different ethnic groups there.

Mother wove a tale of international intrigue set in Singapore with the hero, fittingly enough, an older man, a retired major in the British Army. Although Mother had never been to Singapore, her book is full of details about the different areas of the city and its varied people. She pictured all this so well that a reader who had lived there many years wrote, "It was so true to life, I could almost smell the place reading it." When I asked her how she managed it, never having been there, she said, "I've been in Taiwan, and all those Far Eastern cities look the same." Mystery stories were a new venture for her and she had to fit writing into her other activities, so it was only in 1969 that *The Man on the Raffles Veranda* was published by Doubleday.

The book sold well enough to encourage Mother to do another, this a true labor of love in honor of her Brussels housekeeper, Mademoiselle Nerincx, an indispensable helpmate and eventually a real friend, who had done clandestine work for the Belgian Resistance during the German Occupation in World War II. The heroine of the book was in fact the housekeeper at the American Embassy in Brussels, albeit with a different name. In the book she was the one who noticed that a famous painting of the Madonna being returned to Belgium by the U.S. government was only a copy and who led the search to recover the original. Vivid descriptions of diplomatic life, of Belgium itself, and of the mores of that society provided a good setting for a fast-moving tale. Doubleday published *The Embassy Madonna* in 1971, and Mother soon began work on a third book.

This appeared in 1974 as *The Cuernavaca Question*, inspired by her first and only trip to Mexico a couple of years before with her good friend Alice Acheson, the widow of former Secretary of State Dean Acheson. The pace of the trip had been a little slow for Mother, and she had time to study her surroundings and jot down some observations. On her return she set to work again, this time weaving a tale about a young embassy officer chasing down a ring smuggling drugs into the United States. One problem developed about the title. Mother had proposed "The Cuernavaca Conundrum," but the editor said the word "conundrum" might be misunderstood by contemporary readers, leading them to think the book focused on sex.

In fact, as Mother said, her tales contained very little sex and no tortures, thus limiting sales. Nevertheless, several thousand copies of each were sold, and Mother received many complimentary letters from readers. The books are still good tales, with vivid descriptions of places and people and an especially fine feel for older men and women.

By this time Mother, now seventy-eight years old, decided to stop writing mysteries and turn to a memoir. She had done some work earlier but now she really focused on it. She spent many hours, lying in bed or sitting quietly on her favorite sofa, conjuring up the settings and dialogues of the past with almost total recall. As a former artist, she had good visual memory of the places she had lived, or even just visited, and of the faces and characters of the people she met. She then hand-wrote, edited, and finally typed out pages of her manuscript bit by bit, making her recollections vivid for the generations that would succeed her.

She sent a few early chapters to Doubleday. They replied that it was interesting, but autobiographies were a hard sell and hers needed tightening and freshening up to receive serious consideration. She did a revised draft of much of it and kept working on the rest, but it was a slow process, and even her formidable energy began to flag. The completed second draft went as far as her departure from Brussels in 1949. She did nothing on her time in Moscow, as she had covered those years, 1949–52, in *Postmarked Moscow,* published by Scribner's in 1952, and from which much material in the chapters on Moscow in this book is drawn. She typed a few draft pages on the Taiwan assignment, but she left the bulk of that portion in early, handwritten form or in letters home.

Mother's life was not all work, of course. She normally spent Christmas with me and my family when we were in the United States, Thanksgiving at Marian's, and Easter, plus several weekends, with Deborah's family on Long Island. Each summer she would leave the city for a month or two, visiting friends, staying with Deborah, or renting a place for herself. In 1968 she took a house for June and July in Black Point, our old stomping ground, so my family and I could stay with her during my six weeks' leave from Saigon. Later she grew fond of Maine and actually spent a happy month at the Asticou Inn on Mt. Desert Island in the early 1980s.

Mother's frequent travels abroad during these years included a study cruise around the Greek Islands, visits to friends in England and France, and two delightful stays with Deborah and Peter in Paris while Peter was heading his law firm's office there. She also made more adventurous trips, usually to visit us in our posts abroad. She came to Moscow in the mid-1960s, to India a couple of years later, and even to Somalia in 1974. She was very game, even coming with us in our Land Rover on an excursion into the Somali desert.

In September 1979 Mother visited us in Vienna. We showed her the sights, introduced her to many of our friends, and went with her to Budapest. Our two-day visit there included an accidental walk of two

28. *Lydia with her son, Roger, in Budapest, 1979.*

and a half miles through an island park, dinner at a gypsy restaurant, observation of a Hungarian wedding, and Sunday lunch in a workers' cafeteria, the only place to eat we could find open. *Goulash* being our only word in Hungarian, that is what we got, slopped onto a tin tray that we carried over to a long wooden table, where we sat on a bench next to dirty but polite laborers. Mother soldiered through it all and laughed about it for months afterward.

Mother's final voyage abroad, in March 1982, was a trip to Paris to see Peter and Deborah. They persuaded her to take the expensive supersonic Concorde to shorten the flight and benefit from the expedited processing and special airport lounges for Concorde passengers. Mother reported that she liked all that but found the seats on the plane too narrow. She was not fat, just "matronly," and the seats were in fact quite narrow.

After her Paris stay, Mother came on to Munich, and we joined her to see the city together. We walked around town, went to an opera, and poked into museums. We took Mother to a very fancy restaurant, allegedly the best in Munich, with exquisitely presented food. It was not a great success, as Mother thought our table ill-placed for her ambassador son and "did not like food too much handled." The rest of the visit was fine, however, and after two days we saw her off for Paris and the Concorde home, admiring her spunk at almost eighty-six years of age.

During these years Mother's health was good. She continued to live in her apartment, took walks virtually every day, slept well, and drank very moderately (one cocktail before dinner, perhaps a glass of sherry before lunch, and a little wine with dinner if there were guests). She ate sensibly and gained little weight. She broke bones twice falling down stairs in others' houses, but apart from the occasional bad cold, she seemed to have no illness of any kind.

One spring night in 1984 she awoke with a throat so sore she could hardly breathe. She managed to rouse a neighbor and was rushed to the hospital, where they treated her and released her the next day. It appeared that her bed sheets had absorbed some kind of poison, rat poison perhaps, at the laundry, and that was what caused her distress. The experience damaged her lungs, already weakened because she had smoked virtually her entire adult life. A few weeks later she was diagnosed with lung cancer. She struggled through months of radiation treatment, showing real grit throughout. She even attended her grandson Alan Solbert's wedding on Long Island in September 1984 and the reception at the Solberts' house nearby. She was in a lovely flowered frock, with pale green slippers to match, looking every inch the charming Grande Dame she was.

The disease finally claimed her life on December 3, 1984. She died at home, leaving three children, twelve grandchildren, and four great-grandchildren. She was particularly pleased with the last. "Looks so good on the obituary," she used to say.

Mother was buried with my father in Arlington Cemetery after a memorial service at St. John's Church. She used to laugh about the response of the cemetery authorities when she asked if she could be buried with him. "That's fine, Madame; we just dig a little deeper." She left only a few instructions about the funeral. "The service is to be said at St. John's Church by the rector or any male clergyman of my son's choice. The navy hymn should be played. My name on Alan's tombstone should read 'and his wife,' not 'and his beloved wife.'" I was a little embarrassed when I approached the rector of St. John's about the "male clergyman" instruction, but the rector said there was no problem; he would say the service. There was also a memorial service and reception in New York arranged by Deborah, complete with trumpets to send Mother on her way. Many friends came to the services or sent letters, as Mother had endeared herself to a wide circle in New York as well as Washington.

Mother always said she would be on a pink cloud looking down with pleasure at the activities of her offspring. Given her determination in pursuit of what she really wanted, I imagine she is doing so right now. It is a nice feeling.

INDEX

Index

Page numbers in italics denote illustrations.

ADST-DACOR
Diplomats and Diplomacy Series

Since 1776, extraordinary men and women have represented the United States abroad under all sorts of circumstances. What they did and how and why they did it remain little known to their compatriots. In 1995 the Association for Diplomatic Studies and Training (ADST) and Diplomatic and Consular Officers, Retired, Inc. (DACOR), created the Diplomats and Diplomacy book series to increase public knowledge and appreciation of the involvement of American diplomats in world history. The series seeks to demystify diplomacy by telling the story of those who have conducted our foreign relations, as they lived, influenced, and reported them. *Distinguished Service: Lydia Chapin Kirk, Partner in Diplomacy, 1896–1984*, edited by Roger Kirk, is the thirtieth volume in the series.

Other titles in the series

Architecture of Diplomacy: Building America's Embassies
Jane C. Loeffler
Behind Embassy Walls: The Life and Times of an American Diplomat
Brandon Grove
Born a Foreigner: A Memoir of the American Presence in Asia
Charles T. Cross
Ellsworth Bunker: Global Troubleshooter, Vietnam Hawk
Howard B. Schaffer
Intervening in Africa: Superpower Peacemaking in a Troubled Continent
Herman J. Cohen

In Those Days: A Diplomat Remembers
James W. Spain
Mission to Algiers: Diplomacy by Engagement
Cameron R. Hume
A New Vision for America: Toward Human Solidarity
John Richardson
Plunging into Haiti: Clinton, Aristide, and the Defeat of Diplomacy
Ralph Pezzullo
Saudi Arabia and the United States: Birth of a Security Partnership
Parker T. Hart
Toussaint's Clause: The Founding Fathers and the Haitian Revolution
Gordon Brown
Uncle Sam in Barbary: A Diplomatic History
Richard B. Parker
The United States and Pakistan, 1947–2000: Disenchanted Allies
Dennis Kux
Vietnam and Beyond: A Diplomat's Cold War Education
Robert H. Miller